United States
Department
of Agriculture

Forest Service

Rocky Mountain
Research Station

Proceedings RMRS-P-48CD

July 2007

Southwestern Rare and Endangered Plants:

Proceedings of the Fourth Conference

March 22-26, 2004
Las Cruces, New Mexico

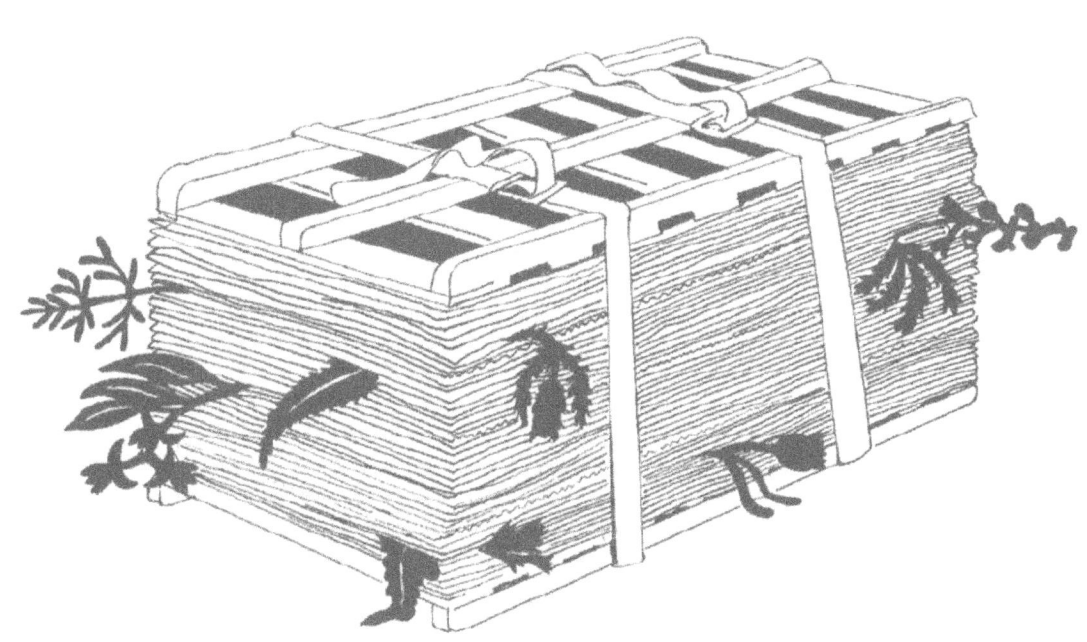

Barlow-Irick, P., J. Anderson and C. McDonald, tech eds. 2007. Southwestern rare and endangered plants: Proceedings of the fourth conference; March 22-26, 2004; Las Cruces, New Mexico. Proceedings RMRS-P-48CD. Fort Collins, CO: U.S. Department of Agriculture, Forest Service, Rocky Mountain Research Station. 135 p.

Abstract

These contributed papers review the current status of plant conservation in the southwestern U.S.

Key Words: plant conservation, conservation partnerships, endangered plants, plant taxonomy, genetics, demography, reproductive biology, biogeography, plant surveys, plant monitoring

These manuscripts received technical and statistical review. Views expressed in each paper are those of the authors and not necessarily those of the sponsoring organizations or the USDA Forest Service.

Cover illustration: Have Plant Press, Will Travel by Patricia Barlow-Irick

USDA Forest Service
Proceedings RMRS-P-48CD

Southwestern Rare and Endangered Plants: Proceedings of the Fourth Conference

March 22-26, 2004
Las Cruces, New Mexico

Technical Coordinators:

Patricia Barlow-Irick
Largo Canyon School
Counselor, NM

John Anderson
U.S. Bureau of Land Management
Phoenix, AZ

Charlie McDonald
U.S. Forest Service
Albuquerque, New Mexico

A Tale of Two Rare Wild Buckwheats (*Eriogonum* Subgenus *Eucycla* (Polygonaceae)) from Southeastern Arizona

JOHN L. ANDERSON

U.S. Bureau of Land Management, 21605 N. Seventh Ave, Phoenix, AZ 85027

ABSTRACT. Unusual soils, compared to surrounding common soils, act as edaphic habitat islands and often harbor rare plants. These edaphic elements can be disjuncts or endemics. Two rare wild buckwheats from southeastern Arizona that grow on Tertiary lacustrine lakebed deposits have been found to be a disjunct, and an endemic. *Eriogonum apachense* from the Bylas area is determined to be a disjunct expression of *E. heermannii* var. *argense*, a Mojave Desert taxon from northern Arizona and adjacent California and Nevada, not a distinct endemic species. At a historical location of *E. apachense* near Vail, Arizona, a new species of *Eriogonum*, also in subgenus *Eucycla*, was discovered growing on mudstones of the Oligocene Pantano Formation. It was also recently found on outcrops of the Plio-Pleistocene Saint David Formation above the San Pedro River near Fairbank, Arizona.

The large North American genus of wild buckwheats, *Eriogonum*, has approximately 255 species. Only *Carex*, *Astragalus*, and *Penstemon* have more. This large number of species in *Eriogonum* is a consequence of extensive speciation (Shultz 1993) with "…about one third of the species uncommon to rare" (Reveal 2001). In the Intermountain West geographic isolation has been the stimulus to speciation, either through habitat or physiographic diversity. This situation is especially pertinent on the Colorado Plateau with its high levels of sedimentary geological diversity and topographic diversity of canyons and mesas. Fifty per cent of Utah endemics occur in the Colorado Plateau; and, thirty-six per cent of Utah endemics grow on clay, silt, mudstones, and shales and 18% on limestone (Shultz 1993). The creosote (*Larrea tridentata* (DC.) Coville) deserts of southern Arizona are in the Southern Basin and Range physiographic province which is characterized by igneous mountains and alluvial basins; and, these unusual edaphic habitats are uncommon there. Though, in a small number of places (Fig. 1) they have been formed by late Tertiary lacustrine basin deposits (Nations et al 1982) where many endemics, disjuncts, and peripherals have been documented (Anderson 1996).

In Arizona there are 23 species in the subgenus *Eucycla* (Nutt.) Kuntze of *Eriogonum* (Reveal 2001). Many of these species are edaphic endemics. The two scientific epithets from subgenus *Eucycla* to be discussed in this paper are *Eriogonum apachense* Reveal (Fig. 2) and *E. terrenatum* Reveal (Fig. 3). The plants named as *Eriogonum apachense*, the Apache wild buckwheat, occur in the San Carlos Basin (Safford Basin) where they grow on late Tertiary white lacustrine limestone deposits above the Gila River (Fig. 4) approximately ten to twelve miles northwest of Bylas, Arizona. The species was described

1

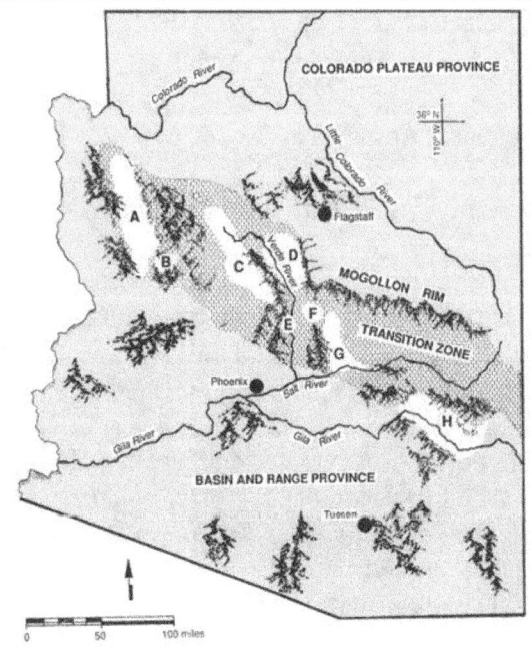

FIGURE 1. Arizona map showing late Tertiary lacustrine basins in central Arizona. A – Big Sandy Basin, B – Burro Creek, C – Chino Valley, D – Verde Valley, E – Lower Verde Valley (Horseshoe reservoir), F- Payson, G – Tonto Basin, and H – San Carlos Basin (from Anderson 1996)

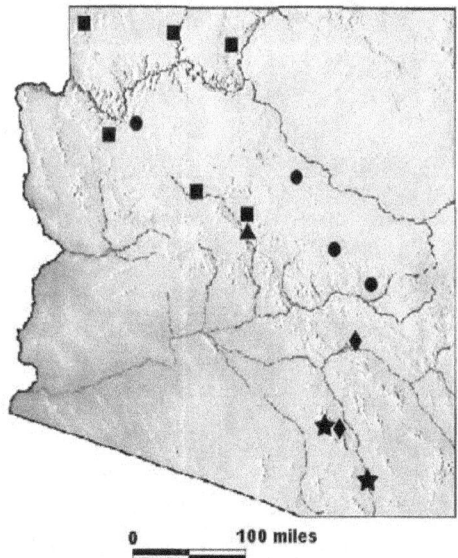

FIGURE 5. Arizona map showing distribution of subject wild buckwheats (*Eriogonum*). *E. apachense* (diamonds), *E. heermannii* var. *argense* (squares), *E. terrenatum* (stars), *E. ericifolium* (triangle), *E. pulchrum* (circles).

FIGURE 2. *Eriogonum apachense* type locality near Bylas, Graham County, Arizona.

FIGURE 3. *Eriogonum terrenatum* at type locality near Fairbank, Cochise County, Arizona.

FIGURE 4. *Eriogonum apachense* on late Tertiary lacustrine habitat in the San Carlos Basin.

FIGURE 6. *Eriogonum heermannii* var. *argense* habitat on Verde Formation in White Hills, Verde Valley, Yavapai County, Arizona.

FIGURE 7. *Eriogonum terrenatum* habitat on Pantano Formation near Vail, Pima County, Arizona.

FIGURE 8. *Eriogonum terrenatum* habitat on middle member of St. David Formation near Fairbank, along the San Pedro River Valley, Cochise County, the type locality. Person on the left is Jack Whetstone, BLM, Sierra Vista, AZ, and person on the right is the author.

as closely related to *Eriogonum heermannii* Dur. & Hilg. and distinguished by "…the narrowly turbinate involucres, truncated outer perianth segments, generally smaller and more slender stature and habit, and the distinct geographical distribution." (Reveal 1969). At that time the nearest known populations of *Eriogonum heermannii* were from approximately 200 miles to the northwest in Mohave and Coconino Counties (Fig. 5).

The subsequent discovery by Bob Denham of plants similar to *Eriogonum apachense* on the Verde Formation in the Verde Valley (Fig. 6), another Late Tertiary lacustrine basin, and by Marc Baker of plants similar to *E. heermannii* var. *argense* Munz along the upper Verde River in the Chino Valley on both sedimentary and igneous habitats brought the two taxa into close geographic proximity of about 25 miles apart. This new information led to a reevaluation of their taxonomic relationship. In October 2003, Marc Baker, James Reveal, and the author visited these wild buckwheat sites in the Chino and Verde Valleys; and, the latter two also visited the type locality of *Eriogonum apachense* near Bylas. (See Appendix One for exact location information on plant sites and collections). Morphological evaluation of live material from these populations (documented by collections: *Reveal 8412*, and *8413* from the Verde Valley and *Reveal 8418* and *8419* from the San Carlos Basin) showed variation among plants in each population in the taxonomic characters (involucre shape, inflorescence branch width, and plant stature) previously used to distinguish the two species. There were no consistent patterns of morphological differences that distinguished between populations as separate species. *Eriogonum apachense* is thus determined to be a disjunct expression of *E. heermannii* var. *argense*. This disjunct distribution pattern is repeated in several other northern taxa from the Colorado Plateau that are disjunct on late Tertiary lacustrine deposits in the Sonoran Desert (Fig. 5); they include *Arenaria eastwoodiae* Rydb., *Astragalus calycosus* Torr. var. *scaposus* (Gray) Jones, *Penstemon thompsonae* (Gray) Rydb., *Physaria newberryi* Gray, and *Streptanthus cordatus* Nutt. ex T. & G. These disjunctions are floristic remnants of the southern expansion of Colorado Plateau pinyon-juniper woodlands into southern Arizona during the last Wisconsin glaciation (Anderson 1996).

Because an historical collection from eight miles south of Vail, Pima County, (*Marcus Jones s.n.* RSA) had also been identified as *Eriogonum apachense* (Reveal 1976), the author searched for it in this area. Outcrops of another sedimentary formation, the Oligocene Pantano Formation, provided potential edaphic habitat for rare plants approximately eight miles southeast of Vail. This population was not relocated; but, conversely, during these searches another *Eriogonum* previously unknown to science was discovered (*Anderson 84-70* ASU, *Anderson 84-71* ASU; *R. Duncan s.n.*, Nov 7 2002, ARIZ, NY, US). These wild buckwheats grow on plum colored sediments of the Upper Pantano Formation (Spence 2002) in the Chihuahuan Desert (Fig. 7). On a field visit with the author in October 2003, Reveal confirmed this *Eriogonum* as a new species (*Reveal 8415* and *Reveal 8416*). (See Appendix One for exact location information on plant sites and collections). Coincidentally, Liz

Makings, a graduate student at ASU working on a master's thesis on a "Flora of the San Pedro Riparian National Conservation Area" (Makings 2003), discovered another population of this same undescribed wild buckwheat (*Makings 1467* ASU) in her study area in 2003. These plants also grow in the Chihuahuan Desert, but on white lacustrine limestones and green claystones (Fig. 8) of the Pleistocene Middle Member of the Saint David Formation (Gray 1967) between the ghost town of Fairbank and the old railroad station of Boquillas in Cochise County. There are two subpopulations here within one square mile with 800-1000 plants total, growing on bluffs above the west side of the San Pedro River. No other populations were found during additional inventories by Jack Whetstone, BLM Sierra Vista, and the author along the San Pedro Riparian National Conservation Area between Sierra Vista and Fairbank. This new species, the San Pedro River Valley wild buckwheat, was named *Eriogonum terrenatum* Reveal (2004) after the type locality near the ruins of the eighteenth century Spanish fort, Presidio de Santa Cruz de Terrenate.

Eriogonum terrenatum is closely related to *E. pulchellum* J. T. Howell which occurs north of the Mogollon Rim in northern Arizona and to *E. ericifolia* Torrey & Gray which is endemic to the lacustrine limestone of the Verde Formation in the Verde Valley near Camp Verde, Yavapai County. It differs from these two species in its larger stature, flowers, and achenes; its involucres campanulate versus turbinate; leaf margins enrolled versus revolute; and consistently white flowers. Other characters of leaf shape and pubescence and flowering stem length are

4

TABLE 1–Comparison of morphological characters in *Eriogonum terrenatum* and its closest relatives.

Characteristic	E. terrenatum	E. pulchrum	E. ericifolium
Plant height	1-4 cm	0.8-1.2 cm	0.5-1.5 cm
Leaf			
shape	linear-oblanceolate to linear-elliptic	oblanceolate to elliptic	linear
length	0.3-0.8 cm	0.5-0.8 cm	0.6-1.5 cm
adaxial surface	thinly floccose to glabrous	floccose	glabrous
edge	enrolled	slightly revolute	revolute
involucre shape	campanulate	narrowly turbinate	turbinate
flowers			
color	white	white to rose	white to pink or rose
size	3.5-4.5 mm	1.5-2 mm	2-3 mm
flowering stem length	0.5-3 cm	1-5 cm	0.3-1 cm
achene	4.0-4.5 mm	1-5 cm	0.3-1.0 cm

intermediate between these two species (Table 1). Previous to this recent fieldwork and the discovery of additional material for comparison, the Vail population of *Eriogonum terrenatum* was treated as *E. ericifolium* by Duncan (2003).

The distributional pattern of the San Pedro River Valley wild buckwheat is similar to that of other rare plants on Late Tertiary lacustrine outcrops in southern Arizona mentioned above (Anderson 1996). Though, *Eriogonum terrenatum* signifies the first such taxon from the Chihuahuan Desert, and not the Sonoran Desert. A list of associated Chihuahuan Desert species for the two *Eriogonum terrenatum* sites appears in Appendix Two.

ACKNOWLEDMENTS

The herbarium curators at ARIZ, ASU, NMSU, and RSA were very helpful in supplying specimens for examination and botanical references from their libraries. Ms. Shannon Doan and Ms. Elizabeth Makings at ASU provided Power Point assistance. Mr. Jack Whetstone at the Sierra Vista BLM provided field assistance. Dr. Vance Haynes at the University of Arizona gave information on the St. David Formation.

LITERATURE CITED

Anderson, J. L. 1996. Floristic patterns on late Tertiary lacustrine deposits in the Arizona Sonoran Desert. Madrõno 43: 255-272.

Duncan, R. B. 2003. Noteworthy Collections – *Eriogonum ericifolium*. Madrõno 50: 53.

Gray, R. S. 1967. Petrography of the upper Cenozoic non-marine sediments in the San PedroValley, Arizona. Journal of Sedimentary Petrology 37: 774-789.

Makings, E. 2003. Flora of the San Pedro Riparian National Conservation Area. Unpublished master's thesis. Arizona State University.

Nations, J. D., J. J. Landye, and R. H. Hevly. 1982. Location and chronology of Tertiary sedimentary deposits in Arizona: a review. Pp. 107-122 *in* R. V. Ingersoll and M. O. Woodburne (eds.), Cenozoic nonmarine deposits of California and Arizona. Pacific Section, Society of Economic Paleontologists and Mineralogists.

Reveal, J. R. 1969. A new perennial buckwheat (*Eriogonum*, *Polygonaceae*) from southeastern Arizona. Journal of the Arizona Academy of Sciences 5:222-225.

_____. 1976. *Eriogonum* (Polygonaceae) of Arizona and New Mexico . Phytologia 34: 428-429.

_____. 2001 onward. *Eriogonoideae* (*Polygonaceae*) of North America north of

Mexico. From website on January 12, 2004: www.life.umd.edu/emeritus/reveal/pbio/eriog/key html.

_____. 2004. New entities in *Eriogonum* (*Polygonaceae: Eriogonoideae*). Phytologia 86: 121-159.

Shultz, L. M. 1993. Patterns of endemism in the Utah flora. Pp. 249-263 *in* R. Sivinski and K.Lightfoot (eds.), Southwestern rare and endangered plants. New Mexico Forestry and Resources Conservation Division Misc. Pub. No. 2. Santa Fe, NM.

Spence, J. E., C. A. Ferguson, S. M. Richard, T. R. Orr, P. A. Pearthree, W. G. Gilbert, and R.W. Krantz. 2002 (revised). Geologic map of The Narrows 7 1/2' Quadrangle and the southern part of the Rincon Peak 7 1/2' Quadrangle, eastern Pima County, Arizona.

APPENDIX ONE

Collections

Eriogonum heermannii Durand & Hilg. var. *argense* (M. E. Jones) Munz

U.S.A. Arizona.

Yavapai Co.: White Hills, along U.S. Forest Service Road 119A, 1 mile north of Middle Verde Road, this junction 3.5 miles northwest of exit 289 on Interstate Highway 17, 2.45 air miles north-northwest of Middle Verde and 6.85 air miles north-northwest of Camp Verde, on calcareous soil of the Verde Formation associated with *Larrea* and *Juniperus*, 3400 ft elev., 34° 39"14"N, 111°54'16"W – T15N, R4E, sec. 35 SW ¼ of the NW1/4. *J. Reveal 8412 with J. Anderson and M. Baker*, October 17, 2003

Yavapai Co.: White Hills, along U.S. Forest Service Road 119A, 1.6 miles north of Middle Verde Road, this junction 3.5 miles northwest of exit 289 on Interstate Highway 17, 2.45 air miles north-northwest of Middle Verde and 6.8 air miles north-northwest of Camp Verde, on calcareous soil of the Verde Formation associated with *Larrea* and *Juniperus*, 3550 ft elev., 34° 39'19"N, 111°53'48"W – T15N, R4E, sec. 35 NE ¼ of the NW1/4. *J. Reveal 8413 with J. Anderson and M. Baker*, October 17, 2003

Graham Co.: Along U.S. Highway 70 near Cottonwood Wash, 11.5 miles northwest of Bylas and 8.3 miles east-southeast of junction of Indian Road 8, San Carlos Indian Reservation, on white lacustrine outcrops associated with *Canotia holocantha* and *Purshia subintegra*, 2840 ft elev., about 33°14'45"N, 110°16'03"W - T2S, R20E, sec. 3. (General area of type locality of *Eriogonum apachense* Reveal, now a synonym of var. *argense*.) *J. Reveal 8418 with J. Anderson* , October 21, 2003

Graham Co.: Along U.S. Highway 70 near Salt Creek, 13.3 miles northwest of Bylas and 6.5 miles east-southeast of junction of Indian Road 8, San Carlos Indian Reservation, on white lacustrine outcrops associated with *Canotia holocantha* and *Purshia subintegra*, 2935 ft elev., about 33°15'30"N, 110°17'40"W - T2S, R20E, sec. 16. (General area of type locality *Eriogonum apachense* Reveal, now a synonym of var. *argense*.) *J. Reveal 8419 with J. Anderson*, October 21, 2003

Eriogonum terrenatum Reveal

U.S.A. Arizona.

Pima Co.: 8.3 miles southeast of Vail exit of I-10 on old highway (frontage Road); T16S R17E S 27 NW ¼; on shaley brown outcrops of the Pantano Formation (Oligocene lacustrine) in eroded area of hillsides and washes, 3520 ft. elev. With *Juniperus, Acacia, Krameria parviflora, Psilostrophe cooperi, Menodora scabra*, and *Dyssodia*. *John Anderson 84-70, 84-71*, Nov 30, 1984

Pima Co.: North of East Marsh Station (or Pantano) Road north of Cienaga Creek, 8.3 miles east-northeast of the Mountain View Exit (Exit 279) along Highway 10, 1.4 air mile northwest of Cross Hill and 6.85 air miles east-southeast of Vail, growing on mudstone and siltstone of the Oligocene Pantano Formation associated with with *Larraea, Juniperus, Tiquilia canescens, Parthenium incanum*, and *Acacia constricta*, 3520 ft elev., 32°01'00"N, 110°36'01"W - T16S, R17E, sec. 27 NW¼ of the NW¼. *J. Reveal 8415 with J. Anderson*, October 20, 2003

Pima Co.: South of East Marsh Station (or Pantano) Road north of Cienega Creek, 8.3 miles east-northeast of the Mountain View Exit (Exit 281) at Interstate Highway 10, 1.1 air mile west-northwest of Cross Hill and 7.1 air miles east-southeast of Vail, growing on plum-colored mudstone and siltstone of the Oligocene Pantano Formation, associated with *Larraea, Juniperus, Tiquilia canescens, Parthenium incanum*, and *Acacia constricta*, 3560 ft elev., 32°00'35"N, 110°35'58"W - T16S, R17E, sec. 27 NE¼ of the SW¼. *J. Reveal 8416 with J. Anderson*, October 20, 2003

Cochise Co.: Contention Uplands, calcareous soils, subshrub 40 cm tall, associated with *Koberlinia spinosa, Ephedra trifurca, Acacia constricta, Yucca elata, Prosopsis velutina, Tiquilia canescens, Thymophylla acerosa, Zinnia acerosa, Pleuraphis mutica*, 3856 ft elev., 31°N 46.482, 110°W 13.299. *E. Makings 1467*, April 10, 2003

Cochise Co.: San Pedro Riparian National Conservation Area, on low eroded bluffs of Pleistocene deposits west of the San Pedro River, southeast of Boquillas (ruins) and southwest of Contention (ruins), about 4.5 air mi NNW of Fairbank and Arizona Highway 82, north of the site of Presidio de Santa Cruz de Terrenate, associated with *Larraea,*

Juniperus, Tiquilia canescens, Parthenium incanum, and *Acacia neovernicosa* and other desert shrubs, 3840 ft elev., N31°46'37", W110°13'33", T19S, R21E, sec. 20 SE¼ of the SE¼. *J. Reveal 8417 with J. Anderson, E. Makings, & J. Whetstone,* October 20, 2003

Appendix Two

Associated Species with *Eriogonum terrenatum*

At the Pantano Formation, near Vail, Pima County, Arizona

Acacia neovernicosa, Krameria erecta, Thymphylla acerosa, Tiquilia canescens, Larrea tridentata, Psilostrophe cooperi, Parthenium incanum, Tridens mutica, Allionia incarnata, Ziziphus obtusifolia, Dasylirion wheerlii, Juniperus coahuilensis, Foquieria splendens, Pleuraphis mutica, Ephedra trifurca, Zinnia pumila, Rhamnus microphylla, Polygala macradenia, Bouteloua eriopoda, Isocoma tenuisecta, Echinocactus erectocentra, Bahia absinthifolia, Agave sp.

At the St David Formation, near Fairbank, Cochise County, Arizona

Acacia neovernicosa, Tiquilia canescens, Sporobolus airoides, Aristida purpurea, Ephedra trifurca, Pleuraphis mutica, Parthenium incanum, Thymophylla acerosa, Dalea formosa, Koberlinia spinosa, Yucca elata, Zinnia pumila, Larrea tridentata, Flourensia cernua, Koberlinia spinosa, Ziziphus obtusifolia, Hymenopappus filifolius var. *pauciflorus*

Penstemon lanceolatus Benth. or *P. ramosus* Crosswhite in Arizona and New Mexico, a Peripheral or Endemic Species?

ANDERSON, J. L.[1], S. RICHMOND-WILLIAMS[2], AND O. WILLIAMS[2].

[1]Bureau of Land Management, 21605 N. Seventh Ave., Phoenix, Arizona 85027, [2]Bureau of Land Management, 1800 Marquess, Las Cruces, New Mexico 88005.

ABSTRACT. The red-flowered member of *Penstemon* sect. *Chamaeleon* from southeastern Arizona and southwestern New Mexico has been treated taxonomically both as part of the Mexican species, *P. lanceolatus* Benth., and as a separate species, *P. ramosus* Crosswhite. Under the former treatment the Arizona and New Mexico populations are peripheral populations of a primarily Mexican species; and, under the latter they represent an endemic species restricted to this area. *Penstemon ramosus* was distinguished from *P. lanceolatus* by branching below the inflorescence and by having narrow, revolute leaves. Morphological examination of herbarium specimens from Arizona, New Mexico, Texas, and Mexico, including duplicates of paratypes cited in the original publication of *P. ramosus*, and of field material in Arizona and New Mexico showed no consistent differences in these characters throughout the entire range. Therefore, Penste*mon ramosus* should be synonymized under *P. lanceolatus*, and Arizona and New Mexico plants that have been distinguished as *P. ramosus* should be treated as peripherals of *P. lanceolatus*.

Peripheral populations of a species are those that occur at the edge of the range of the species. Depending on the connectivity of habitat and topography, these peripheral populations may be continuous with the main body of the species, or fragmented from it. The degree of habitat change may depend on the extent of the overall range of the species. Wide ranging species could have very different environmental conditions at the geographic extremes of their range. In addition, if the habitat conditions, for instance climate and topography, have been altered at the edge of the range, peripheral populations may start to evolve different adaptive characters through incipient speciation; or, isolated peripheral populations may diverge from the rest of the species through founder effects. Also, disjunctions may be an artifact of lack of collections, especially in remote areas.

In the case of *Penstemon lanceolatus* Benth. and *P. ramosus* Crosswhite, the former taxon has been treated as a wide ranging species with scattered occurrences from central Mexico north to southern Texas, New Mexico, and Arizona (Straw 1959, 1992; Kearney and Peebles 1960; Nisbet and Jackson 1960). More recently, Crosswhite (1966) named the peripheral populations of Arizona and New Mexico as a separate species, *Penstemon ramosus*, which became, in consequence, a narrow endemic species; and as a result, it is considered a BLM Las Cruces Field Office sensitive species, a Region 3 Forest Service sensitive species, and a New Mexico State species of concern (Figure 1). Accordingly, the taxonomic status of *Penstemon ramosus* as either an endemic species or the northwesterly peripheral populations of a more widespread *P. lanceolatus* will effect its conservation status vis-à-vis a sensitive species. Kartez (2003) cites *Penstemon ramosus* for the United States and not *P. lanceolatus*

These two beardtongues are in *Penstemon* section *Chamaeleon* Crosswhite, which is "…separated from other sections by the peculiarly flattened and twisted anther sacs which are usually sharply toothed or stoutly hispid at the suture…" (Crosswhite 1966). Although flower color in species of section *Chamaeleon* may be either red or blue-purple, both *P. lanceolatus* and *P. ramosus* have red flowers. The type collection (Fig. 2) of *Penstemon lanceolatus* (*Hartweg 184* GH, NY) is from Aguas Calientes, Mexico. It was named by Bentham in 1839 (Bentham 1970 reprint). The type material upon which Crosswhite (1966) based *Penstemon ramosus* is a collection ("…on a bluff of the Gila River in extreme southwestern New Mexico, near the border of Arizona…", August 30, 1880, *Greene 281* (GH)) used by Greene (1881) as the type of *P. pauciflorus*, a later homonym of *P. pauciflorus* Buckley. In his publication Crosswhite

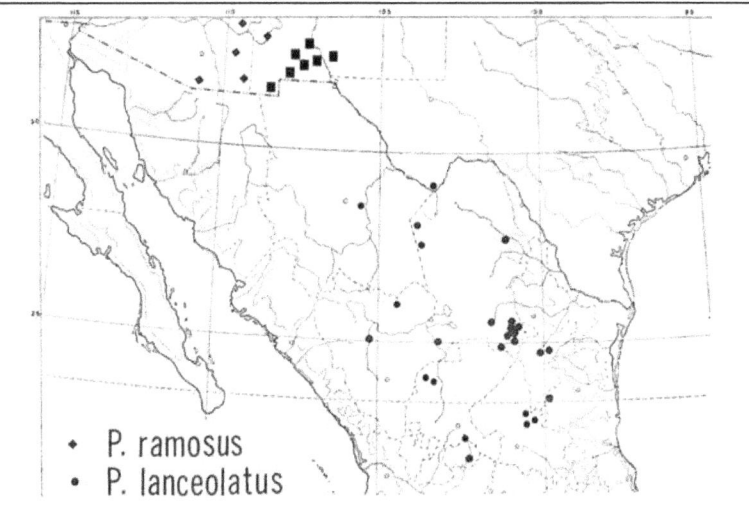

FIGURE 1. Map of the Southwest showing locations of *Penstemon lanceolatus* (circles) and *P. ramosus* (diamonds old records and squares new records) as separate species.

• P. ramosus
• P. lanceolatus

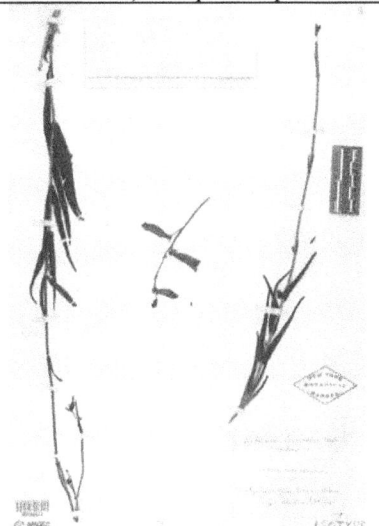

FIGURE 2. Type specimen of *Penstemon lanceolatus, Hartweg 184* (NY).

FIGURE 3. Duplicate of paratype of *Penstemon ramosus, Peebles and Loomis 5847* (ARIZ).

(1966) only cited this one population of *Penstemon ramosus* from New Mexico (two others by allusion) and four others from Arizona (Fig. 3) which made *P. ramosus* appear geographically isolated from the rest of *P. lanceolatus* . Crosswhite (1966) morphologically distintguished *Penstemon ramosus* from. *P. lanceolatus* based on the characters in Table 1

TABLE 1□*Comparison of morphological characters used by Crosswhite (1966) to separate* Penstemon ramosus *from* P. lanceolatus.

Penstemon ramosus	Penstemon lanceolatus
Stems branched below the inflorescence	Stems unbranched below the inflorescence
Leaves linear, 1-6 mm wide	Leaves lanceolate 4-8 mm wide
Leaves revolute	Leaves not revolute

METHODS

At present, there are several more herbarium collections on hand than were available to Crosswhite and, accordingly, more locations are known for *Penstemon ramosus*. For that reason additional existing material is available for comparison of the two taxa. In 2003 we studied thirty eight herbarium collections of both beardtongues at ARIZ, ASU, and NMSU (Table 2) including duplicates of paratypes for *Penstemon ramosus*: *Maguire 11723*, *Maguire 11181*, and *Peebles and Loomis 5847* (all ARIZ) cited by Crosswhite (1966). Specimens were primarily examined for the specific key characters cited by Crosswhite (1966) of inflorescence branching ("ramosus" means branched), leaf width, and revolute leaf edge; in addition, other taxonomically important characters in *Penstemon* were looked at. In June 2003 we visited several of these new herbarium collection locations in southwestern NM, obtained mostly from records of the NM Heritage Program Database. These sites included the Sierra de las Uvas Mountains in Dona Ana County, the Cooke's Range, Florida Mountains, and Tres Hermanas Mountains in Luna County, and the Alamo Hueco Mountains in Hidalgo County. The fieldwork was conducted under extreme drought conditions that affected the results of number of plants found. (Sites were also visited in AZ, but, due to extreme drought conditions, no beardtongue plants were seen). Exact locations, habitat data, and associated species are given in the Appendix.

TABLE 2—List of herbarium specimens examined.

ARIZ	ASU	NMSU
Maguire 11723	Lehto 4034 (first)	Whitefield s n.
Maguire 11181	Lehto 4034 (duplicate)	Weber s.n.
Peebles and Loomis 5847	Pinkava et al 5813	Todsen 8406-1
Loomis and Peebles 5430	Pinakava et al 6124	D. L. Anderson 6184
Walker s n.	Pinkava and Reeves 13158	Spellenberg et al 5436
Zimmerman 2337	Pinkava et al 9490	Columbus 1299
Worthington 19804	Lehto et al 21802	Todsen s n. (Sierra Co.)
Maguire 11547	Engard 707 and Gentry	Todsen s n. (Hidalgo Co.)
Mearns 2353	Pinkava 13245	Worthington 21968
Warnock 904		
Stanford et al 28		
Rodriguez 919		
Shreve 8544		
Stanford et al 538		
Engard and Gentry 23216		
Walker s n.		
Lundell 5057		
Stanford 612		
Hinton 21892		
Starr 581		

Thirty eight *Penstemon* herbarium specimens were examined morphologically (see Table 2 above). Twenty one specimens from Arizona and New Mexico have been annotated as *Penstemon ramosus* and seventeen from Mexico and Texas as *P. lanceolatus*. Of these thirty eight only three specimens have branched stems: one each from New Mexico, Tres Hermanas Mountains (*Worthington 19804* ARIZ); Texas, Big Bend area (*Warnock 904* ARIZ), and Mexico, Coahuila-Sierra San Marcos (*Pinkava 13158* ASU); the few other specimens with branched stems have had the main stem clipped by herbivory with resultant side branching.

A close assessment of the leaves of these thirty eight specimens showed that, if not flat, they are usually conduplicate, but seldom revolute; and, in those specimens with some revolute leaves, this character state is mixed with conduplicate leaves (*Maguire 11723* ARIZ; *Weber s.n.* NMSU; *Todsen s.n.* Hidalgo Co. NMSU; Worthington 21698 NMSU). Average width of leaves is 3-6 mm from narrowly linear to narrowly lanceolate; there is a tendency to narrower leaves in Arizona and New Mexico and wider leaves in Mexico, but there is overlap in leaf width on individual plants and throughout the overall geographic range.

The three duplicates of paratypes of *Penstemon ramosus* examined all had unbranched stems similar to *P. lanceolatus* and linear leaves with a combination of leaf edge forms (Figure 3).

Comparison of other *Penstemon* taxonomic characters, such as, for instance, flower color and shape, anther dehiscence type and denticulation, staminode pubescence and position, calyx shape, and inflorescence glandularity, confirmed no differences between the two taxa.

From June 17-20, 2003, the authors and Douglas Newton, Arizona Native Plant Society volunteer, visited locations of newer records of *Penstemon ramosus*. At the Sierra de las Uvas Mountains we found twenty-five plants on the rocky, lower slopes of Sierra Alta Peak growing on volcanic tuff in juniper-grassland (Figure 4). One plant had one faded flower and several capsules. Some plants were branched due to herbivory, the others plants had unbranched stems and leaves that were either conduplicate or involute. In the Cooke's Range we found only one plant, but it was in full bloom; a single stem was vouchered. This plant was growing in a rocky, igneous basin with pinyon-juniper woodland and chaparral. At Mahoney Park in the Florida Mountains we again found about twenty-five plants, half adult with some in fruit, and half juveniles. This population was growing on limestone hills in Chihuahuan Desertscrub (Figure 5). None of these plants had branched stems and the leaves were conduplicate or involute (Figure 6). At South Peak of the Tres Hermanas Mountains we located just two plants growing on a granite boulder covered hillside with juniper, chaparral, and grassland species. We searched the Thicket Spring area of the Alamo Hueco Mountains without success. Most sites, except Mahoney Park, have been heavily grazed which may have impacted the results of numbers of plants found.

Earlier in June, 2003, Richmond-Williams found a single unbranched plant in flower in Sierra County, Tierra

FIGURE 5. *Penstemon* habitat in limestone hills at Mahoney Park in the Florida Mountains, Luna County, NM.

FIGURE 6. *Penstemon* plant showing conduplicate leaves from the Florida Mountains, Luna County, NM.

FIGURE 4. *Penstemon* plant with unbranched stems on volcanic tuff at Sierra Alta Peak in the Sierra de las Uvas, Dona Ana County, NM. Note single flower on left most stem.

Blanca Canyon, in rocky soils with juniper-grassland. Additional new *Penstemon* locations not visited include: Hidalgo County, the Banner Mine in the Pyramid Mountains, the Big Hatchet Mountains, and the Dog Springs Mountains; Dona Ana County, Summerford Mountain in the Dona Ana Mountains and the San Andres Mountains in White Sands Missile Range; Sierra County near Caballo Dam; and Grant County near Red Rock. Interestingly, the last named location may be near the type locality of the species named by Greene (1881) as *Penstemon pauciflorus.*

DISCUSSION

Penstemon is one of the "macro-genera" cited by Shultz (1993) with a high number of species and endemics in the Utah flora. Its center of diversity is in the Intermountain Region and its high level of endemism is due to "…edaphic endemism and geographic isolation…" (Shultz 1993). This specialized habitat pattern important to the speciation of narrow endemics is not shared by *Penstemon lanceolatus* and *P. ramosus.* These taxa grow on similar common edaphic and vegetative habitat throughout their range: a foothill zone of desert mountains from the upper edge of Chihuahuan Desertscrub, semi-desert grassland, and chaparral, to the lower edge of pinyon-juniper-oak woodland; each locality may be a combination of species from all of these communities (see Appendix). These biotic communities extend throughout this geographic range (Brown 1982). Soil habitats are diverse, including granite, igneous, limestone, and alluvium, but not specialized edaphic habitats; the common denominator on herbarium labels is "rocky". Even with these generic habitat types and accordingly large areas of potential habitat, the beardtongues in question are usually described as uncommon on herbarium labels. Although they have large showy red flowers, they are vegetatively quite cryptic in appearance which may have caused them to be overlooked in the field. Their foothill habitat has been heavily impacted by overgrazing in the past and that may have had an effect on their "uncommonness".

Based on our examination of more recent herbarium specimens and live field material during visits to several new locations, the *Penstemon* specimens, including duplicates of paratypes of *P. ramosus*, showed no consistent differences in the characters used by Crosswhite (1966) to distinguish *Penstemon ramosus* from *P. lanceolatus*, or in other *Penstemon* taxonomic characters as well. Although Crosswhite (1966) lists revolute leaves as a key character of *Penstemon ramosus* (p. 340), his description of the species calls the leaves involute (p. 342). This difference confuses the use of this morphological character in defining and distinguishing the two *Penstemon* taxa. Also, the branched stem specimen from Texas (*Warnock 904* ARIZ) is annotated by Crosswhite as *Penstemon lanceolatus* (Figure 7), which seems to further blur

their distinction as different taxa. In the original description of this *Penstemon* by Greene (1881), he states "...stems 2 feet high, suffrutescent at base, and with a few strict branches..." suggesting that his plants were unbranched. In his *Penstemon* treatment for the Chihuahua Desert Flora, Straw (1992), also, treats *Penstemon ramosus* in synonymy with *P. lanceolatus*.

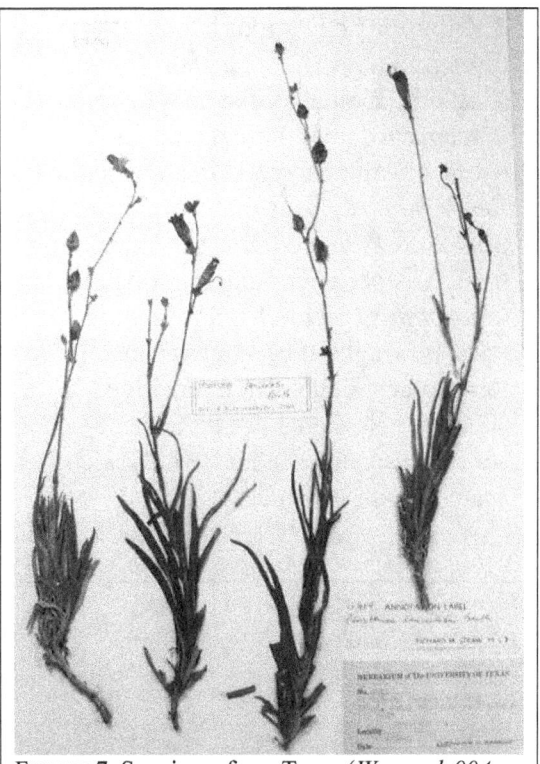

FIGURE 7, Specimen from Texas (*Warnock 904* ARIZ) with branched stems and annotated as *Penstemon lanceolatus* by Crosswhite (see center label).

The additional recent collections from several different mountain ranges in southwestern New Mexico have established a more continuous distribution between southeastern Arizona and central Mexico. The formerly "disjunct" populations in Arizona and New Mexico named as *Penstemon ramosus* are now shown to be more closely connected to the remainder of the range of *P. lanceolatus*

13

in Texas and Mexico. Additional *Penstemon* surveys are recommended in the desert mountains of Chihuahua and western Texas to determine further connectivity in range.

Based on the lack of confirmed morphological differences and lack of geographical or ecological isolation potentially leading to speciation (as a result of greater connectivity of distribution and similar habitat types discussed above), *Penstemon ramosus* should be treated as a synonym under *P. lanceolatus*; and, the Arizona and New Mexico plants included in an endemic *Penstemon ramosus* that were formerly treated as *P. lanceolatus* should again be treated as peripheral populations of *P. lanceolatus* (Figure 8). *Penstemon ramosus* ought to be removed as a BLM Las Cruces Field Office sensitive species, a Region 3 Forest Service sensitive species, and a New Mexico State species of concern.

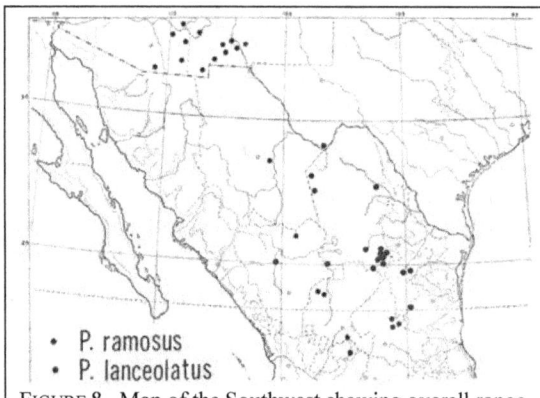

FIGURE 8. Map of the Southwest showing overall range of *Penstemon lanceolatus* based on the results of this study.

ACKNOWLEDGMENTS

The herbarium curators at ARIZ, ASU, NMSU, and RSA were very helpful in supplying specimens for examination and botanical references from their libraries. Ms. Shannon Doan at ASU provided Power Point assistance and found the slide of the type specimen of *Penstemon lanceolatus* at NY. Greg Gallegos with the Las Cruces BLM provided computer assistance. Doug Newton of the Arizona Native Plant Society assisted in fieldwork. Dr. Richard Straw gave provided helpful discussions on his *Penstemon* research for the Chihuahuan Desert.

LITERATURE CITED

Bentham, G. 1970 (reprint of 1839). Plantae Hartwegianae with an introduction by R. McVaugh. J. Cramer, Germany.

Brown , D. E., ed. 1982. Biotic communities of the American Southwest---United States and Mexico. Desert Plants 4:1-342.

Crosswhite, F. S. 1966. Revision of *Penstemon* section *Chamaeleon* (Scrophulariaceae). Sida 2:339-346.

Greene, E. L. 1881. New plants of New Mexico and Arizona. Bot. Gaz. 6:217-219.

Kartesz, J.T. 2003. A Synonymized Checklist and Atlas with Biological Attributes for the Vascular Flora of the United States, Canada, and Greenland. Second Edition. In: Kartesz, J.T., and C.A. Meacham. Synthesis of the North American Flora, Version 2.0-BLM.

Kearney, T. H. and R. H. Peebles. 1960. Arizona flora. 2nd ed. Supplement by J. T. Howell and E. McClintock. University of California Press, Berkeley.

Nisbet, G. and R. Jackson. 1960. The genus Penstemon in New Mexico. Univ. Kans. Sci. Bull. 41:691-759.

Shultz. L. 1993. Patterns of endemism in the Utah flora. Pp. 249-263 *in* R. Sivinski and K. Lightfoot (eds.), Southwestern rare and endangered plants. New Mexico Forestry and

Resources Conservation Division Misc. Pub. No. 2. Santa Fe, NM.

Straw, R. M. 1959. Los *Penstemon* de Mexico. I. Sobre la confusion entre *Penstemon lanceolatu*s y *Penstemon imberbis*. Biol. Soc. Mex. 24:39-52.

_____. 1992. Penstemon. Pp. xx-xx *in* J. Henrickson & M. C. Johnston 1992 (eds.), A flora of the Chihuahuan Desert Region. Unpublished ms.

APPENDIX

Dona Ana County: Sierra de las Uvas Mountains, lower north-northwest facing slopes of Sierra Alta Peak, growing on volcanic tuff in juniper-grassland; with *Juniperus monosperma, Rhus microphylla, Dasylirion wheeleri, Brickellia californica, Artemisia ludoviciana, Aloysia wrightii, Heterotheca villosa, Opuntia phaecantha, Pleuraphis mutica, Bouteloua gracilis, Bouteloua eriopoda,* and *Sporobolus cryptandrus*; T20S R3W S14; 0300382 N, 3605575 E; approx. twenty-five plants.

Dona Ana County: Cooke's Range, basin below Cooke's Town, growing in igneous derived soils with scattered granitic boulders in chaparral with scattered pinyon and juniper; with *Cercocarpus montanus, Quercus turbinella, Nolina microcarpa, Parthenium incanum, Rhus aromatica* var. *trilobata, Fallugia paradoxa, Fendlera rupicola, Krascheninnikovia lanata, Bouteloua curtipendula, Bouteloua hirsuta, Bouteloua eriopoda, Bouteloua gracilis*; 5900 ft elevation; T20S R8W S19 SW; 0245771 N, 3604236 E; only one plant (in flower).

Luna County: Florida Mountains, Mahoney Park, growing on toeslopes of east and north-facing limestone hills with Chihuahuan Desertscrub; with *Juniperus monosperma, Nolina texana, Dasylirion wheeleri, Rhus aromatica* var. *trilobata, Rhus microphylla, Krameria erecta, Cercocarpus montanus, Yucca baccata, Thymophylla pentachaeta, Tecoma stans, Fouquieria splendens, Garrya wrightii, Dalea Formosa, Eriogonum jamesii, Hymenoxys scaposa, Escobaria orcuttii, Bouteloua curtipendula, Bouteloua eriopoda, Aristida purpurea*; 5220 feet elevation; T25S R8W S35; 0251114 N, 3552652 E; and 5390 feet elevation; 3552177 N, 0251651 E; approx. twenty five plants total in two colonies.

Luna County: Tres Hermanas Mountains, growing on steep granitic boulder covered north-facing slopes of South Peak; with *Juniperus monosperma, Quercus turbinella, Mimosa biuncifera, Ericameria laricifolia, Rhus microphylla, Dasylirion wheeleri, Aloysia wrightii, Parthenium incanum, Aristida purpurea, Stipa* sp.; 5205 feet elevation; T27S R8W S31; 0244301 N, 3533460 E; only two plants found.

Further Elucidation of the Taxonomic Relationships and Geographic Distribution of *Escobaria sneedii* var. *sneedii*, *E. sneedii* var. *leei*, and *E. guadalupensis* (Cactaceae)

Marc A. Baker

Main Campus, College of Liberal Arts and Sciences, School of Life Sciences, PO Box 74501, Tempe, Arizona 85287-4501

ABSTRACT. Individuals of *E. sneedii* var. *sneedii* were found to occur in greater abundance within the Guadalupe Mountains than was previously recorded. No additional populations morphologically intermediate between *E. guadalupensis* and *E. sneedii* were found. Taxonomic affiliation and geographic distribution among three *Escobaria* taxa were readdressed with phenetic analyses. Principle components analysis (PCA) showed moderate resolution between individuals representing *E. guadalupensis* and *E. sneedii*. Resolution was poor between those of *E. sneedii* var. *sneedii* and *E. sneedii* var. *leei*. Results from discriminant analysis (DA) correctly classified individuals within populations of *E. guadalupensis*, *E. sneedii* var. *sneedii* and *E. sneedii* var. *leei* 100, 79.6, and 86.4 percent, respectively. The taxonomic recognition of *E. sneedii* var. *leei*, as separate from *E. sneedii* var. *sneedii* is tenuous.

INTRODUCTION

Escobaria sneedii Britton & Rose and its relatives are endemic to various isolated mountain ranges of the Chihuahuan Desert. They are popular in horticulture because their diminutive size and cold-tolerance. Two taxa, *E. sneedii* var. *sneedii* and *E. sneedii* var. *leei* (Rose *ex* Bödecker) D. R. Hunt are given special status legal protection by the United States Government. *Escobaria sneedii* var. *sneedii* is listed as Endangered and *E. sneedii* var. *leei* is listed as Threatened (U. S. Fish & Wildlife Service 1993).

According to Benson (1982), *Escobaria sneedii* includes two varieties, *E. sneedii* var. *sneedii* and *E. sneedii* var. *leei*. Benson's classification is monothetic in nature and his segregation of *E. sneedii* from other species is based on a single unique character: profuse branching of immature stems. Because of the danger in monothetic groups being artificial, especially those relying on a single character (Sneath & Sokal 1973), Zimmerman's (1985) treatment of the *E. sneedii* complex represents a more natural grouping. Using a more polythetic approach, Zimmerman expands this circumscription of *E. sneedii* to include all *Escobaria* with evenly radiating central spines in conjunction with small, cespitose stems that lack a medullary system. In his broader view, he recognizes a total of nine varieties. His classification is based on a number of shared character states and it is unnecessary for any one taxonomic variety to possess any single state. In addition, the classification of any one population may depend on the mean value for some or all character states and some taxa may only be differentiated using a combination of such means. Thus, identification at the varietal level based on a single individual within *E. sneedii* may not always be possible.

Soon after the completion of Zimmerman's monograph, a closely related taxon, *Escobaria guadalupensis* Brack & Heil, was described by Heil & Brack (1986). Heil & Brack (1986) separate *E. guadalupensis* from *E. sneedii* based on its lack of dimorphic, profusely branching stems. In the broad sense of *E. sneedii* (Zimmerman 1985), *E. guadalupensis*, therefore, would not be excluded.

According to Zimmerman (1985, 1993), known populations of *E. sneedii* var. *sneedii* are restricted to the Franklin Mountains area of Texas and New Mexico between El Paso and Las Cruces. All known populations of *E. guadalupensis* occur within a narrow geographical range, mostly at higher elevations, in the Guadalupe Mountains of Texas within the Guadalupe Mountains National Park. All known populations of *E. sneedii* var. *leei* occur at low elevations in the vicinity of Carlsbad Caverns National Park (CCNP), New Mexico. In contrast, Heil and Brack (1985) define the distribution of *E. sneedii* var. *leei* as confined to areas within the eastern half of CCNP and define all related populations within the western half as *E. sneedii* var. *sneedii*. Although they report a small degree of sympatry between the two varieties, they find no evidence for hybridization between the two taxa. They separate the two taxa based on spine orientation, *E. sneedii* var. *leei* having deflexed spines and *E. sneedii* var. *sneedii* having spreading spines. An alternate view suggests (Zimmerman 1993) that differences in morphology among populations of *E. sneedii* within CCNP may due to introgression stemming from hybridization between *E. sneedii* var. *leei* and *Escobaria guadalupensis*, or that these intermediate

forms represent ancestral populations from which both *E. sneedii* and *E. guadalupensis* have radiated. The smaller stems and tightly compacted appressed-spines of *E. sneedii* var. *leei*, for instance, could be adaptations to arid conditions at lower elevations and the larger stems, and longer, spreading spines of *E. guadalupensis* may be adaptations to more mesic conditions and differences in herbivore strategy at higher elevations.

Chromosome number determinations have all been diploid ($n= 11$) within the *E. sneedii* complex (Pinkava et al. 1985, Weedin & Powell 1978, Weedin et al. 1989, Zimmerman 1985, Baker & Johnson 2000) and, therefore, polyploidy does not appear to be a genetic barrier.

In light of controversy over the circumscriptions of these taxa, Baker and Johnson (2000) undertook phenetic analyses to elucidate diagnostic characters and to determine the taxonomic status of individuals within three unplaced populations. Discriminant analysis (DA) correctly classified individuals of *E. guadalupensis* 100 percent, while there were more misclassifications for the two varieties of *E. sneedii*. In two of the Guadalupe Mountains populations, about one-third of the individuals were classified as *E. sneedii* var. *sneedii* and about two-thirds as *E. sneedii* var. *leei*. For Cottonwood Canyon West, about 70 percent of the individuals were classified as *E. sneedii* var. *sneedii* and about 30 percent as *E. guadalupensis*. In part, the results of Baker and Johnson (2000) supported Zimmerman's hypothesis that the unidentified populations of *E. sneedii*-related individuals within the Guadalupe Mountains of New Mexico represented intermediates between *E. guadalupensis* and *E. sneedii*.

Individuals of these same populations, however, were morphologically indistinguishable from those 200 km distant and near the type locality of *E. sneedii* var. *sneedii*. Although this scenario may initially seem contradictory to the concept of genetic drift, the lack of morphologic and taxonomic separation owing to geographic isolation is not an unusual phenomenon in evolution. Populations may be geographically isolated for long periods of time without diverging. enough to be recognized taxonomically (Stebbins 1950). Recently, Thompson (1997) refuted her initial hypothesis that geographically proximate populations of *Lobelia* would cluster in terms of phenetic structure. In fact, it has long been accepted by systematists that adaptive radiation through climatic and edaphic conditions is a more powerful process of differentiation than is genetic drift from spacial isolation (Stebbins 1950). In this sense, it would not be unusual for populations of *E. guadalupensis* and *E. sneedii* var. *leei*, which occur within areas of climatic and edaphic extremes, to have evolved more rapidly from ancestral populations within the Guadalupe Mountains than have the geographically isolated populations of *E. sneedii*. Also, it is more parsimonious for two extreme morphotypes to radiate by peripheral and ecological isolation, than for the two extremes to hybridize and give rise to a wide-ranging intermediate (Barlow-Irick 1995). Zones of intergradation, such as those represented by some of the Guadalupe Mountains populations of *E.*

sneedii, are common occurrence during the divergence of population systems (Grant 1971).

The main objective of this study was to survey within the Guadalupe Mountains for populations of the *Escobaria sneedii/E. guadalupensis* complex occurring geographically intermediate to the western and eastern clusters of known populations, and to further assess taxonomic relationships using the morphological criteria established by Baker and Johnson (2000).

METHODS

Surveys were conducted within the Guadalupe Mountains during June 2001 between latitude 32° 04' and 32° 10'N and longitude 104° 33' and 104° 42'W (Fig. 1).

A total of 95 individuals were measured for the four characters diagnostic within the taxonomic group (Baker & Johnson 2000). The new data were incorporated into the Baker and Johnson (2000) data set and analyzed using algorithms within the SYSTAT7 statistical package of SPSS7 and SPSS7 version 10.0. Data were transformed as necessary in an attempt to meet assumptions of homogeneity of variance.

Apriori analyses (individuals ungrouped) were performed using principal components analysis. The original Bishop's Cap population was excluded from the PCA analysis. Posterior analyses (individuals pre-grouped) were performed using discriminant functions.

RESULTS

Of the five areas searched, five populations were found, filling in geographical gaps among previously known populations (Table 1, Fig. 1). The primary plant associates for each population are given in Appendix 1. Populations of *E. sneedii* ranged between 4,200 ft (1280 m) and 6,500 ft (1980 m) elevation and were fairly evenly distributed over at least 80 mi² (207 km²) of habitat within the Guadalupe Mountains, between upper Cottonwood Canyon, where *E. guadalupensis* forms occur, and Walnut Canyon, where *E. sneedii* var. *leei* forms occur. Roughly extrapolating from population densities, it is estimated that there are an average of at least 1,000 individuals per square mile (2.59 km) or a total of ca. 80,000 individuals in this area of the Guadalupe Mountains.

The first factor of the PCA accounted for 55.7 percent of the total variation and the second factor for only 19.7 percent (Table 2). Figure 2 represents a scatterplot of factor 1 vs. factor 2. Although individuals are well-grouped

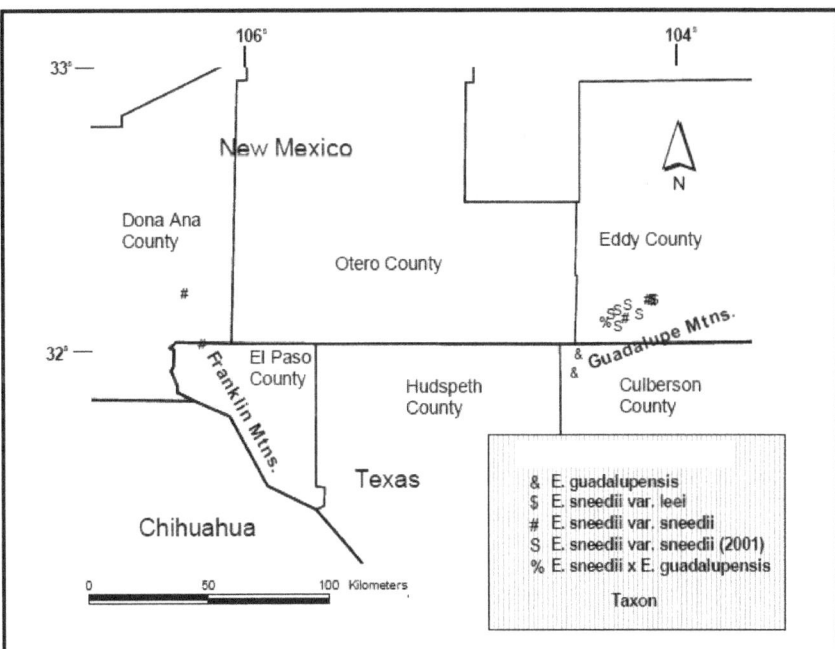

FIGURE 1. Locations of study populations of *Escobaria* in the Franklin and Guadalupe Mountains, NM and TX.

Table 1. Locations of 2001 populations for *Escobaria sneedii*.

Site	Elevation	Longitude / Latitude	N	Habitat	Voucher Number
Bear Canyon	1815m	32° 09'N 104° 36'W	20	limestone shelves in transition scrub, steep NW-facing hillside	*MB14106*
Putman Canyon	1890-1950m	32° 07'N 104° 39'W	25	limestone shelves in transition scrub, SE-NE-facing hillsides	*MB14107*
Cottonwood Canyon East	1980m	32° 06'N 104° 41'W	15	limestone shelves in transition scrub, NW-facing hillside	*MB14111*
Slaughter Canyon	1280-1465m	32° 06'N 104° 33'W	50	south to SW-facing limestone hillside of mostly rounded bedrock, desert scrub	*MB14115*
Double Canyon	1495-1675m	32° 04'N 104°39'W	50	east-facing hillside of mostly exposed rounded and weathered limestone, desert scrub	*MB14119*

19

within taxa, the three groups were not separate from one another. Individuals of *E. sneedii* var. *sneedii* and *E. sneedii* var. *leei* showed considerable overlap. As expected, individuals of the Cottonwood West population were plotted among those of both of *E. sneedii* var. sneedii and *E. guadalupensis*.

Results similar to those of the PCA were obtained from Discriminant analysis. Table 4 presents predicted group membership among the three taxa, which excluded the Bishop's Cap and the Cottonwood Canyon West populations. As with the Baker and Johnson (2000) study, individuals within the *E. guadalupensis* populations were classified correctly 100 percent. Individuals within the *E. sneedii* var. sneedii and *E. sneedii* var. *leei* populations were correctly classified 79.6 percent and 86.4 percent, respectively. Since individuals of the Bishops cap and Cottonwood Canyon West populations were left ungrouped, the DA grouped these individuals according to one of the three defined taxa. For the Cottonwood Canyon West population, 41.2 percent were classified as *E. guadalupensis* and 51.8 percent of the individuals were classified as *E. sneedii* var. *sneedii*. Within the Bishop's Cap population 30 percent were classified as *E. guadalupensis* and 70 percent of the individuals were classified as *E. sneedii* var. *sneedii*.

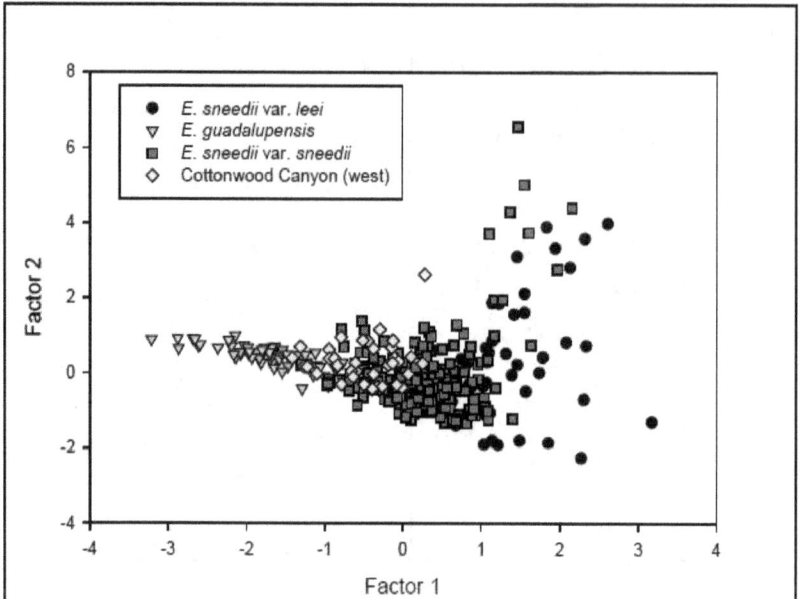

FIGURE 2. Scatterplot of PCA factor one vs. factor two, by taxon. Individuals of Cottonwood Canyon West population plotted separately

TABLE 2. PCA component loadings for each character, by factor.

Character	Factor 1	Factor 2
Inner central spine length	-0.9	0.2
Maximum stem diameter	-0.8	0.0
Number of radial spines per areole	0.7	-0.4
Number of immature stems	0.6	0.8
Percent of total variance explained	55.7	19.7

DISCUSSION AND CONCLUSIONS

The range of *E. sneedii* within the Guadalupe Mountains was found to be much more extensive than was previously recorded. Morphology, as based on the characters used in this study, of most *E. sneedii* individuals within the Guadalupe Mountains was indistinguishable from those in the Franklins Mountains (type locality). The exceptions being the Cottonwood Canyon West and the two Walnut Canyon Populations.

TABLE 3. Classification Results from discriminant analysis. Cottonwood Canyon West and Bishops Cap individuals grouped according to one of the three defined taxa.

| Taxon | Predicted Group Membership | | | |
	E. guadalupensis	*E. sneedii* var. *sneedii*	*E. sneedii* var. *leei*	Total
By number of individuals				
E. guadalupensis	32	0	0	32
E. sneedii var. *sneedii*	9	187	39	235
E. sneedii var. *leei*	0	8	51	59
Cottonwood Canyon West	14	20	0	34
Bishops Cap	7	3	0	10
By percent of individuals				
E. guadalupensis	**100**	0	0	100.0
E. sneedii var. *sneedii*	3.8	**79.6**	16.6	100.0
E. sneedii var. *leei*	0	13.6	**86.4**	100.0
Cottonwood Canyon West	41.2	58.8	0	100.0
Bishops Cap	70	30	0	100.0
81.0% of original grouped cases correctly classified. Box's M = 458.4, Approx. F = 22.4				

Analyses herein did not indicate that populations within each taxon were morphologically distinct from those of the other taxa. However, when populations of intermediate morphology were excluded from the analysis, DA classified correctly nearly all individuals of *E. guadalupensis* from those of *E. sneedii*. As with the Baker and Johnson (2000) data, the Cottonwood Canyon West population appeared to be taxonomically intermediate between *E. guadalupensis* and *E. sneedii*. The Bishop's Cap population was somewhat more problematical. It was excluded in the present PCA and left ungrouped in the DA because the sample size was low (N = 10) and because a recent visit to the site recorded individuals morphologically intermediate between those of typical *E. sneedii* and *E. tuberculosa* (Engelm.) Britton & Rose (personal observation). Thus, the large stems and long spines of the Bishop's Cap *E. sneedii* individuals (Baker & Johnson 2000) may be a product of hybridization with a taxon outside the scope of the present study.

The taxonomic recognition of *E. sneedii* var. *leei,* as separate from that of *E. sneedii* var. *sneedii,* was shown to be tenuous. Within populations classified as *E. sneedii* var. *sneedii*, 16.6 percent of the individuals were misclassified as those belonging to *E. sneedii* var. *leei*, and within populations of *E. sneedii* var. *leei*, 13.6 percent of the individuals were misclassified as those belonging to *E. sneedii* var. *sneedii*. Populations of *E. sneedii* var. *leei* were restricted to a single, small canyon that is not geographically distant from populations currently classified as *E. sneedii* var. *sneedii*.

With respect to the taxonomic status of *E. guadalupensis*, the data herein added little to that of the Baker and Johnson (2000) study. Further work is needed to assess the geographic extent of morphological intermediacy between *E. guadalupensis* and *E. sneedii*.

Of the three taxa, individuals of *E. sneedii* var. *sneedii* were the most abundant, geographically widespread, and morphological variable and intermediate. For these reasons, *E. sneedii* probably represents the ancestral form that gave rise to *E. guadalupensis* to the west and *E. sneedii* var. *leei* to the east. The Franklin Mountains' *E.*

sneedii may represent an incipient population that dispersed from the Guadalupe Mountains or residual populations of a once much larger distribution.

ACKNOWLEDGEMENTS

Funding was provided by Carlsbad Caverns National park under the aid and direction of Renee West and Diane Dobos-Bubno. The removal of areoles from *E. sneedii* var. *sneedii* was done under U. S. Fish and Wildlife Service Permit no. 841795.

LITERATURE CITED

Baker, M. A. and R. Johnson. 2000. Morphometric Analysis of *Escobaria sneedii* var. *sneedii*, *E. sneedii* var. *leei*, and *E. guadalupensis* (Cactaceae). Systematic Botany 25(4): 577-587.

Barlow-Irick, P. 1995. Endangered species survey of eight proposed project sites within Carlsbad Caverns National Park, Eddy Co., New Mexico. Unpublished paper on file at: Carlsbad Caverns National Park, Carlsbad, New Mexico.

Benson, L. 1982. The cacti of the United States and Canada. Stanford, California: Stanford University Press.

Grant V. and K. A. Grant. 1971. Natural Hybridization between the cholla cactus species *Opuntia spinosior* and *Opuntia versicolor*. Proceedings of the National Academy of Science 68: 1993-1995.

Heil, K. and S. Brack. 1985. The cacti of Carlsbad National Park. Cactus and Succulent Journal 57: 127-134.

_____. 1986. The cacti of Guadalupe Mountains National Park. Cactus and Succulent Journal 58: 165-177.

Pinkava, D. J., M. A. Baker, B. D. Parfitt, M. W. Mohlenbrock, and R. D. Worthington. 1985. Chromosome numbers of some cacti of western North America - v. Systematic Botany 10: 471-483.

Sneath, P. H. A. Sokal. R. R. 1973. Numerical taxonomy. San Francisco: W. H. Freeman and Company.

Stebbins, G. L. 1950. Variation and Evolution in Plants. New York & London: Columbia University Press.

Thompson, S. W. 1997. Phenetic analysis of morphological variation in the *Lobelia cardinalis* complex (Campanulaceae: Lobelioideae). Systematic Botany 22: 315-331.

United State Fish and Wildlife Service. 1993. Plant taxa for listing as Endangered or Threatened Species: Notice of Review. Federal Register 58: 51144-51190.

Weedin, J. F. and A. M. Powell. 1978. Chromosome numbers in Chihuahuan Desert Cactaceae. Trans-Pecos, Texas. American Journal of Botany 65: 531-537.

_____, _____, and D. O. Kolle. 1989. Chromosome numbers in Chihuahuan Desert Cactaceae. II. Trans-Pecos Texas. Southwestern Naturalist 34: 160-164.

Zimmerman, A. D. 1985. Systematics of the genus *Coryphantha* (Cactaceae). Austin, Tx: University of Texas at Austin. Dissertation.

_____. 1993. [Letter to K. Lightfoot] On file at: Forestry and Resources Conservation Division, Santa Fe, New Mexico.

Plant associates within 2001 populations for *Escobaria sneedii*.

Site	Associates
Bear Canyon	*Agave lechuguilla, Cercocarpus montanus, Chrysactinia mexicana, Dalea formosa, Dasylirion leiophyllum, Echinocereus triglochidiatus* var. *gurneyi, Heterotheca villosa, Juniperus deppeana, Muhlenbergia pauciflora, Nolina micrantha, Opuntia engelmannii, Parthenium incanum, Petrophyton caespitosum, Quercus pungens, Rhus trilobata,* and *Yucca baccata.*
Putman Canyon	*Acacia greggii, Agave lechuguilla, Cercocarpus montanus, Chrysactinia mexicana, Dasylirion leiophyllum, Echinocereus triglochidiatus* var. *gurneyi, Eriogonum jamesii, Evolvulus nuttallianus, Fendlera rupicola, Garrya wrightii, Hesperostipa neomexicana, Hedyotis nigricans, Juniperus scopulorum, Muhlenbergia emersleyi, M. pauciflora, Opuntia engelmannii, Pinus ponderosa, Quercus pungens, Rhus microphylla,* and *Yucca baccata*
Cottonwood Canyon East	*Arbutus xalapensis, Agave lechuguilla, A. parryi, Chrysactinia mexicana, Cercocarpus montanus, Dasylirion leiophyllum, Echinocereus triglochidiatus* var. *gurneyi, Fendlerella utahensis, Garrya wrightii, Hedeoma plicata, Hesperostipa neomexicana, Juniperus deppeana, Muhlenbergia pauciflora, Nolina micrantha, Opuntia engelmannii, Petrophyton caespitosum, Pinus edulis, P. ponderosa, Quercus pungens, Talinum pulchellum, Vitis arizonica* and *Yucca baccata*
Slaughter Canyon	*Acacia roemeriana, Agave lechuguilla, Aloysia wrightii, Aristida purpurea, Berberis trifoliata, Bernardia obovata, Bouteloua eriopoda, Condalia ericoides, Dalea formosa, Dasylirion leiophyllum, Echinocereus stramineus, E. triglochidiatus* var. *gurneyi, Escobaria strobiliformis, Fouquieria splendens, Juniperus pinchotti, Krameria grayi, Muhlenbergia pauciflora, Opuntia engelmannii, O. macrocentra, Quercus pungens, Rhus microphylla, Thelocactus bicolor, Tridens muticus,* and *Yucca faxoniana*
Double Canyon	*Acacia roemeriana, Agave lechuguilla, Aristida purpurea, Artemisia ludoviciana, Dalea bicolor, Dalea formosa, Dasylirion leiophyllum, Echinocereus triglochidiatus, Eriogonum hieracifolium, Escobaria strobiliformis, Fouquieria splendens, Juniperus pinchotti, Muhlenbergia pauciflora, Parthenium incanum, Quercus pungens,* and *Rhus microphylla*

Determining the Population Boundaries of a Narrowly Endemic Perennial Plant, Lane Mountain Milk-Vetch, in San Bernardino County, California.

DAVID CHARLTON,

Charis Corporation, 222 East Main Street Suite 216 Barstow California 92311
760-256-7033

ABSTRACT. The Lane Mountain milk-vetch (*Astragalus jaegerianus*) is a federally endangered species. It was first discovered in 1939 by Edmund Jaeger in the central Mojave Desert of California. This plant species was not collected again until the army became interested in expanding Fort Irwin's western boundary in the 1980's. Following its rediscovery, volunteers eventually found a few scattered plants in three populations within a 10-mile radius. Army-funded surveys since 1990 defined four generally distinct populations. The most extensive survey, in conjunction with a GIS analysis of potential habitat within 50 miles of the core populations, occurred in 2001. A total of 387 transects were surveyed within twelve 7.5 minute quadrangles and nearly 4,000 plants were found on 21,000 acres. The 2001 survey established that the milk-vetch is restricted to only 4 populations and that it has specific soil and elevation requirements. Ecological studies regarding moisture-holding capacity of the substrate, seed bank availability, seed germination, resprout frequency and pollination ecology have also been conducted. A population genetic study is underway.

INTRODUCTION

The management of approximately 100,000 acres of Bureau of Land Management (BLM) land was transferred to US Army in 2003 as part of the proposed expansion of the National Desert Training Center at Fort Irwin (NTC). Two federally listed resident species occur on this property the desert tortoise and the Lane Mountain milk-vetch (*Astragalus jaegerianus* Munz). The project received a no jeopardy opinion from the US Fish and Wildlife Service (USFWS 2004). Mitigation measures are being developed at present.

HISTORY

The milk-vetch is named after its discoverer, Edmund Jaeger, the Riverside City College biology professor who was a botanical explorer during the 1930-60's and is responsible for the publication of some of the most informative popular books ever written on desert ecology. Based on Jaeger's herbarium specimen label locations, the region southwest of Fort Irwin was visited in 1941 by two of the nations top botanists and collections were made by Rupert Barneby, the *Astragalus* expert, and Phillip Munz the expert on the Southern California flora. No further collecting of this species occurred until 1985 when the expansion was first proposed and the Army sponsored botanical surveys.

Between 1939 and 1984 approximately 100 plants were found in three populations. The milk-vetch had a patchy distribution over a 10-mile long area, occurring on rocky rises within the central Mojave Desert. Repeated searches for this species by small groups and individuals over the next 10 years turned up very few plants. Two systematic surveys by UCLA in the late 1990's (Prigge et al. 2000) found approximately 850 plants.

The Lane Mountain milk-vetch was recommended for listing as an endangered species by the USF&WS in January 1975 with the enactment of the Endangered Species Act. It, along with 1,700 other plants, made the USFWS list in June of 1976. In 1980, the Lane Mountain milk-vetch was included in the updated notice of review as a Category 1 listing. In 1983, a supplemental notice of review changed it to a Category 2; but, nine years later it was included in a listing package with six other species of milk-vetch. In 1998, following two public comment periods, it was granted endangered species status (USFWS 1998).

DESCRIPTION

The Lane Mountain milk-vetch is a vining perennial that usually grows within other shrubs. It appears to be a Pleistocene relic with very few related species. For this reason, Barneby (1964) put it in its own section. The milk-vetch's cryptic nature and scattered and limited distribution have made it very difficult to detect. In low rainfall years, it barely grows 3 inches tall before it flowers and can only be observed beneath other shrubs. In high rainfall years it overtops the host shrubs making it much easier to observe, especially when in flower or fruit. The small pink flowers with purple nectar guides are scattered on long stems, but the brown-purple pendulous leathery pods can be quite dense, making the plant most observable in either flower or fruit.

HABITAT

Early physiological studies have shown that the rocky ridges where the milk-vetch occurs stays moister than the surrounding loamy alluvial fan soils. It is assumed that rainwater is trapped in cracks in the rocks and is available to the plants later in the season. Field observations show shrubs growing on the rocky soils still contain leaves or are flowering in early summer when adjacent plants on alluvial fans are dormant. Field data and observations show that the shrubby vegetation on the rises is much smaller in stature and much more diverse in species than the surrounding deep sandy soils in the swales. The host shrubs often grow in multispecies clumps on the rocky soils. Mine digs near known populations often have a caliche layer several feet below the soil surface that may also trap water. Milk-vetch is also more common growing in nearly leafless shrub species with photosynthetic stems such as Mormon tea (*Ephedra nevadensis*) and turpentine broom (*Thamnosma montana*). It also occurs in common low growing species such as burrobush (*Ambrosia dumosa*) with only two occurrences within the much taller but co-dominant creosote bush (*Larrea tridentata*).

METHODOLOGY

In 2000-1 a massive effort was made to determine the boundaries of the populations (Charis 2002). A survey team was assembled that consisted of 35 field members. Organization, the development of field forms, and a survey scheme were complicated by the scope of the project. No one had experience working with a crew that large. Almost 750,000 dollars were spent over two seasons. The field crews were organized with botanists experienced with the milk-vetch as team leaders, a range of botanists some with graduate degrees, interested novices, and people with no field experience or particular interest in plants. The teams were split into 4 crews of 5-7 with 3 fulltime weekday crews and a part time crew with weekday volunteers working on the weekends. Surveying began in the center of one of the known populations and more plants were found the first day than were expected during the whole field season. The same surveyors consistently found the most plants, while others consistently found the fewest. The best surveyors were a grocery store stocker and a foreign born ecologist with exceptional eyesight.

At first, surveys were contiguous and plants were continually found for several weeks. Progress was very slow because staying accurately on compass readings and waiting while field forms were filled out slowed the pace. After several weeks of surveying, the field forms were changed to take less time and surveys were moved from contiguous to being separated by a half-mile to 1 mile. The presence or absence of milk-vetch plants was a factor in determining the location of the next day's surveys.

The location, phenology, host shrub species, height, and presence of seedlings were documented in the field forms. Several field forms were developed including site forms, plant location forms, GPS log number forms, etc.

All GPS units were numbered and plant identification numbers were sequentially based on each units identification number. It was necessary to download at least every 4 days and the GPS

log form identified the last number downloaded before previous results were deleted. The corners of the transects were recorded but errors in either the recording of data or in the points kept by the GPS units occurred. By cross-referencing during the data verification phase, error conflicts were rectified. GPS numbers were difficult to read in the field during the sunny late afternoons especially if the GPS surface was scratched. Individual recorders found and maintained the best contrast settings.

The second year surveys, conducted in 2002-03, consisted of a much smaller group of surveyors (Charis 2003b). Two botanists spent all spring driving roads within a 50-mile radius looking for and surveying potential habitat. The one survey crew concentrated on the perimeters of the existing populations. A few new plants were found and the population boundaries were modified slightly. Poor rainfall in some areas made surveys at some populations impossible. In some cases, plants sprouted and went dormant before the survey began. In normal years, the plants do not begin blooming until mid-April when both surveys began.

RESULTS OF OTHER SURVEYS

We were asked by the BLM to document the number of Mojave fishhook cacti (*Sclerocactus polyancistrus* (Engelmann & Bigelow) Britton & Rose) observed during the surveys. Because of the large amount of

TABLE 1 Results of Phenology Data

	Beginning	Ending
Flowering	April 7	May 19
Mature Fruits Present	April 20	May 30
Pods Dehiscing	May 13	June
Plant Become Dormant	May 21	June 30

milk-vetch data, surveyors did not have the time to continue taking data on the cacti. We did document which transects contains the 4,000 plants observed during the survey.

Although field crews saw copious amounts of milk-vetch seed fall and build up at the base of the plant, observations were not made on the fate of fallen seed. It was assumed that they were scattered by wind, because evidence of seed predation was never observed. Surveyors documented seedlings under 76 shrubs for a total of 386 seedlings.

In a sample survey of 50 plants in 2001-2002, approximately 75 percent of the known plant locations from 2000-01 were relocated the next year from remaining skeletons. By 2002-03, very few of the skeletons were left. It is assumed that rabbits or rodents ate some of the dried skeletons. The skeletons were too intertwined in the shrubs to break off and blow away. Several-year old skeletons changed in color from tan to gray. Occasionally, old stems indicated the location of previous plants and careful inspection would show whether these plants were still alive. Very few apparently dead skeletons were observed during the surveys. Previous individual monitoring of plants tagged by the USF&WS at the Coolgardie Mesa population and by UCLA in the Brinkman Wash population, showed that many plants did not sprout in poor rainfall years and that plants previously not observed sprouted.

RESULTS

Eventually, approximately half the land within the delineated population boundaries was surveyed and approximately 5,000 more plants were documented. The results of the survey delineated 4 distinct subpopulations occurring at a 45-degree angle from the southwest to the northeast. Extensive efforts to find plants in adjacent areas within a 50 square-mile areas were negative. It was assumed that rolling topography, diverse shrub vegetation, granitic substrate, and elevation were primary indicators of potential habitat.

None of the portions of the known populations surveyed by UCLA in 1998-99 were resurveyed. By using similar methodology it was possible to combine data sets. Data on nearly 6,000 plants is now known. Thirty different shrub host plants were documented, many milk-vetch plants occurred in a shrub species only once or twice. One-fifth of all milk-vetch plants were found in turpentine broom. Milk-vetch was densest in areas where shrub diversity was high and several species of shrubs often occurred together. Three quarters of all milk-vetch plants occurred in one host plant but one-fifth had two host plants. The rest had multiple host shrubs, no host plants, or were in dead shrubs.

Patterns of habitat preferences within the rises were not found. Plants generally were more common in the more mesic microclimates such as the north side in some areas, but were more common on the ridge crests or at the foot of the south-facing slope of other rises. It is of interest, that 88 percent of the plants occurred between 1,025 and 1,175 meters (3,365 - 3,854 ft) elevation. The total elevation range for the milk-vetch was between 945 and 1,280 meters (3,100 - 4,200 ft) amsl.

The geology of the known habitat was complicated, with milk-vetch plants occurring mostly in light-to-extremely dark-colored granitic substrate (diorite to gabbro). Occasionally, milk-vetch plants also occur in Pleistocene relic reddish-clay soils and a few plants occurred on Lane Mountain, a Tertiary rhyolitic dome. A comparison can be made between the geology and soil type within the population boundaries and within a 50-mile (80.5 km) radius of the populations. Note the important differences in Tables 2 and 3.

Soil surveys in the region are only a level three, in which, the boundaries of individual soil series is not determined. Electronic soil map polygons include the three major soil series occurring within the polygon and possibly an estimate of the percentage of one of the three. The milk-vetch plants were limited to two soil polygon types. The Cajon-Wasco-Rosamond and Calvista-Trigger-rock outcrop types. All these soil series are common and widespread in inland Southern California.

The milk-vetch responds to rain and has been observed sprouting any time between January and March and after summer rains. Plants will stay small and abort flowers if not enough rainfall occurs. Rainfall episodes of over an inch, every 3-4 weeks, between December and March are ideal. The second year studies had to be postponed one year due to lack of rainfall in 2001-2002. In 2002-2003, only three scattered storms occurred between December and April. Most areas received rainfall from only one of the storms, and plant growth

of milk-vetch and shrubs was poor, although wildflower displays were excellent. Areas within the milk-vetch population boundaries that received precipitation from two or all three storms had good milk-vetch growth.

The surveys began in mid-April when the milk-vetch is in full bloom. The plants remain in flower for approximately one month and then quickly set fruit. The pendulous pods split only on the distal end and the small but numerous seed pour on the ground under the nurse shrub. The seed is then scattered by strong winds that can occur in mid to late summer. Seed predation by insects or birds was never observed.

Although pollinators were also not observed during the first year, one of the crew leaders conducted a pollination study two years later and easily identified several pollinators (Charis 2003c). The major pollinator is a Megachilid bee, *Anthidium dammersi*. This species is attracted to most pin-purple flowered plants.

MANAGEMENT CONSIDERATIONS

Of the four populations the eastern most and smallest is on Fort Irwin property, but is adjacent to the NASA Goldstone Deep Space Complex. It has been fenced off-limits. Army

TABLE 2. Geology bedrock types within the population boundaries and within a 50-mile radius

Bedrock	% Population Boundary	% 50-mile adjacent area
Granitic	90	32
Diorite	5	4
Gabbro	4	Trace
Disturbed/undetermined	1	45

TABLE 3. Relationships between soils within the milk-vetch populations and adjacent habitat.

Soil series map polygon	% within population boundaries	% in adjacent area
Cajon-Wasco-Rosamond	5	16
Calvista-Trigger-rock outcrop	95	11
Nickel-Arizo-Bitter	0	25
Upspring-Sparkhule-rock outcrop	0	10

maneuvers do not occur here because of potential dust interference with NASA research at Goldstone. The largest population, the Coolgardie Mesa population, is located on BLM and private land and would be best managed under the proposed West Mojave Coordinated Management Plan. There are presently three main threats to the Coolgardie population development on private land, OHV travel, and mining. The Coolgardie population is shaped like a donut and a portion of the hole is presently used by off-road vehicles, primarily during spring break. Dry sieve gold mining also takes place within population boundaries on private property. The other populations within the expansion area will be managed by the Fort Irwin Natural Resources Management Plan and within the mitigation measures to be developed under the Biologic Opinion.

The two middle populations are located within the proposed Fort Irwin expansion area. One of the populations is in the middle of a proposed battle corridor. A small portion of the other is located in an area that would receive moderate to heavy traffic. The rest of the second population is proposed to be fenced and posted off limits. The populations will be located in a no dig zone (Charis 2003a).

In January of 2004, Ray Bransfield of the USFWS issued a preliminary jeopardy opinion for the desert tortoise and the Lane Mountain milk-vetch. Minor changes were proposed for the fencing of the one population to reduce the jeopardy opinion. This was later followed by a no jeopardy opinion in April. Critical habitat was delineated in April that is slightly larger than the population delineations that followed minimum convex polygons of the

outermost plants. It is now up to the army to modify the project and develop mitigation measures for the desert tortoise and milk-vetch before training on the expansion will proceed.

The army is modifying it's Integrated National Resources Management Plan to include the milk-vetch populations within the expansion area. This will reduce the need to delineate critical habitat on the army post. Also the expansion Environmental Assessment is going through the public comment time during May 2004.

DISCUSSION

The Lane Mountain milk-vetch is not as rare at once thought. The four populations occur within 21,000 acres. The total range of the species is restricted to a very small portion of the central Mojave Desert. Plants occur only on a portion of the rises within the population boundaries. There are significant differences in the habitat and vegetation between the western most and eastern most populations.

How many plants are there? The unsurveyed half within the population boundaries is lower quality habitat. It was avoided in the first place because there was a high change plants would not be found. These areas often occurred in valleys that lacked rolling hills and diverse vegetation. Only the small rises within those areas will contain small populations of plants. Conclusions that only half the population was counted because only half the area was surveyed should prove to be false. If past experience with desert cymopterus (*Cymopterus deserticola* Brandeg.) holds true, the number of plants that sprout is proportional to the amount of rainfall. In studies at Edwards AFB a seven-fold increase in plant numbers occurred between average and above average years. In high rainfall years, many more plants should occur in the areas already surveyed than in the areas not surveyed.

Above average rainfall has not occurred in this century. The two milk-vetch survey years were slightly above normal and slightly below normal in rainfall. At 2,500 feet (762 m) elevation average rainfall is about 4.5 inches (11.4 cm). At 3,500 to 4,500 feet (1067-1372 m) elevation, the elevation range of this species, rainfall is relatively higher. In the past, high rainfall is approximately 10 inches (25.4 cm) at 2,500' (762 m). Therefore it is possible for as much as 15 inches (38.1 cm) of rain to fall in milk-vetch habitat during an exceptional season. More plants should be expected to occur during high rainfall events, although the actual number of plants should be slightly higher than documented because some were missed by surveyors.

It is extremely difficult to estimate the actual population of plants. The fact that no surveys have occurred during exceptional rainfall years means that population levels could increase dramatically when such an event should occur. The number of plants missed during the surveys should be minor because when potential habitat was located everyone began looking more carefully. When a plant was found the other surveyors would mill about looking for plants while they were waiting for other pairs to complete the field forms. This resulted in 100 percent coverage of the adjacent habitat.

This plant is so cryptic that it can be missed simply by looking from the wrong angle. Also, much of the fieldwork continued after the plants were dormant. In June, some plants would

shrink and disappear while others would dry leaving skeletons that were very easy to see and document. Although many plant had disappeared by the time the survey was completed, the largest number of plants found in one day occurred in late July, while counting only dormant plants.

In order to model potential habitat for the Lane Mountain milk-vetch based on habitat features, three geospatial variables were used; elevation, soils, and geology. The range of features were rated as high, medium, and low. A multiplier of 3 was given to the dataset rated high, a 2 to the medium dataset, and a 1 for low. A 0 was given to areas and features without habitat/plants. A total of 9 points was possible, with the highest number representing the best habitat. The existing population boundaries were located within areas with 7-9 points. Several areas northwest, southeast, and south of the existing populations also had high numbers but plants were not found during scouting surveys.

Why the narrow range? One variable in the area not looked at was the variation in precipitation. Rainfall gauges and weather stations are located in Barstow, 15 miles south of the populations, Daggett 15 miles east of Barstow, and several sites located on Fort Irwin west and northwest of the plants. The variation in rainfall records between the various Fort Irwin sites and between the Barstow and Daggett sites, show that a great variation in local rainfall exists. The curious angle in which the plant populations occur may be related to storm tracks. The storms pass through the Cajon Pass, which is a separation point between the San Gabriel, and San Bernardino Mountains created by the San Andreas Fault. That, combined with the prevailing westerly winds, may result in the most reliable rainfall occurring in the region where the milk-vetch grows.

BIBLIOGRAPHY

Bagley, M. 1989. Sensitive plant species survey on a portion of the proposed Fort Irwin, NTC expansion area, San Bernardino County, California. Report prepared for Michael Brandman and Associates, Santa Ana, California. Submitted to U.S. Army Corps of Engineers, Los Angeles District.

_____ 1998. Draft status report for Lane Mountain milk-vetch (*Astraglus jaegerianus*). Prepared for the Bureau of Land Management. California Desert District, Riverside. California.

Barneby, R. C. 1964. Atlas of North American Astragalus. Mem. New York Bot. Garden. 13:1-1188.

Charis Professional Services, 2002. Distribution and abundance of Lane Mountain milk-vetch (*Astragalus jaegerianus* Munz) report of spring-summer survey.

_____ 2003a. Supplemental Draft Environmental Impact Statement for the Proposed Addition of Maneuver Training Land at Fort Irwin, CA. Unpublished report prepared for the U.S. Army National Training Center, Fort Irwin, California.

_____ 2003b. Lane Mountain Milk-vetch Population Survey, July 2003. Prepared for US Army National Training Center, Fort Irwin.

_____ 2003c. Lane Mountain Milk-vetch Pollination Report, August 2003. Prepared for US Army National Training Center, Fort Irwin.

Prigge, B. A., M. R. Sharifi, and D. Morafka. 2000. Lane Mountain milk-vetch surveys (Progress Report III). Prepared for the National Training Center, U.S. Department of the Army Contract No. DSCA05-99-P-0759.

U. S. Fish and Wildlife Service (USFWS) 1998. Endangered and threatened wildlife and plants; determination of endangered or threatened status for five desert milk-vetch taxa from California. Federal Register 63.

193; 6 October, 1998: 53596-53615 Primary author: D. Steeck.

_____ 2004. Biological Opinion for the Proposed Addition of Maneuver Training Lands at Fort Irwin, California (1-8-03-F-48). Primary author: Ray Bransfield.

Interagency Rare Plant Team Inventory Results - 1998 through 2003.

DEBORAH J. CLARK[1] AND DAVID A. TAIT[2]

[1]Bureau of Land Management, 150 East 900 North, Richfield, UT 84701
[2]U.S. D. A. Forest Service, Fishlake National Forest, 115 East 900 North, Richfield, UT 84701

ABSTRACT. Fishlake National Forest, Dixie National Forest, Bureau of Land Management - Richfield Field Office, and Capitol Reef National Park became partners in an Interagency Agreement to inventory and monitor threatened, endangered, and sensitive plant species shared by these agencies. From 1998 to 2003, the Interagency Rare Plant Team surveyed and recorded over 650 new locations for 32 TES plant species, covering more than 70,000 acres of federally managed lands. Geographical Information System and Global Positioning System technologies were used to predict and map all known and newly discovered occurrences of rare plants in the study area. Sufficient population numbers and occurrence data were gathered during the course of this study to pursue delisting of one of the federally listed threatened species and has allowed the Utah Natural Heritage rarity status of seven sensitive species to be downgraded. Knowledge gained about these species and their habitat requirements has helped determine which species are truly rare and in need of additional conservation actions. In addition, results from this study help determine which species and populations should be monitored to find out if specific human activities are affecting them and will enable federal land managers to ensure that those plants are protected.

INTRODUCTION

The Bureau of Land Management Richland Field Office (BLM), U. S. D. A. Forest Service, Dixie National Forest (DNF) and Fishlake National Forest (FNF), and Capitol Reef National Park (CARE) share management responsibilities for many of the same Threatened, Endangered & Sensitive plant species (TE&S). To enable each of these agencies to better manage their shared TE&S species, they decided to create an interagency botany position and hire an employee to act as team leader for an interagency rare plant team. A BLM employee was hired for the team coordinator position and stationed at CARE. As funding allows, additional seasonal employees are hired to assist the interagency botanist with surveys and monitoring for shared TE&S species throughout their ranges, regardless of agency boundaries. Through the interagency agreement, agencies are able to pool funding so limited TE&S funding is more efficiently used to hire a multi-agency team.

The study area is located in south central Utah, in the Northern Colorado Plateau region. It extends from Hanksville (along Highway 24) west to Loa, north into the San Rafael Swell and south through the Waterpocket Fold and encompasses approximately 3,000 square miles. Unique geological conditions in combination with the arid climate and great elevation range within the study area have created microhabitats that support over 40 rare and endemic plant species. The study area includes lands on DNF and FNF that are over 11,000 feet elevation and extends down through CARE onto BLM to approximately 4,000 feet elevation. Plant communities range from high mountain grasslands, spruce/fir forests, and aspen woodlands down through pinyon-juniper woodlands, sagebrush, shadscale grasslands, and sparsely vegetated badlands.

Eight federally listed and one candidate for federal listing species were selected as the primary focus for surveys; *Cycladenia humilis var. jonesii* (Jones cycladenia) (FWS 1986), *Erigeron maguirei* (Maguire's daisy) (FWS 1985b, FWS 1996), *Pediocactus despainii* (San Rafael cactus) (FWS 1987), *Pediocactus winkleri* (Winklers cactus) (FWS 1998), *Sclerocactus wrightiae* (Wright's fishhook cactus) (FWS 1979), *Spiranthes diluvialis* (Ute ladies-tresses) (FWS 1992b), *Townsendia aprica* (Last Chance townsendia) (FWS 1985a), *Schoencrambe barnebyi* (Barneby's reed-mustard) (FWS 1992a), and *Aliciella cespitosa*, formerly *Gilia caespitosa* (Rabbit Valley gilia) (FWS 1985c). Table 1 shows the distribution of each of the above species by agency.

An additional 30+ sensitive species occur within the study area. They are ranked as sensitive by the agencies and the Utah Natural Heritage Program (UNHP). The majority of species are ranked by UNHP as Global 1 or 2/State 1 or 2. This ranking is defined as (1) critically endangered throughout its range, with 5 or fewer occurrences known; and (2) endangered throughout its range, imperiled globally/statewide because of rarity with only 6 to 20 known occurrences.

The study area encompasses CARE, which has been a magnet for recreational activities for many years. The park itself is primarily an undeveloped area that receives almost three-quarters of a million visitors each year. Many of these visitors hike established trails or explore the backcountry. Lands adjacent to the park are managed by the U.S.D.A. Forest Service and BLM and offer hiking, camping, off-highway vehicle use, and horseback riding opportunities. Many of the areas that have high recreational use also have rare plant populations within or adjacent to them. Therefore, the whereabouts of rare plants in areas of high use and whether the plants are being affected by human activities is essential information for federal land managers. Four of the federally listed plant species occur in the northern portion of the park and on adjacent BLM lands and are in active cattle grazing allotments. For these four

Table 1. Federally protected plants by agency distribution

Species	Status	Agencies Found On			
		CARE	BLM	DNF	FNF
Cycladenia humilis var. jonesii	Threatened	X	X		
Erigeron maguirei	Threatened	X	X		X
Aliciella cespitosa	Candidate	X	X	X	X
Pediocactus despainii	Endangered	X	X		X
Pediocactus winkleri	Threatened	X	X		
Schoencrambe barnebyi	Endangered	X	X		
Sclerocactus wrightiae	Endangered	X	X		
Spiranthes diluvialis	Threatened	X	X		
Townsendia aprica	Threatened	X	X	X	X

species, it is essential for park and BLM management to know the whereabouts of these plants and whether cattle grazing may affect them.

METHODS

The primary purposes of this study are to (1) conduct intensive surveys for the target species on potential habitat within the study area, (2) determine potential for impacts by visitor, recreational or livestock use if possible, and (3) implement monitoring programs for species most likely to be affected by human impacts.

Prior to each field season, representatives of the participating agencies and the interagency botanist meet to discuss priorities for surveys and monitoring. A list of species and areas to be surveyed is selected for the upcoming field season. The list usually contains several of the target species plus a few sensitive species that an agency needs more information about. When an agency receives funding to conduct rare plant inventories adjacent to, but outside the primary study area they present this information at the annual meeting. These additional survey areas are discussed and if agreed upon by the group, then the team conducts surveys outside the primary study area. This cooperation and flexibility of the group has allowed the team to survey the Tushar Mountains on FNF, outside the primary study area for several endemic species. Findings from these additional surveys are included in this paper. Following this meeting, the interagency botanist compiles all available information and location data on the species selected for the season's fieldwork. This information is entered into Geographic Information System (GIS). It is then overlaid with geologic formations, slope, aspect, and elevation to create a profile of potential habitat by species. In addition to accurately depicting known and potential habitats, this analysis refines the range of the target species and helps resource managers plan how many people will be needed to accomplish the surveys. Depending on funding availability for the upcoming season, one or more seasonal employees are hired to assist the interagency botanist with surveys and monitoring.

After completing this initial work, the interagency rare plant team conducts surveys in potential habitat for the target species. Surveys begin in the early spring at lower elevations and as the season progresses the team moves to higher elevations, thus ensuring proper search times for each species. During the appropriate blooming time for each species, areas are surveyed by walking wandering transects through all accessible areas and/or by using binoculars to search cliffs. If an area contains potential habitat for two or more species and those species bloom at different times, then that area is searched multiple times to ensure surveys are as thorough as possible for each species. All areas surveyed are noted on topographical maps, regardless of whether the target or any sensitive species were found. This information is then entered into GIS so resource managers can quickly see if an area has been surveyed and whether TE&S plants were found.

For each new occurrence of a species, team members complete a modified version of the UNHP Site Visit Account Survey Form, take photographs, and map its location on 7.5' quadrangle maps. Wherever possible, a Global Positioning System (GPS) is used to map the precise location of each new occurrence. All new localities are then entered into a master database and GIS that are shared by the participating agencies. This ensures long-term retrieval capabilities for current and future resource managers.

RESULTS

Surveys have been conducted since 1998 by the interagency botanist, a seasonal team leader hired by CARE, and numerous seasonal team members hired by each of the agencies. If additional people were needed to survey specific areas, CARE, BLM or Forest Service staff assisted on an as needed basis. Surveys typically begin in early April and continue into September. During the last six years, the interagency rare plant team has surveyed and recorded over 650 locations for 32 TE&S plant species. Twenty-three of the sensitive species known to occur in the study area were found and recorded (Table 2).

Because the target species are shared by the agencies and findings benefit the entire group, interagency cooperation in the form of funding, vehicles, and hiring employees from different agencies to all work on the same team has been significant. Additionally, since BLM, FNF and DNF administered lands generally occur at different elevation ranges and have a slightly different suite of sensitive species, this enables the team to efficiently survey on BLM and lower elevation areas in CARE early in the spring, then shift to the Forest Service and higher elevation areas in CARE later in the summer. Often surveys on CARE and BLM are completed by the end of June so if the Forest Service has priority species that occur outside the primary study area, i.e.

Boulder Mountain on DNF for *Potentilla angelliae* and the Tushar Mountains on FNF for a suite of endemic species, the team is able to assist the Forest Service with these additional needs.

To date, the team has surveyed over 70,000 acres of federally managed lands. This includes approximately 29,000 acres on Capitol Reef National Park, 17,000 acres on Bureau of Land Management, 11,000 acres on Dixie National Forest and 13,000 acres on Fishlake National Forest. The effort has resulted in a dramatic increase in number of individual plants known for several species (Table 3).

Calendar years 2000, 2002 and 2003 were difficult periods to survey for plants since they were extremely dry years. Many of the plants targeted for surveys either didn't bloom or if they did bloom it was for a short time period. To compensate for this, the team moved to higher elevations sooner than originally planned and adjusted the list of species to look for those species that came up and bloomed despite the drought.

Habitat modeling information proved very useful in selecting potential habitat to survey. Approximately 90% of areas selected for surveys using elevation and geological formation contained sites with one or more of the target species. In addition to using geology and elevation range for selecting potential habitats, associate plant species lists for each sensitive species location were compiled. This information used in conjunction with geology and elevation assists field surveyors in targeting the best survey locations. Review of all past reports and findings show that aspect and slope were not as critical in the analysis for selecting potential habitat

TABLE 2. Threatened, Endangered and Sensitive plants recorded during this study. Rarity status rankings are those designated following 2002 survey results.

Scientific Name*	Common Name	Rarity/Legal Status
Aliciella cespitosa (*Gilia caespitosa*)	Rabbit Valley Gilia	**Candidate for listing** G2/S2
Aliciella tenuis (*Gilia tenuis*)	Mussentuchit Gilia	G1/S1
Astragalus consobrinus	Bicknell Milkvetch	G2G3/S2S3
Astragalus harrisonii	Harrison's Milkvetch	G2G3/S2S3
Astragalus laccoliticus	Caineville Milkvetch	G2?/S2?
Castilleja parvula var. parvula	Tushar paintbrush	G2/S2
Cirsium eatonii var. harrisonii	Eaton's thistle	G4G5T1Q/S1
Cycladenia humilis var. jonesii	Jones cycladenia	**Threatened** G3G4T2/S2
Cymopterus beckii	Pinnate spring-parsley	G1/S1
Draba sobolifera	Creeping draba	G2/S2
Erigeron abajoensis	Abajo daisy	G1G2/S1S2
Erigeron awapensis	Awapa daisy	G1Q/S1
Erigeron maguirei	Maguire's daisy	**Threatened** G2/S2
Eriogonum corymbosum var. revealianum	Reveal's buckwheat	G5T3/S3
Habenaria zothecina	Alcove bog-orchid	G2/S2
Hymenoxys acaulis var. nana	Cushion golden-flower	G5T1T2/S1S2
Lomatium junceum	Rush lomatium	G3/S3
Opuntia basilaris var. heilii	Heil's beavertail	G5T2T3/S2S3
Pediocactus despainii	San Rafael cactus	**Endangered** G2/S2
Pediocactus winkleri	Winklers cactus	**Threatened** G1/S1
Penstemon cespitosus var. suffruticosus	Tushar penstemon	G5T2/S2
Physaria acutifola var. purpurea	Ryberg's twinpod	G5T2/S2
Potentilla angilliae	Angel's cinquefoil	G1/S1
Salix arizonica	Arizona willow	G2G3/S2
Schoencrambe barnebyi	Barneby plains-mustard	**Endangered** G1/S1
Sclerocactus wrightiae	Wright's fishhook cactus	**Endangered** G2/S2
Senecio castoreus	Beaver Mountain groundsel	G1/S1
Sphaeralcea psoraloides	Psoralea globemallow	G2/S2
Spiranthes diluvialis	Ute's ladies-tresses	**Threatened** G2/S1
Thelesperma windhamii (*T. subnudum var. alpinum*)	Alpine greenthread	G2/S2
Townsendia aprica	Last Chance townsendia	**Threatened** G2/S2
Xylorhiza confertifolia	Henrieville woody-aster	G2G3/S2S3

*Scientific names generally follow Welsh (1993).

TABLE 3. Increase in Number of Plants Known

Scientific Name	Common Name	Number's Known Prior to 1998*	Number's Known by 2003*
Aliciella cespitosa (*Gilia caespitosa*)	Rabbit Valley Gilia	4,700	25,200
Aliciella tenuis (*Gilia tenuis*)	Mussentuchit gilia	1,000	10,600
Cymopterus beckii	Pinnate spring-parsley	2,000	32,000
Erigeron maguirei	Maguire's daisy	5,000	27,000
Hymenoxys acaulis var. nana	Cushion golden-flower	2,000	11,500
Pediocactus winkleri	Winklers cactus	5,000	6,500
Potentilla angelliae	Angel's cinquefoil	2,000	19,000
Schoencrambe barnebyi	Barneby's Reed-mustard	2,000	3,800
Thelesperma windhamii (T. subnudum var. alpinum)	Alpine greenthread	2,000	34,000
Townsendia aprica	Last Chance Townsendia	6,000	21,000

* all numbers are approximate

areas, with one exception. Slope and aspect were found to be essential for selecting potential habitat for *Schoencrambe barnebyi*. Initial surveys for this species focused in the Moenkopi formation with no regard for slope or aspect. After two years of surveying, Barneby's reed-mustard has only been found on steep, north-facing slopes in the Moenkopi formation.

Sufficient data was gathered during the course of this study to pursue delisting of *Erigeron maguirei*, a federally listed Threatened species. The interagency team is currently working with the U. S. Fish and Wildlife Service on a proposal to delist this species. Another significant result of this study is that the rarity status of six other species can be downgraded (Table 4). UNHP is responsible for maintaining the rarity status lists for Utah and is continually reviewing information submitted regarding status changes. Some of the species listed in Table 4 have already been downgraded, as noted in Table 2; others are still under review.

Results from this study have helped determine which of the target species should be monitored to find out if any human activities affect them. The team has initiated and is maintaining monitoring plots for *Pediocactus despainii, P. winkleri, Sclerocactus wrightiae, Townsendia aprica* and *Aliciella cespitosa*. These plots were established both for gathering life history information and determining if human activities or livestock grazing may affect these species.

Since agencies are required to spend time and money managing species that are federally listed or on sensitive species lists, it behooves them to know which species are truly rare and in need of protection. Findings from this study are helping the agencies refine their sensitive species list and focus their limited management dollars on the species most in need. Knowledge gained from this study is invaluable for resource managers making management decisions and ensuring that plants are protected. Another benefit of this agreement is that information gathered during this study enables the participating agencies to meet Congress' intent under the Endangered Species Act and to comply with federal management policies.

Table 4. Proposed status changes for seven TE&S species.

Scientific Name	Common Name	Rarity/Legal Status	Proposed Status Changes
Aliciella cespitosa	Rabbit Valley Gilia	**Candidate** - G1/S1	**Candidate** -G2/S2
Cymopterus beckii	Pinnate spring-parsley	G1/S1	G2G3/S2S3
Erigeron maguirei	Maguire's daisy	**Threatened** -G2/S2	G2G3/S2S3
Hymenoxys acaulis var. *nana*	Cushion golden-flower	G5T1/S1	G5T3/S3
Lomatium junceum	Rush lomatium	G2/S2	G3/S3
Pediocactus winkleri	Winklers cactus	**Threatened** - G1/S1	**Threatened** -G2/S2
Thelesperma windhamii (*T. subnudum var. alpinum*)	Alpine greenthread	G5T1/S1	G5T2/S2

LITERATURE CITED

U.S. Fish and Wildlife Service. 1979. Endangered and Threatened Wildlife and Plants; Ruling to list *Sclerocactus wrightiae* as Endangered under the authority of the Endangered Species Act. October 11 1979. Federal Register. 44 FR 58866-58868

_____ 1985a. Endangered and Threatened Wildlife and Plants; Ruling to list *Townsendia aprica* as Threatened under the authority of the Endangered Species Act. August 21, 1985. Federal Register. 50 FR 33734-33737

_____ 1985b. Endangered and Threatened Wildlife and Plants; Ruling to list *Erigeron maguirei* as Endangered under the authority of the Endangered Species Act. September 5, 1985. Federal Register. 50 FR 36089-36092

_____ 1985c. Endangered and threatened wildlife and plants; review of plant taxa for listing as endangered or threatened species. 27 Sept. 1985. Federal Register 50(188):39526-39584

_____ 1986. Endangered and Threatened Wildlife and Plants; Ruling to list *Cycladenia humilis var. jonesii* as Threatened under the authority of the Endangered Species Act. June 4, 1986. Federal Register. 51 FR 86 16526

_____ 1987. Endangered and Threatened Wildlife and Plants; Ruling to list *Pediocactus despainii* as Endangered under the authority of the Endangered Species Act. September 16, 1987. Federal Register. 52 FR 34914-34917

_____ 1992a. Endangered and Threatened Wildlife and Plants; Ruling to list *Schoencrambe barnebyi* as Endangered under the authority of the Endangered Species Act. January 14, 1992. Federal Register. 57 FR 1398-1403

_____ 1992b. Endangered and Threatened Wildlife and Plants; Ruling to list *Spiranthes diluvialis* as Threatened under the authority of the Endangered Species Act. January 17, 1992. Federal Register. 57 FR 2048-2054

_____ 1996. Endangered and Threatened Wildlife and Plants; Ruling to reclassify and down list *Erigeron maguirei* as Threatened under the authority of the Endangered Species Act. June 19, 1996. Federal Register. 61 FR 31054-31058

_____ 1998. Endangered and Threatened Wildlife and Plants; Ruling to list *Pediocactus winkleri* as Threatened under the authority of the Endangered Species Act. August 20, 1998. Federal Register. 52 FR 34914- 34917

Welsh, S. L. et al. 1993. A Utah Flora, second edition, revised. Brigham Young University Press, Provo, Utah. 986 pp.

Dune Communities of SE Colorado: Patterns of Rarity, Disjunction and Succession

T. Kelso[1]*, N. Bower[2], P. Halteman[1], K. Tenney[2], AND S. Weaver[3]

*Author for correspondence
[1] Dept of Biology, Colorado College, Colorado Springs, CO 80903
[2] Dept of Chemistry, Colorado College, Colorado Springs, CO 80903
[3] Dept of Geology, Colorado College, Colorado Springs, CO 80903

ABSTRACT. Dune communities occur across the western Great Plains and in isolated spots in eastern Colorado. They are biologically important due to their endemic nature, their rapid succession, and their ephemeral abundance in response to climate, grazing practices, and ranchland management. The abundance of these terrestrial islands has changed considerably over scales from tens to thousands of years. The Colorado dune communities have high conservation value due to their unusual biota and diminished presence. They also are of value as sentinel communities for more wide-scale biotic change in surrounding grasslands. These communities have not received detailed documentation of their interactive biotic and geological profiles in recent years. This study provides such a profile for an isolated dune complex in El Paso County, Colorado where we examine their plant species, vegetation patterns, and geochemical characteristics. Dune communities are threatened in part because of ranchland practices that seek to diminish their presence. We identify here areas of mutual interest and potential collaboration between ranchers and biologists that might serve to mitigate conflicts between conservation goals for a unique biota and the practical exigencies of ranchland management in semi-arid grasslands.

INTRODUCTION

Dune "blowouts" occur as craters of unstable sand in dune fields around the globe. Across arid grasslands of southeastern Colorado, New Mexico and the western Great Plains, dune extent has varied over scales that range from thousands of years to less than a decade, responding to patterns of temperature, precipitation and aeolian activity as well as land use practices. Reports from nineteenth century explorers suggest that dunefields were then considerably more extensive than today (Muhs and Holliday, 1995), although expansion occurred during the 1930's and 1950's (McGinnies and others, 1991) due to drought and inappropriate agricultural practices.

Signature vegetation patterns with unique elements of the grasslands flora (Rydberg, 1895; Pool, 1914; Rameley, 1939) occur across blowouts on their slopes, crests, and crater bottoms. Although not species-rich, blowout communities are of conservation concern in Colorado (Colorado Natural Heritage Program, 1999; 2001) due to their infrequency and the habitat endemism of the biota, in which some members are rare. Others exemplify disjunctions in distribution where substantial populations appear only in habitat islands across an intervening matrix of more vegetated grasslands on stabilized soils. From a ranching point of view, however, blowout communities are problematic. They are prone to spreading and thus diminish range already limited in quality and quantity. For decades, ranchers have expended considerable effort to eradicate blowouts with attempts at revegetation and sand control. The prospect of a continuing drought and its related economic stresses have understandably exacerbated these concerns.

As land management practices have aimed at dune minimization conservation interest in these restricted communities has risen (Colorado Natural Heritage Program 2001) for several reasons. In addition to their unique biota, dune communities may be highly sensitive indicators of short and longterm climate change (Muhs and Maat, 1993; Muhs and Holliday, 1995; Muhs and others, 1996; Muhs and others, 1999, Swinehart, 1998). Early studies on plant succession in dune communities of Nebraska (Weaver, 1965, 1968; Weaver and Albertson, 1954) and northern Colorado (Ramaley, 1939) described species-specific phases that reflected interactive aspects of vegetation, climate and soil stabilization. In light of increasing concern about global warming and ecological impacts of climate change on grassland communities, the rapid succession on dune complexes in response to seasonal moisture and wind (McGinnies and others, 1991) suggests the potential to use dunes as sentinel communities for other more subtle changes in surrounding grasslands. Monitoring small-scale community changes could provide an early opportunity to detect wider scale changes and implement management strategies for grassland

systems under climatic and grazing stress.

Our study focused on a dune complex ca 50 km southeast of Colorado Springs Colorado in the Chico Basin region of El Paso County (Fig. 1). We held the following objectives:

- ❏ To document plant community stratification across the Chico Basin dunes and the dominant plant species that represent different stages of succession here.

- ❏ To document the regional dune flora with particular attention to the abundance and ecology of rare species.

- ❏ To provide a detailed topographic profile of the dune complex.

- ❏ To assess differences of soil texture on different dune faces that correlate with vegetation zonation.

- ❏ To provide a botanical and geological baseline for comparison with other dune complexes in southeastern Colorado and long term monitoring.

- ❏ To provide a vegetation-based system of assessment for dune succession to assist local ranchers in understanding the dynamics of local dune communities.

- ❏ To suggest strategies that might balance conservation of dune biota with the management needs of ranchers.

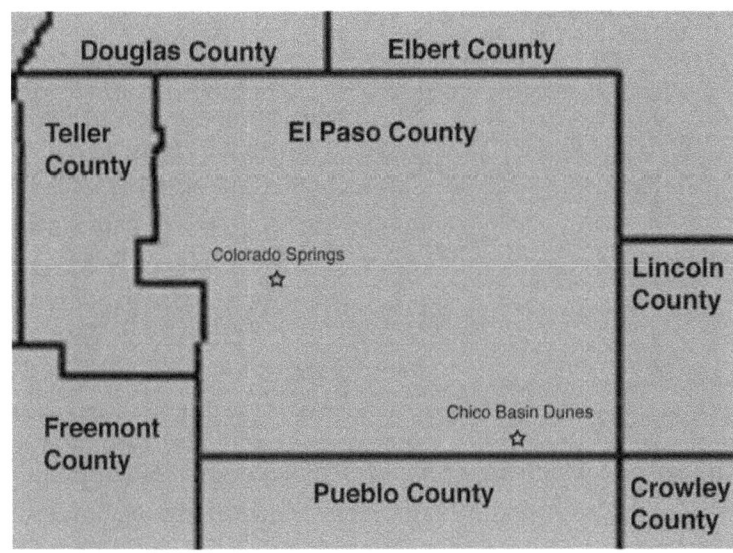

FIGURE 1. Location of Chico Basin dune system in El Paso County.

METHODS

Study Site. The dominant vegetation of the Chico Basin region contains a complex of sand-sage and shortgrass prairies underlain by deep aeolian sands (Natural Resources Conservation Service, 2004). The area has been recognized by the Nature Conservancy as a significant conservation region for southeastern grasslands (The Nature Conservancy, 1998); it contains a number of potential conservation sites with high biotic values for the county (Colorado Natural Heritage Program, 2001) . One of those sites is the dune complex. Given a history of intensive grazing, most of the grasslands have been impacted from their historical composition and the dunes are surrounded by dense stands of sand-sage with a few interspersed native grasses. Current grazing practices implemented over the past four years restrict cattle access to the dunes. The open sand complexes here occur in a three-dune cluster over a regional sand sheet of ca 1000 ha overall; the dunes are isolated from other large complexes in northeastern Colorado by ca 270 km, although a few minor blowouts occur within 20 km.

This dune system consists of three blowout complexes; our primary study site was the largest and most northerly of them, covering about four km2 with several connected parabolic dunes. Open craters occur primarily on the north and northwest faces, the direction of prevailing winds in the winter. Like other parabolic dune systems, these show long trailing edges in the windward direction (Pye and Tsoar, 1990) with dune movement to the south. Aerial photographic records shows progressive dune stabilization and steadily increasing vegetative cover across the regional sand sheet from 1955 to the present; where significant blowouts were numerous across the landscape in the 1950's, the Chico complex is the only one remaining now.

Vegetation Sampling. We visited the site regularly from May to October 2003 for botanical surveys; preliminary surveys had been conducted on other dunes and blowouts in the area in 1999, 2000, and 2001. Vegetation stratification and dominant species across different dune faces were assessed throughout the growing season with voucher specimens deposited in the Colorado College Herbarium (COCO). Overall conditions with respect to rainfall and temperature in 2003 were consistent with 30-year averages after the exceptional drought year of 2002 (Table 1).

41

TABLE 1. Summer temperature and precipitation for Pueblo, CO. Data from www.crh.noaa/gov/pub/climate indicate short and longterm means for the months of June-August

Year	Daily Mean °F	Total Precipitation (inches)
1999	75.3	5.03
2000	74.2	4.88
2001	74.2	5.80
2002	76.5	1.57
2003	75.0	5.21
mean 1971-2000		5.64

Soil Sampling and Topographic Mapping. A baseline profile of the dune using a Trimble GPS unit was conducted in October, 2003 and soil samples corresponding to different dune aspects were collected and plotted at that time. Soil analyses were performed in the laboratory at Colorado College in the winter of 2003-2004. Physical fractionation was achieved with a series of sieves (Tyler #10, 25, 40, 50, 60, 70, 120, 140, and 230). The smallest particle size fraction (<63µ) was subsequently chemically fractionated and analyzed; the results of that analysis will be reported elsewhere. The particle size distributions were analyzed using cluster analysis (Minitab 13, 2000) to produce dendrograms (Fig. 2) and Excel to produce a histogram (Fig. 3) of particle sizes.

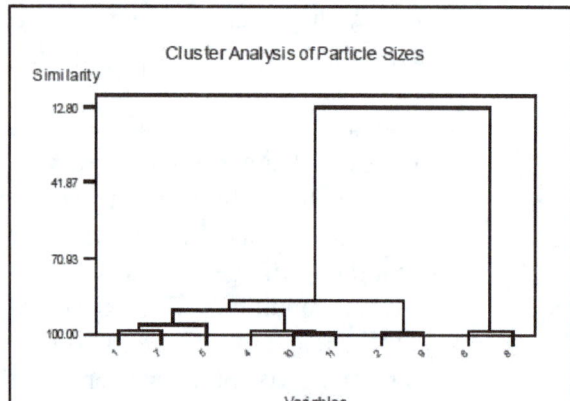

FIGURE 2. Cluster analysis of soil particle sizes for samples taken in the Chico Dunes.

Soils. The results of the soil particle size fractionation are presented in Fig. 3. The samples collected from the most exposed locations (6, 8) were generally on the windward side of the dunes, or in saddles between ridges. These locations are the most barren of vegetation and have the largest mean particle sizes. Samples from the leeward side of the dunes have on average a finer grain size and a more bimodal distribution of grain sizes. These sites (2, 9) exhibit more plant cover than that found on the windward sites. The third group (1, 5, 7) exhibits the greatest plant cover with samples taken from enclosed bowls and leeward sites. The final group of samples (4, 10, 11) is from locations on the south and northeast edge of the complex (4 and 10, respectively) where the underlying plain is not covered by loose sand, and from an extradunal site (11) a few kilometers west. These last sites exhibit the regionally abundant sand-sage and shortgrass cover.

Flora and Vegetation. The Chico Basin dune flora is relatively small. Our survey documented ca 50 species, representing 19 families (Appendix A). Almost half of the flora is composed of habitat specialists of deep open sandy soils; two species (*Chenopodium cycloides* and *Oxybaphus carletonii*) carry conservation tracking status with the Colorado Natural Heritage Program. We identified five vegetation zones representing different slope positions and aspects (Table 2). Dune zonation correlates with wind exposure and the concomitant different degrees of soil stability and textural profiles; they represent different successional stages of dune vegetation, with Zones I, II, and

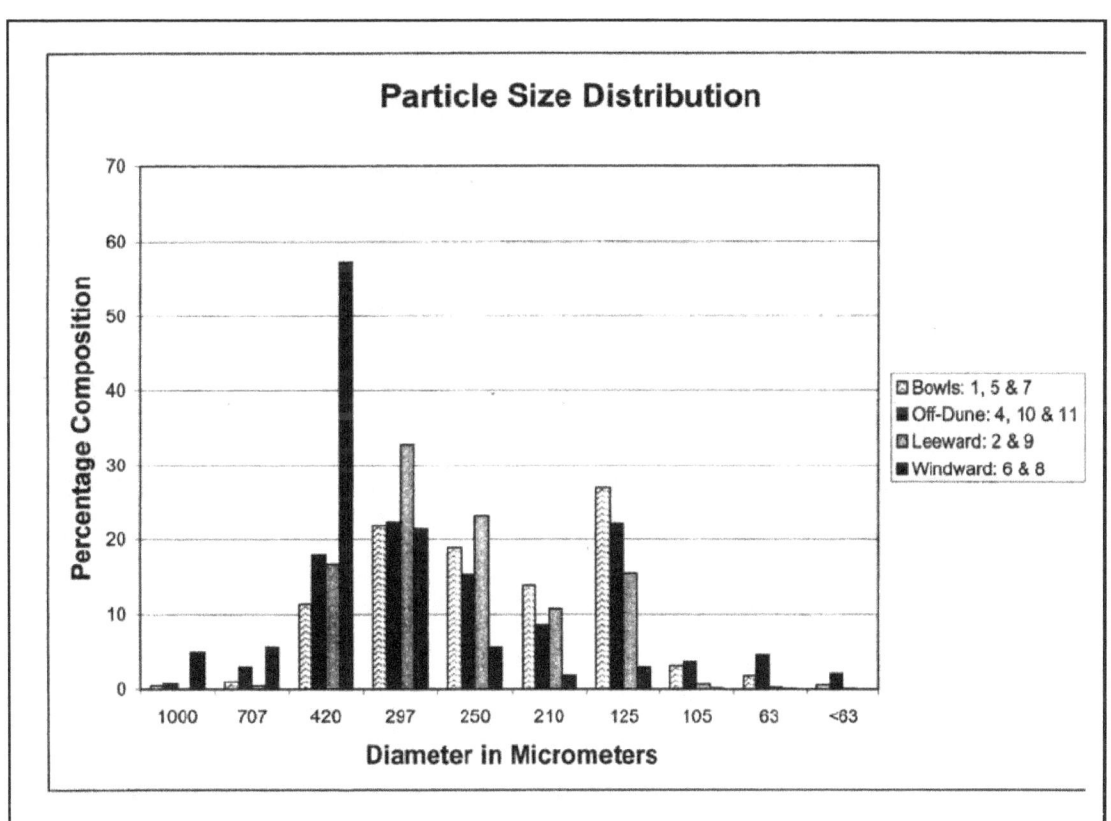

FIGURE 3. Histogram of particle sizes fractions for samples taken from the Chico Basin.

TABLE 2. Vegetation patterns occurring on the Chico Basin Dunes.

Location	Topography/ Cover	Dominant Species	Other Species
I. Dune Crests	Slope: 0 -<5% Cover 40-50%	*Redfieldia flexuosa, Psoralidium lanceolatum Muhlenbergia pungens*	Sporadic annuals
II. Windward Craters	Slope: 18-33% Cover <10%	*Psoralidium lanceolatum, Muhlenbergia pungens*	*Euploca convolvulacea, Palafoxia sphacelata, Helianthus petiolaris*
III. Upper Leeward Slopes	Slope: 0 -10% Cover 50-75%	*Andropogon hallii, Oryzopsis hymenoides, Sporobolus giganteus, Sporobolus cryptandrus*	*Polanisia jamesii, Oenothera latifolia, Cenchrus longispinus, Asclepias arenaria, Ipomopsis longiflora, Helianthus petiolaris*
IV. Interdunal Leeward Swales and Lower Leeward Slopes	Slope: 0- <10% Cover 50-75%	Mixed forbs, graminoids, and suffrutescents	*Corispermum* spp., *Chenopodium* spp., *Nuttalia nuda, Ambrosia* spp., *Helianthus petiolaris, Physalis pumila, Machaeranthera* spp., *Ipomopsis longiflora, Chamaesyce missurica, Oligosporous filifolius, Aristida* spp.
V. Interdunal Windward Swales	Slope: 0- <10% Cover 20-40%	*Psoralidium lanceolatum, Helianthus petiolaris, Corispermum* spp., *Muhlenbergia pungens*	Sporadic annuals; outer crater edges on windward side transitioning into *Oligosporous filifolius –Aristida* spp. community

inner Zone V being in early succession (soil samples 6 & 8), Zones II and IV in intermediate succession (soil samples 1, 2, 5, 7 & 9), and outer Zone V (soil samples 4, 10) in late succession.

DISCUSSION

Dune Flora. Regional differences in climate and the surrounding source floras provide minor floristic differences between these dunes and those documented in the early studies of Ramaley (1939) and Poole (1914). These differences may also reflect the shifts in plant community composition that plains grasslands underwent following the droughts of the 1930's and 1950's (Weaver and Albertson 1954). Since the studies were done, additional decades of intensive grazing impact coupled with periods of drought decreased components of native grasses such as little bluestem (Schizachyrium scoparium) and increased the density of sand-sage (Oligosporous/Artemisia filifolius) shrubland across the plains (Weaver and Albertson 1954). However, with the exception of small differences in composition, the dune vegetation here generally correlates to that seen on other Great Plains dune systems as profiled by Weaver (1965), McGinnies et al. (1991), Ramaley (1939) and Poole (1914).

Vegetation Patterns and Soils. As in other plains dune systems, pioneer stages are dominated by a few rhizomatous species, notably blowout grass (Redfieldia flexuosa), lemon scurfpea (Psoralidium lanceolatum) and sand muhly (Muhlenbergia pungens), followed by intermediate stages where these species drop out and the vegetation is dominated by tall bunchgrasses, tap-rooted perennials and annuals. Later succession brings the incursion of bunchgrasses such as three-awn (Aristida spp.) and sand-sage. On the Chico Basin dunes, early succession occurs in Zones 1, 2 and inner portions of 5 (Table 2). These zones on dune crests and craters have highly unstable soils dominated by the rhizomatous species with a few seasonally abundant annuals. Soils of early successional zones are dominated by larger particle sizes as would be expected where active ablation occurs (Fig. 4, samples 6 & 8, mode at 420 μ). Intermediate successional phases seen in Zones 3 and 4 (leeward slopes and swales) hold the greatest diversity of plant species; these soils have with the greatest percentage of intermediate particle sizes (Fig. 3, samples 1-5, 7, mode at 300 μm). Outer Zone 5 (leeward interdunal swales transitioning into shrub-grassland) is in late successional stage. Soils here are dominated by finer particle sizes (Fig. 3, samples 4, 9-11, mode at 125 μ). Approximately one third of the study site lies in each of the early, middle, and late successional stages.

Much of the dune complex has some plant cover during the growing season. The greatest cover occurs in June when annuals appear and in August-September with late summer moisture initiating a resurgence in flowering, seed head development of grasses, and appearance of late season species typical of dunes. This progression makes estimates of vegetative cover quite variable according to the month of the year. In winter and early spring, the dunes appear to hold much less vegetative cover overall than they do in the growing season; even within this season, apparent cover varies according to the degree to which certain temporally sensitive species are present.

Plant Diversity and Succession. Leeward swales and slopes representing intermediate stages of succession have the highest plant diversity. This diversity correlates with a larger percentage of mid-range soil particle sizes, in comparison to late succession where finer particle sizes dominate the soils and to early succession where larger particle sizes dominate. Wind protection, mid- range of particle sizes and downslope position may contribute to species diversity here by positively influencing soil water availability and substrate stability. This leeward flora includes large populations of *Chenopodium cycloides* (sand goosefoot), a rare dune endemic for Colorado and New Mexico (conservation rating S1 and S2, respectively) and habitat specialists such as sand bluestem (*Andropogon hallii*), sand milkweed (*Asclepias arenaria*) and sand gilia (*Ipomopsis longiflora*). Other examples include wooly indigo bush (*Dalea villosa*), James' clammyweed (*Polanisia jamesii*) and broad-leaved evening primrose (*Oenothera latifolia*). While these do not generally carry ratings for immediate conservation concern, substantial populations are restricted to the occurrence of deep, open dune soils. As dune control has made such habitats increasingly sporadic and diminished in extent, populations of such endemics become restricted in numbers. Here they are abundant throughout the complex but notably lacking in the surrounding communities and regionally uncommon. Although zoological surveys were not part of this study, we consistently observed a diversity of vertebrates and invertebrates. Tiger beetle (*Cicindela*)

species are often associated with dune complexes and at least two species of tiger beetles are already known from the Chico dunes; other may occur here as well (Bleed and Flowerday 1998; Colorado Natural Heritage Program 2001). Some of the dune fauna may be of conservation interest as they are in other dune complexes (Bleed and Flowerday 1998).

Dune Succession and Management. The overall stability of any dune complex can be assessed by the relative amount of each successional zone that occurs; the clarity of these species-specific zones also makes it easy to track annual changes in dune systems. For management purposes, dunes with large areas in early succession are more likely to be expansive than those with more area in intermediate and late stages that indicate stabilizing soils. Expansive dune complexes benefit from grazing control at least in the growing season and/or revegetation with stage-appropriate species such as the rhizomatous species in *Redfieldia*, *Muhlenbergia*, and *Psoralidium*.

Allowing some open dune complexes to persist could be an effective way of providing nearby source material for introduction or reintroduction of stabilizing species in the event of dune reactivation. This could be particularly important after successive drought years that diminish or eliminate soil seed banks and as long distances between open dune fields make seed dispersal more difficult. Nearby blowout complexes, even small ones, may provide a source for seeds or rhizomatous genets. As vegetation of any sort slows sand movements, even annual species may enhance the rate of succession on dune fields and provide ecological benefits. Thus, an argument can be made for allowing small dune complexes to persist at different stages and for grazing restrictions to allow stabilizing species to become established.

Small regional source complexes not only have the potential to enhance cover on problematic complexes, they also provide signals of regional change that may be occurring at a more subtle level. Reversion to earlier successional stages in a small, easily monitored complex, for example, would suggest imminent regional dune reactivation and grazing practices adjusted accordingly. Dune endemic species may be particularly well adapted to living in relatively small colonies and thus maintenance of even small blowout communities promotes persistence of their biota.

CONCLUSIONS

Dune blowout complexes are unique systems that have not received as much biological attention as they might merit, in part because of their arguably problematic nature, and in part because of a flora that can lack visual appeal and is often taxonomically challenging. However, dunes command interest due to their signature flora and fauna, some components of which are rare and many endemic. Plant-animal interactions as well as dune invertebrate diversity and ecology remain poorly known. Dune systems have diminished in recent years due to active eradication programs and these communities are increasingly disparate. They carry the potential to serve as indicators for other regional ecological changes. However, the merits of dune conservation must be balanced with the management concerns that recognize a region under economic and climatic stress. Given that major dune reactivation would pose a significant

threat, concerns about dune stability are fully justified. However, dune conservation is not incompatible with dune control; collaboration between ranchers and biologists can accommodate different objectives. Detailed surveys and monitoring, using dune assessment for strategic management, and viewing at least modest dune complexes for their potential as early warning signals for system dynamics and as revegetation sources may promote collaboration towards the compatible goals of promoting grassland health and stabilizing an intriguing biota as well.

ACKNOWLEDGMENTS

We wish to acknowledge with gratitude the assistance of Duke Phillips in providing us access to the Chico Basin dunes and to other ranchers in eastern El Paso, Pueblo, and Crowley Counties for offering perspectives, insights and the opportunity to explore this landscape. John Valentine of the NRCS provided aerial photography and grassland expertise, and valuable geological information on dune fields of eastern Colorado was provided by Dan Muhs and Rich Madole of the U.S. Geological Survey, and by Paul Myrow of the Colorado College Geology department. Field and laboratory assistance was provided by Jonathan Lowsley, John Putnam, George Maentz, and Scott Reis. Funding was provided by the Carter Fund for Botanical Research at Colorado College and the National Science Foundation through CSIP grants 9352208 and CSI-97500.

Literature Cited

Bleed, A.S. and Flowerday, Editors. 1998. An Atlas of the Sand Hills, 3rd edition.

Colorado Natural Heritage Program, 1999. Conservation Status Handbook, vol. 3 Colorado State University, Fort Colllins, CO. 258 p.

_____, 2001. Survey of Critical Biological Resources, El Paso County, Colorado.

Colorado State University, Fort Colllins, CO. 288 p.

Great Plains Flora Association. 1986. Flora of the Great Plains. University Press of Kansas, Lawrence. 1392 p.

Mcginnies, W.J., Shantz, H.L., and Mcginnies, W.G. 1991. Changes in vegetation and land use in eastern Colorado: a photographic study, 1904-1986. U.S. Dept. of Agriculture, Agricultural Research Service ARS-85. 165 p.

Muhs, D. R. and Holliday, V.T. 1995. Evidence of active dune sand on the Great Plains in the 19th century from accounts of early explorers. Quaternary Research. 43; 198-208.

Muhs, D.R. and Maat, P.B.. 1993. The potential response of eolian sands to greenhouse warming and precipitation reduction on the Great Plains of the U.S.A. Journal of Arid Environments. 25; 351-261.

Muhs, D.R, Stafford, T.W., Cowherd, S.D., Mahan, S.A., Kihl, R., Maat, P.B., Bush, C.A., and Nehring, J. 1996. Origin of the later Quaternary dune fields of northeastern Colorado. Geomorphology. 1l7; 129-149.

Muhs, D.R., Swinehart, J.B., Loope, D.B., Aleinikoff, J.N., and Been, J. 1999. 200,000 years of climate change recorded in eolian sediments of the high plains of eastern Colorado and western Nebraska in D.R., Lageson, A.P. Lester, and B.D.

Trudhill, editors. Colorado and Adjacent Areas: Boulder, Colorado, Geological Society of America Field Guide 1: 71-91.

Natural Resources Conservation Service, 2004. Electronic Field Office Technical Guide, Ecological Site Description RO69XY019CO. www.nrcs.usda.gov/efotg [2004, March 1]

Poole, R.J. 1914. A study of the vegetation of the sandhills of Nebraska. Minnesota Botanical Studies. 4; 189-312.

Pye, K. and Tsoar, H. 1990. Aeolian Sand and Sand Dunes. Unwin Hyman, London. 396 p.

Ramaley, F. 1939. Sand-hill vegetation of northeastern Colorado. Ecological Monographs. 9; 1-51.

Rydberg, P.A. 1895. Flora of the sand hills of Nebraska. U.S. National Herbarium III, 3:133-203.

Swinehart, J.B. 1998, "Windblown Deposits", pp. 43-55 in Bleed, A.S. and Flowerday, Editors. An Atlas of the Sand Hills, 3rd edition. Conservation and Survey Division, Institute of Agriculture and Natural Resources, University of Nebraska, Lincoln. 260 p.

The Nature Conservancy, 1998. Eco-region Based Conservation in the Central Shortgrass Prairie. The Nature Conservancy of Colorado, Boulder, CO. 92 p.

Weaver, J.E. 1954. North American Prairie. University of Nebraska Press, Lincoln, NE. 348 p.

_____. 1965. Native Vegetation of Nebraska. University of Nebraska Press, Lincoln, NE. 185 p.

_____. 1968. Prairie Plants and Their Environment. University of Nebraska Press, Lincoln, NE. 276 p.

_____. and Albertson, F.W. 1956. Grasslands of the Great Plains. Johnson Publishing Co., Lincoln, NE. 394p.

Weber, W.A. and R.C. Wittman. 2001. Colorado Flora: eastern slope. Third Edition. University Press of Colorado.

Appendix A. Plant Species of Chico Basin Ranch: northern sandhills open dune communities.

Nomenclature follows Weber & Wittmann (2001), unless otherwise noted; commonly recognized alternative genera are given in parentheses. Species with an asterisk * are ecological specialists to sandy soils.

Amaranthaceae
Amaranthus arenicola I.M. Johnston*

Asclepiadaceae
Asclepias arenaria Torrey*

Asteraceae
Ambrosia acanthicarpa Hooker
Ambrosia artemisiifolia L.
Ambrosia psilostachya DC
Cirsium undulatum (Nuttall) Sprengel
Erigeron bellidiastrum Nuttall*
Helianthus petiolaris Nuttall
Heterotheca canescens (DC) Shinners
Machaeranthera bigelovii (Gray) Greene
Machaeranthera linearis Greene*
This taxon is delineated by the Great Plains Flora (1986) as a morphologically distinctive member of *Machaeranthera* that is known only from deep sandy soils. Our material fits the description of this taxon with narrow upright rayflowers and single stems; it is easily distinguished from more characteristic *M. bigelovii* that occurs around the dunes.
Oligosporus [*Artemisia*] *filifolius* (Torrey) Poljakov*
Palafoxia sphacelata (Nuttall) Cory*

Boraginaceae
Euploca convolvulacea Nuttall*
Oreocarya [*Cryptantha*] *suffruticosa* (Torrey) Greene

Cactaceae
Opuntia macrorhiza Engelmann

Capparaceae
Polanisia jamesii (Torrey & Gray) Iltis*

Chenopodiaceae
Chenopodium cycloides Nelson*
Chenopodium leptophyllum (Nuttall) Watson
Corispermum americanum (Nuttall) Nuttall*
Corispermum villosum Rydberg*
Cycloloma atriplicifolium (Sprengel) Coulter*

Cyperaceae
Mariscus schweinitzii (Torrey) Koyama*

Euphorbiaceae
Chamaesyce missurica (Rafinesque) Shinners
Croton texensis (Klotsch) Muller-Argoviensis*

Fabaceae
Astragalus ceramicus Sheldon*
Dalea villosa (Nuttall) Sprengel*
[*Lupinus pusillus* Pursh]
This species was not found in the primary dune complex but occurred in small blowout craters in the surrounding 3 km so is included here as part of the dune community flora.
Psoralidium [*Psoralea*] *lanceolatum* (Pursh) Rydberg

Fumariaceae
Corydalis curvisiliqua Englemann

Loasaceae
Nuttallia nuda (Pursh) Greene

Nyctaginaceae
Abronia fragrans Nuttall*
Oxybaphus glaber Watson
[*Oxybaphus carletoni* (Standley) Weatherby]
This species was not found in the primary dune complex but occurred in small blowout craters in the surrounding 3 km so is included here as part of the dune community flora. Taxonomic disagreement occurs as to whether or not this is a recognizable taxon at the species level, but the dune forms in our region are sufficiently distinctive from *O. glaber* that we recognize it as such here.

Onagraceae
Oenothera albicaulis Pursh
Oenothera latifolia (Rydberg) Munz.*

Poaceae
Andropogon hallii Hackel*
*Aristida divaricata** Humboldt & Bonpland
Aristida purpurea Nuttall
Chondrosum [*Bouteloua*] *hirsuta* (Lagasca) Sweet
Calamovilfa longifolia (Hooker) Scribner*
Cenchrus longispinus (Hackel) Fernald*
Muhlenbergia pungens Thurber*
Redfieldia flexuosa (Thurber) Vasey*
Sporobolus giganteus Nash*
Triplasis purpurea (Walter) Chapman*

Polemoniaceae
Ipomopsis longiflora (Torrey) V. Grant*
Polygonaceae
Eriogonum annuum Nuttall*
Eriogonum effusum Nuttall

Santalaceae
Comandra umbellata (L.) Nuttall

Solanaceae
Physalis pumila Nuttall ssp. *hispida* (Waterfall) Hinton*

Geologic Associations of Arizona Willow in the White Mountains, Arizona

Jonathan W. Long and Alvin L. Medina

Rocky Mountain Research Station, U.S. Forest Service
2500 South Pine Knoll Drive, Flagstaff, AZ 86001

ABSTRACT: The Arizona willow (*Salix arizonica* Dorn) is a rare species growing in isolated populations at the margins of the Colorado Plateau. Although its habitat in the White Mountains of Arizona has been mischaracterized as basaltic, the area is actually a complex mixture of felsic, basaltic and epiclastic formations. Comparing the distribution of the Arizona willow to mapped geologic formations revealed that occupied sites are strongly associated with felsic, coarse-textured Mount Baldy formations. The most robust subpopulations are located in three glaciated reaches, but about half occur in exposures of the Sheep Crossing Formation. Other sites occur in areas mapped as Quaternary basalt, but these lie either downstream from Mount Baldy formations or where basalt and porous cinders form a relatively thin mantle over the Mount Baldy formations. Glacial deposits, the Sheep Crossing Formation, and large alluvial deposits have high hydrologic conductivity that may favor the willow. Despite its affinity for the Mount Baldy formations, the Arizona willow is not a strict substrate specialist, since it has survived when transplanted into basaltic areas in Arizona and it grows in different substrates in New Mexico and Utah. Nonetheless, understanding the geologic associations of this rare plant can help to explain its distribution and to design appropriate conservation measures.

INTRODUCTION

Mount Baldy stands out at the second highest mountain in Arizona (3476 m) and as a refuge for rare species. The mountain represents the only known habitat in Arizona and the southernmost habitat overall for the Arizona willow (*Salix arizonica* Dorn). Because geology has tremendous influence over climate, topography, hydrology, and soil chemistry, it is essential to interpreting plant biogeography. However, many ecologists trying to explain the distribution of plants in the White Mountains have discounted or misrepresented the geologic variation of the area. For example, Sivinski and Knight (1996) concluded that substrate specialization was not an important factor governing plant endemism in the Mogollon Province, which extends from New Mexico to the White Mountains, because the area was "almost entirely volcanic in origin." The conservation agreement for the Arizona willow asserted that all but one population of this plant in New Mexico and Arizona occur on "basaltic (volcanic) soils" (AWITT 1995). Similarly, a conservation assessment characterized the habitat of the Mogollon Paintbrush (*Castilleja mogollonica* Pennell), which co-occurs with Arizona willow, as "basalt-derived" (Bainbridge and Warren 1992). Failure to recognize the potential confounding effects of geologic variation can result in faulty inferences concerning the distribution and status of species.

STUDY AREA

Mount Baldy has been studied and mapped by geologists beginning well over a century ago, when G. K. Gilbert described Mount Baldy as "massive eruptions of trachyte," from which, "stretch, in every direction, long slopes of sanidin-dolerite [basalt]" (Gilbert 1875). Gilbert's description of two distinctive lithologies has remained accurate to the present day, yet one of the first regional maps lumped the two types into "Quaternary-Tertiary basalt" (Wilson and Moore 1960). Melton (1961) was the first to describe numerous glacial deposits on Mount Baldy, while Finnell et al. (1967) observed that the volcano was composed of three major groups of volcanic rocks with different compositions. However, Merrill's dissertation (1974) was the first work to map various felsic volcanic, mafic volcanic, and epiclastic formations around the entire mountain.

A variety of volcanic and epiclastic flows created the White Mountains of Arizona. Between 23 to 12 million years ago, volcanic and volcaniclastic eruptions of predominantly andesitic to basaltic-andesitic petrology flowed across a wide area in east-central Arizona (Berry 1976). Atop this surface, felsic lava flows built the Mount Baldy volcano to an elevation of nearly 4000 m (Merrill 1974; Nealey 1989). The Sheep Crossing Formation resulted from volcaniclastic processes that caused colluvium and tuff to accumulate in the valleys at the base of the volcano (Merrill 1974). Starting approximately nine million years ago and continuing into the Quaternary, basaltic flows partially covered the older volcanic deposits (Merrill 1974; Condit 1984).

During the Quaternary Ice Ages, four distinct glacial events sculpted the two major peaks of the volcano, Mount Baldy and Mount Ord (Merrill 1974). The earliest glaciation was the most extensive, shaping five valleys that flowed in directions to the north, west, and east. The glaciers sculpted out U-shaped valleys and deposited small amounts of till on the slopes of the two peaks. Most of the material loosened by the glaciers was transported far away from the mountains where the streams were less steep (Merrill 1974). A very small glacier occurred on Mount Ord within the past 3000 years, while periglacial activity formed talus deposits in northeastern drainages of the Mount Baldy volcano and also shaped south-facing slopes (Merrill 1974).

METHODS

We prepared a composite geology map of the Mount Baldy area based on the maps by Merrill (1974), Wrucke and Hibpshman (1981), Condit (1984), and Nealey (1989). Onto this map, we plotted the reported locations of Arizona willow subpopulation (fig. 1). We identified subpopulations based on groups that occurred on separate drainages, or that occurred on the same drainage but were separated by at least 500 meters of apparently unoccupied habitat. For each subpopulation, we identified the geologic formations at the site. We also determined whether the watershed above the site was derived from felsic Mount Baldy formations or from basaltic formations. To compare the association between the Arizona willow and particular formations, we summed both the number of populations on each type and the estimated total numbers of Arizona willow on each type.

This overlay approach has several limitations. First, while all large stands of Arizona willow have probably been identified, small plants may have been missed. Consequently some subpopulations may not have been identified in small side drainages. Second, recent human impacts such as reservoir construction has altered plant distributions. However, in the dammed drainages where it occurs, the plant is still found above and below the reservoirs. Third, the geologic maps available for the area may be inexact, especially in describing drainage bottoms. Maps sometimes overrepresent younger formations that may

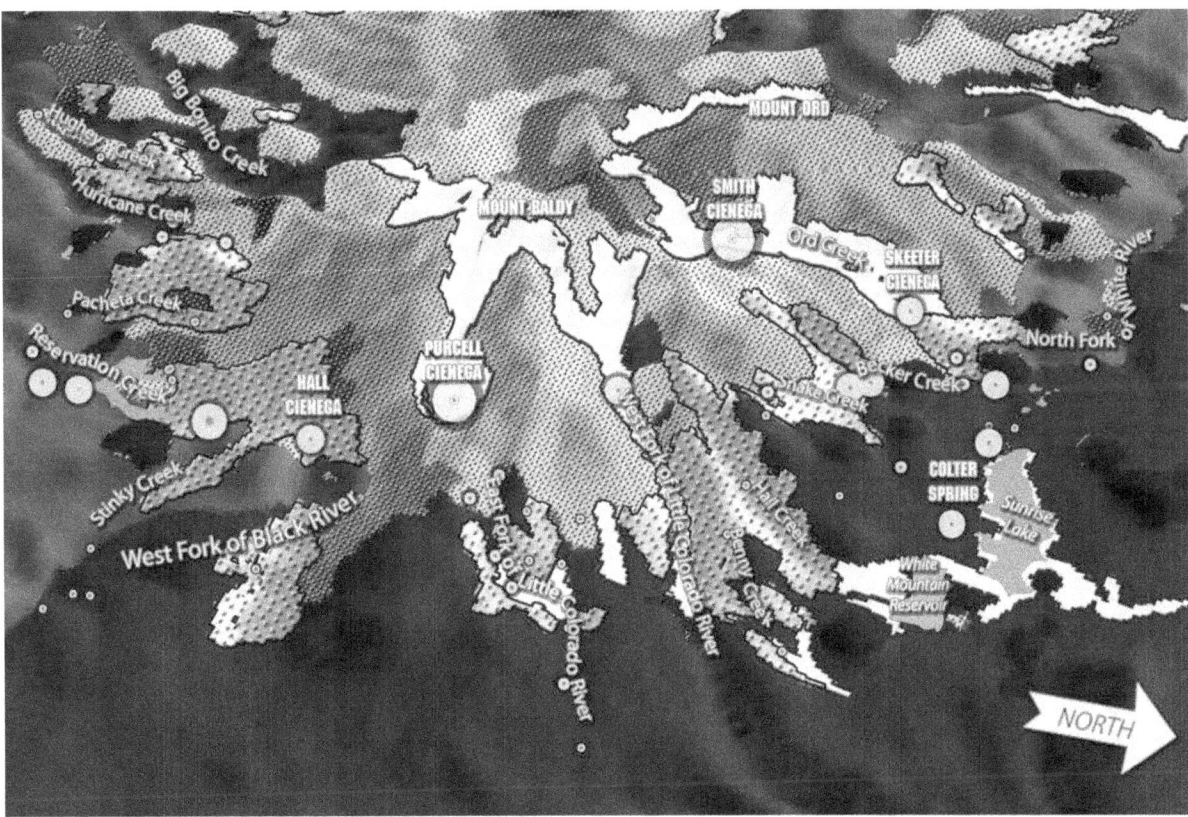

FIGURE 1: Three-dimensional view of geologic formations on the eastern face of Mount Baldy, overlaid by subpopulations of Arizona willow (outlined circles in proportion to estimated size). Fine stippling designates felsic volcanic rocks, coarse stippling designates the Sheep Crossing Formation, white designates glacial and alluvial formations, and dark gray and black designate older and younger basaltic formations, respectively.

have been eroded and replaced with alluvium from older, upstream formations. Despite the limitations of the approach, the results offer valuable insights into relationships between plants and the rocks beneath them.

Enumerating subpopulations of Arizona willow is difficult because individual plants are hard to separate. We used the estimates in the Arizona Willow Conservation Agreement (AWITT 1995) and the White Mountain Apache Tribe's Ecosystem Management plan for Arizona willow habitat (WMAT 1995). Both approaches applied a rule of counting plants separately where their stems were spaced more than 1 meter apart. However, estimated sizes of the largest subpopulations are likely to have large error terms due to the difficulty in counting the prostate form of this clonal

species. The enumerations of both subpopulations and individual plants are used only to demonstrate geologic associations of the plant in relative terms.

RESULTS

Subpopulations occur in a 500 m elevation range, with the highest subpopulation in Smith Cienega (3050 m) and the lowest subpopulation in Hughey Creek (2550 m). Subpopulations are found between 2600 m and 2900 m in all three major watersheds draining Mount Baldy (White River, Black River, and Little Colorado River). Sub-populations occur in drainages that flow north, south, and east, but not in any drainages that flow primarily westward, except for a single plant on a slope above the North Fork of the White River (fig. 1).

The subpopulations are concentrated on landforms derived from the Mount Baldy volcanics (fig. 2), and most of the estimated individuals occur in glaciated reaches (fig. 3). The three largest and densest populations are located in large glaciated meadows (fig. 1 and fig. 3). These populations have been estimated in the hundreds to thousands (AWITT 1995). Large populations also occur in the glaciated valley of the West Fork of the Little Colorado River and in the extensive alluvial deposits along the East Fork of the Little Colorado River.

Nearly half of the populations occur in exposures of the Sheep Crossing Formation (fig. 2), primarily in the upper member of that formation. The Sheep Crossing Formation is texturally indistinguishable from glacial tills in the area, although it was deposited millions of years earlier from debris fans and mudflows from Mount Baldy (Merrill 1974). The only extensive outcrops of the Campground Member that are not associated with the Arizona willow

are all located on the western half of Mount Baldy. Several other populations occur in areas mapped as basaltic, but in valleys downstream from Mount Baldy formations where the felsic substrates naturally deposit. All of these are located within 3.8 kilometers downstream from exposures of the Sheep Crossing Formation.

A few populations occur in areas mapped as basalt and are not downstream of exposures of Mount Baldy formations (fig. 3). These populations occur in the Snake Creek watershed and an adjacent tributary that flows into White Mountain Reservoir. This area has a more complex geology than superficial mapping suggests. The younger basalts, including highly porous cinders, form a relatively thin mantle over the older formations, including the Sheep Crossing Formation, as shown in cross-sections by Merrill (1974). Colter Spring (fig. 1), the location of the holotype specimen of Arizona willow, is a prominent example of one of the many springs in this area.

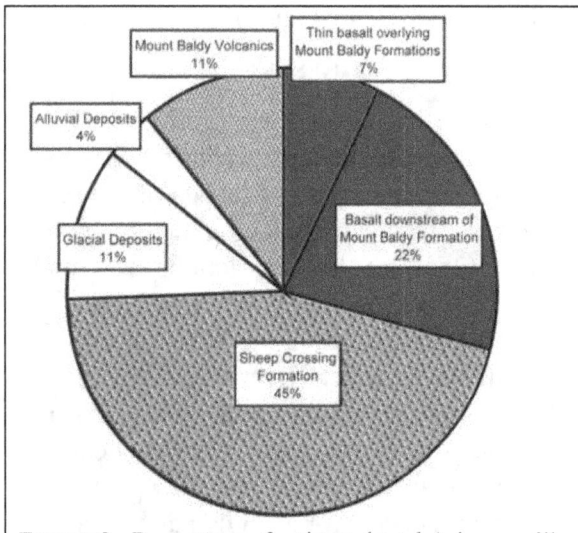

FIGURE 2: Percentage of estimated total Arizona willow subpopulations located on particular geologic formations.

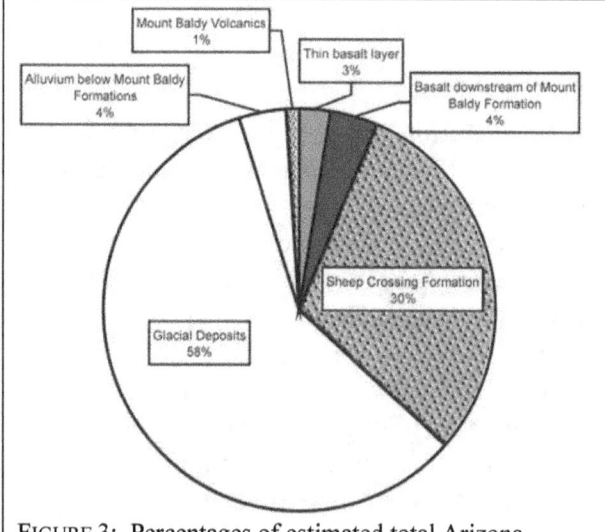

FIGURE 3: Percentages of estimated total Arizona willow individuals located on particular geologic formations

DISCUSSION

Many factors, including elevation, temperature, aspect, soil texture, soil chemistry, and past glaciation, could constrain the distribution of Arizona willow. Due to the evolutionary history of Mount Baldy, most of these factors are inherently correlated and therefore difficult to separate (Long et al. 2003). However, a combination of lithology and topography, or a "lithotopo type" (Montgomery 1999), is largely sufficient to explain the distribution of the species. Specifically, the willow inhabits areas where deposits of felsic Mount Baldy rocks have collected in wide valleys on the lower flanks of the volcano. Climatic regimes may further constrain the downstream and upstream limits of Arizona willow habitat, since there are alluvial deposits further downstream and at least one glacial deposit (Bull Cienega on Ord Creek) that are not inhabited by the plant. However, the distribution is not determined simply by elevation, because streams with spring flows at suitable elevations in basaltic areas have no evidence of Arizona willow, including Soldier Creek to the north, Big Bonito Creek to the Southwest, and Burro Creek to the east.

Influence of Geology on Edaphic Conditions

Differences in geology exert a variety of influences on soils that could account for differences in the suitability of habitat for Arizona willow. However, the most basic difference is soil texture. In Arizona, the substrates occupied by Arizona willow are derived from Mount Baldy formations, which are felsic rocks with greater than 50% silica content (Merrill 1974; Nealey 1989). As such silica-rich volcanics weather, they form relatively deep, acidic soils with low clay content and low organic matter content (Freeman and Dick-Peddie 1970). Riparian meadow soils derived from the Mount Baldy

formations generally have more sand, less clay, less silt, and lower pH than soils derived from basaltic formations (Long et al. 2003). In Utah, all but one of eighteen Arizona willow populations sampled by Mead (1996) had over 30% sand in the uppermost mineral soil horizon (excluding sites that lacked mineral soils due to thick cover of peat). Coarse-textured soils may create more favorable habitat for the Arizona willow by increasing hydrologic conductivity and aeration.

Botanists have noted associations between soil aeration and growth of many willow species. Tall-growing willows of many species are associated with well-aerated mineral soils, while prostrate forms often occur in poorly-drained bogs with abundant fine organic matter (Brinkman 1974). In some cases (e.g., *Salix myrtillifolia* Anderss.), the tall- and low-growing forms of a single willow species have been so distinctive that the two forms were even classified as subspecies (Dorn 1975). For the Arizona willow, taller specimens were observed in microsites where they were sheltered from ungulate grazing (AWITT 1995). However, the occurrence of the prostrate growth form in lightly grazed areas was hypothesized to reflect the influence of finer-textured, less aerobic soils (AWITT 1995). Examining sites in Utah, Mead (1996) concluded that the tallest Arizona willows, and 75% of all stands with an average height greater than 100 cm, grew on Tertiary volcanic parent materials in alluvial flood plains with mineral soils. He also found that peat depth was negatively associated with Arizona willow height. Wetland successional processes such as the accumulation of fine sediments and decomposition of organic matter may reduce gas exchange and stimulate growth of bacteria, both of which promote anaerobic conditions (AWITT 1995).

More complex differences in soil chemistry also could affect the physiology of the willow, yet it demonstrates considerable tolerance. Soil analyses revealed that Arizona willow sites in Utah are highly variable in chemical constituents, none of which seem to be constraining the species (Mead 1996). An isolated subpopulation has persisted at a site with high surface soil pH and low nutrient concentrations on the East Fork of the Sevier River (Mead 1996), demonstrating the species has the capacity to colonize a wide range of coarse substrates. Consequently, substrate preferences of the willow are more likely to be attributable to hydrologic properties than to chemical differences, although it is impracticable to entirely separate these attributes. Furthermore, while most transplants of Arizona willow into purely basaltic areas in the White Mountains apparently died (AWITT 1995), some have survived in Burro Creek (Granfelt 2003). Thus, available evidence suggests that the Arizona willow prefers coarse-textured soils, but it is not a strict substrate specialist.

Topography may reinforce lithology in maintaining favorable hydrologic conditions for Arizona willow. While basalt flows are typically flat, felsic volcanics form steep domes (Stokes 1986). Glaciers, mudflows, and landslides sculpt such steep landforms to form extensive deposits of gravels, sands, and boulders. Rinne (2000) reported that streams draining the Mount Baldy volcano, including glaciated drainages and those below the Sheep Crossing Formation, had higher concentrations of fine gravels than streams in areas of younger basalts. High permeability of the Sheep Crossing Formation relative to the surrounding volcanic formations enables it to serve as a thin aquifer (Merrill 1974), storing and conducting shallow groundwater to seeps and springs at the base of the mountain where the willows congregate. The Arizona willow most likely draws its water from the hyporheic zone rather than from runoff, as has been shown for its cousin and common associate, the serviceberry willow (*Salix monticola* Bebb) (Alstad et al. 1999).

Drainage Connections

Lithology and topography are not sufficient to explain the distribution of the plant, however, because there are extensive exposures of felsic rocks, glacial deposits, and Sheep Crossing Formation on the western slopes of Mount Baldy that are unoccupied. Aspect may partly explain this pattern, since the last major glaciation formed only a small glacier on the west-facing slope (at the head of the East Fork of the White River), while large glaciers occurred in three north- and east-facing drainages. This pattern suggests that north- and east-facing drainages were colder and/or moister. However, Arizona willow occurs in several south-facing drainages (e.g., Hurricane, Hughey, and Pacheta Creeks, fig. 1), indicating that the plant can tolerate warmer, drier aspects. Consequently, topographic barriers and drainage connections may explain why the plant does not occur on the western slopes of Mount Baldy. Subpopulations along Ord Creek are blocked from drainages to the west by the 300 m tall ridge extending from Mount Ord (fig. 1). Similar topographic obstacles may explain the southwestward limit on Arizona willow populations. The next drainage west of Hughey Creek is Big Bonito Creek, whose canyon has incised about 150 meters below the Mount Baldy formations into pre-Mount Baldy volcanic rocks.

We hypothesize that Arizona willow came to the White Mountains via the Little Colorado River, and that low drainage divides and headwater stream transfers facilitated extension to the White and Black River watersheds. The drainage divides between the North Fork of the White River and the Little Colorado River and between the Little Colorado River and the West Fork of the Black River are both very low (<30 m), as are most of the divides between smaller tributaries in that area. Consequently, the eastern flank of Mount Baldy is a relatively gentle landform with shallowly incised streams. The steeper canyons of the North Fork of the White River and Big Bonito Creek may have captured streams on the edge of this plateau after the Arizona willow had become established there. Snake Creek and Becker Creek turn abruptly west to meet the North Fork of the White River, which has incised 150 m over the past 1.5 million years (Condit 1984). Behnke (1979) presumed that headwater transfers were important mechanisms in distributing fish species in the White Mountains.

The Role of Glaciation in Forming Arizona Willow Habitat

Some ecologists have argued that Pleistocene glaciation was a primary factor controlling the distribution of *Salix arizonica* and other willow species in the Southwest (Price et al. 1996). However, alpine conditions such as high elevation, cold temperatures, and increased precipitation not only are associated with past glaciation, but are also intrinsic to the volcanic formations that cap many of the plateaus and peaks of the Southwest. Given this inherent correlation and the limited fossil evidence of pre-glacial conditions, it is difficult to determine the role of glaciation in distributing the modern flora. Glaciation directly affected only five drainages in the White Mountains (Merrill 1974), and Arizona willow occurs in only three of the five. However, the climatic effects of glacial

periods are evident well beyond these drainages. During the last glacial maximum, which ended about 14,000 years ago, temperatures were at least 5° C lower, precipitation may have been 20 to 25% higher, and tree-line was at least 800 m lower (Merrill 1974). Conditions were even colder during the previous two glacial periods (Merrill 1974). Consequently, almost all of the present habitat occupied by Arizona willow would have been above tree-line during the three major glacial episodes.

The environmental conditions associated with glaciation interacted with the pre-glacial landscape to produce the habitats presently occupied by the willow. For many willow species, factors that promote early seral conditions such as an open canopy and mineral soils may provide the best opportunity for seedling establishment. Consequently, the retreat of glaciers would have created optimal habitat for the Arizona willow within the occupied drainages, while periglacial activity such as frost action and rock glaciers formed talus piles in other drainages, notably Becker Creek (Merrill 1974). Heavy snows and rock slides rejuvenate willow shrubs and promote a more stable age structure of ramets (Price et al. 1996). Extensive reworking of these glacial and proglacial deposits would have created good habitat for willow colonization, as demonstrated by the strong correlations between willow pollen and influxes of sediment in Holocene records of willows reported from the San Juan Mountains of Colorado (Andrews et al. 1975).

Implications for Sustainability of Arizona willow subpopulations

In the White Mountains, Arizona willow is presently well-distributed throughout the glacial tills and exposed Sheep Crossing Formation except on the western slopes of Mount Baldy and Mount Ord. The distribution does not suggest that Arizona willow habitat has been eliminated from a broader area that includes purely basaltic drainages, as some other researchers have suggested (AWITT 1995). Researchers have reported death of individual plants and extirpation of small populations following severe infections of a fungus (*Melamspora epitea*) (AWITT 1995). Differences in habitat quality associated with geologic variation may influence the vulnerability of particular subpopulations. The White Mountains have experienced significant warming and drying in the past decade, resulting in severe defoliation of spruce trees in high-elevation forests (Lynch 2004). This period coincides with the reports of deteriorating Arizona willow habitat. Lower elevation subpopulations more commonly assume the tall growth form, which is associated with lower water tables (AWITT 1995; Mead 1996). Consequently, subpopulations that occur at lower elevations in basaltic areas may more vulnerable to drought, disease, insects, and ungulate impacts due to naturally warmer and drier conditions. The glacial deposits that harbor the largest subpopulations of Arizona willow are colder and wetter. These subpopulations are mostly in the prostrate form, similar to low-growing willow species that are accustomed to alpine environments. Because they occur at higher elevations, these populations may be better buffered from the impacts of warming.

Other ecologists have observed that extensive coarse-textured alluvial and colluvial deposits may have special biological significance because they maintain extensive hyporheic exchange zones (Jensen and Goodman 2001). This association may help to understand the distribution of the Arizona willow and the Mogollon paintbrush. However,

consideration of other rare plants in the White Mountains demonstrates that rare plant-geology associations are often individualistic. For example, the Bebb willow (*Salix bebbiana* Sarg.) is most commonly found in basaltic meadows (Long et al. 2003), and it overlaps with Arizona willow only at the lower edge of the latter's range (Granfelt 2004). While the conservation agreement for the Arizona willow (AWITT 1995) states that the willow "occurs in the same ecosystem" as the endemic Mogollon clover (*Trifolium neurophyllum* Greene), others have observed the clover only in association with basaltic soils (Ladyman 1996). On the other hand, the Mogollon clover's close relative, the pygmy clover (*Trifolium longipes* Nutt. var. *pygmaeum* (Gray) J. Gillett), does co-occur with Arizona willow in both Arizona (JWL, personal observation) and in Utah (Mead 1996). Gillet (1969) suggested that because the two closely related clovers are both found in the White Mountains, they would be likely to hybridize. However, geologic segregation might reduce the potential for interbreeding.

The Arizona willow's association with epiclastic formations on the flanks of Mount Baldy has important implications for conservation of the species. Monitoring of the species' status should distinguish between subpopulations in marginal habitats at low elevations in basaltic areas and subpopulations in the preferred lithotopo type. Low elevation populations will probably continue to suffer under a warmer, drier climate, while the glaciated meadows will serve as refugia for this ancient species. Efforts to stimulate reproduction or expand populations of this plant will be more likely to succeed in areas with sandy-gravelly substrates and abundant groundwater supplies. Efforts to conserve the biodiversity of the White Mountains and other high-elevation landscapes of the Southwest should consider fine-scale geology variation on the distribution and demographics of rare species.

LITERATURE CITED

Alstad, K. P.; J.M.Welk, S.A.Williams; and M.J.Trlica. 1999. Carbon and water relations of *Salix monticola* in response to winter browsing and changes in surface water hydrology: an isotopic study using delta 13C and delta 18O. Oecologia 120: 375-385.

Andrews, J. T., P. E. Carrara, F. B. King, and R. Stuckenrath. 1975. Holocene environmental changes in the alpine zones, Northern San Juan Mountains, Colorado, evidence from bog stratigraphy and palynology. Quaternary Research 5: 173-197.

AWITT (Arizona Willow Interagency Technical Team) 1995. Arizona willow conservation agreement and strategy.Ogden, UT: US Forest Service, Intermountain Region, Ogden, Utah; US Forest Service, Southwest Region, Albuquerque, NM; National Park Service, Rocky Mountain Region, Denver, CO; USFWS, Mountain-Prairie Region, Salt Lake City, UT; USFWS, SW Region, Albuquerque, NM.

Bainbridge, S. J. and P.L. Warren. 1992. Status report, April revision: *Castilleja mogollonica* (Mogollon paintbrush).: U. S. Fish and Wildlife Service Ecological Services.

Behnke, R. J. 1979. Monograph of the native trouts of the genus Salmo of Western North America. U.S. Forest Service Rocky Mountain Region, U.S. Dept. of Agriculture, Denver: 163 p.

Berry, R. C. 1976. Mid-Tertiary volcanic history and petrology of the White Mountain volcanic province, southeastern Arizona. Princeton University. Ph.D. dissertation.

Brinkman, K. A. 1974. *Salix* L. willow. In C. S. Schopmeyer editor. Seeds of woody plants in the United States. Washington, DC: U.S. Department of Agriculture, Forest Service: 746-750.

Condit, C. D. 1984. The geology of the western part of the Springerville volcanic field, east-central Arizona. University of New Mexico. Ph. D. dissertation.

Dorn, R.D. 1975. A systematic study of *Salix* section *Cordatae* in North America. Canadian Journal of Botany 53: 1491-1522.

Finnell, T.L., C.G. Bowles, and J.H. Soulé. 1967. Mineral resources of the Mount Baldy Primitive Area, Arizona. Bulletin 1230-H. Washington, DC: U. S. Geological Survey.

Freeman, C.E. and W.A. Dick-Peddie. 1970. Woody riparian vegetation in the Black and Sacramento Mountain Ranges, Southern New Mexico. The Southwestern Naturalist 15: 145-164.

Gilbert, G. K. 1875. Report on the geology of portions of New Mexico and Arizona. U.S.Geographical and Geological Surveys West of the 100th Meridian (Wheeler) 3: 503-567.

Gillett, J. M. 1969. Taxonomy of Trifolium (Leguminosae) II: The *T. longipes* complex in North America. Canadian Journal of Botany 47: 93-113.

Granfelt, C. 2003. [Phone conservation with J. W. Long]. 11-12-2003.

_____ 2004. [Phone conservation with J. W. Long]. 4-19-2004.

Jensen, M. E. and I. A. Goodman. 2001. Effectiveness of direct and indirect biophysical criteria in the hierarchical classification of drainage basins. Journal of the American Water Resources Association 37: 1155-1167.

Ladyman, J. 1996. Distribution and biology of *Trifolium longipes* subsp. *neurophyllum* (Greene). In Maschinski, J.; H. D. Hammond; and L. Holter (eds.) Southwestern rare and endangered plants, second conference: proceedings; 9-11-1995; Flagstaff, AZ: 262-269

Long, J. W., A. Tecle, and B. M. Burnette. 2003. Geologic influences on recovery of riparian wetlands on the White Mountain Apache Reservation. Journal of the Arizona-Nevada Academy of Science 35(2): 45-59.

Lynch, A. M. 2004. Fate and characteristics of *Picea* damaged by *Elatobium abietinum* (Walker) (Homoptera: Aphididae) in the White Mountains of Arizona. Western North American Naturalist 64(1): 7-17.

Mead, L. L. 1996. Habitat characteristics of Arizona willow in Southwestern Utah.Provo, UT: Brigham Young University. Unpublished master's thesis.

Melton, M.A. 1961. Multiple Pleistocene glaciation of the White Mountains, Apache County, Arizona. Bulletin of the Geological Society of America, 72:1279-1282.

Merrill, R. K. 1974. The late Cenozoic geology of the White Mountains, Apache County, Arizona.Tempe, AZ: Arizona State University. Ph.D. dissertation.

Montgomery, D. R. 1999. Process domains and the river continuum. Journal of the American Water Resources Association 35(2): 397-410.

Nealey, L. D. 1989. Geology and petrology of the Late Cenozoic Mount Baldy trachytic volcanic complex, White Mountains volcanic field, Apache and Navajo Counties, Arizona.Albuquerque, NM: University of New Mexico. Ph.D. dissertation.

Price, P. W., T. G. Carr; and A. M. Ormond. 1996. Consequences of land management practices on willows and higher trophic levels. In Maschinski, J., H. D. Hammond, and L. Holter (eds.) Southwestern rare and endangered plants, second conference: proceedings; 9-11-1995; Flagstaff, AZ: 219-223

Rinne, J. N. 2000. Effects of substrate composition on Apache trout fry emergence. Journal of Freshwater Ecology 16(3): 355-365.

Sivinski, R. and P. Knight. 1996. Narrow endemism in the New Mexico Flora. In Maschinski, J., H. D. Hammond, and L. Holter (eds.) Southwestern rare and endangered plants, second conference: proceedings; 9-11-1995; Flagstaff, AZ: 286-296

Stokes, W.L. 1986. Geology of Utah. Salt Lake City, UT: Utah Museum of Natural History, University of Utah and Utah Geological and Mineral Survey Department of Natural Resources. 280 p.

Wilson, E.D. and R.T. Moore,. 1960. Geologic map of Navajo and Apache Counties, Arizona. Tucson: Arizona Bureau of Mines, map.

WMAT (White Mountain Apache Tribe) 1995. Arizona willow management plan: An interim approach to high-elevation riparian and cienega ecosystem management on the Fort Apache Indian Reservation.Whiteriver, AZ: White Mountain Apache Tribe Game and Fish Department.

Wrucke, C.T. and M.H. Hibpshman. 1981. Status of mineral resource information for the Fort Apache Indian Reservation, Arizona. Administrative Report BIA-77. US Geological Survey and US Bureau of Mines.

Relationships Between Rare Plants of the White Mountains and the Late Cenozoic Geology of the Colorado Plateau

Jonathan W. Long

Rocky Mountain Research Station, U.S. Forest Service
2500 South Pine Knoll Drive, Flagstaff, AZ 86001

ABSTRACT. A complex geologic history has shaped the distribution of Arizona willow (*Salix arizonica* Dorn) and the Mogollon paintbrush (*Castilleja mogollonica* Pennell). These subalpine plants do not appear to be strict substrate specialists, but they do seem to favor coarse-textured and well-watered soils. Most of their occupied habitats were shaped by Quaternary glaciations, but are ultimately derived from felsic substrates formed before the Pliocene period. Populations of Arizona willow have been identified in the White Mountains of Arizona, the High Plateaus of Utah, and in the Southern Rocky Mountains of New Mexico and Colorado. Species closely related to the Mogollon paintbrush also occur in the Utah plateaus and the Southern Rocky Mountains. Genetic dissimilarity among these populations suggest that these taxa likely share an evolutionary history that extends into the Neogene, when tributaries of the ancestral Colorado River connected young volcanic highlands on the margins of the Colorado Plateau. This history points to the likelihood of additional populations of Arizona willow in the San Juan Mountains, and it suggests that these plants have survived dramatic changes in their environments. These patterns demonstrate the value of analyzing geology at a detailed level when interpreting habitat preferences and distributions of rare species.

INTRODUCTION

A few species are endemic to only the White Mountains of Arizona, but the list has grown shorter in recent years. The Arizona willow (*Salix arizonica* Dorn) was thought to be a member of this select group until Robert Dorn reidentified a specimen in the Rocky Mountain Herbarium that had been collected in 1913 from southern Utah. This realization led to the recognition of Arizona willow populations in southern Utah, northern New Mexico, and southern Colorado (Thompson et al. 2003). The scattered populations in these four states represent the known distribution for the species (Fig. 1).

The Mogollon paintbrush (*Castilleja mogollonica* Pennell) is another rare plant that is endemic to the White Mountains of Arizona, but whose status as a separate species has been questioned. Pennell first described this yellow-bracted paintbrush as a separate species (Pennell 1951). Holmgren (1973) placed it in the Septentrionales group, which includes the yellow-bracted sulphur Indian paintbrush (*C. sulphurea* Rydb.) as well as several endemic species of the Southwest (Fig. 2). National plant databases (the USDA's PLANTS National Database and the University of North Carolina's Biota of North America Program) currently hold that *C. mogollonica* is a synonym for *C. sulphurea*, which is

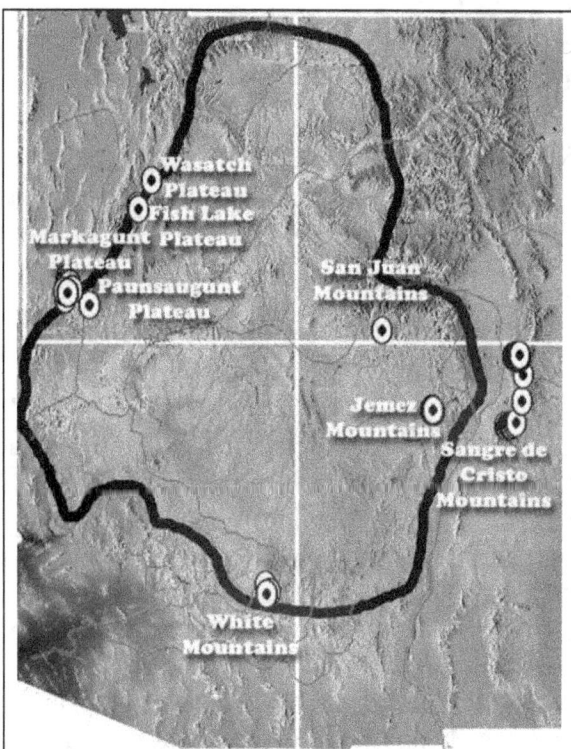

FIGURE 1: Distribution of Arizona willow in the Colorado Plateau region.

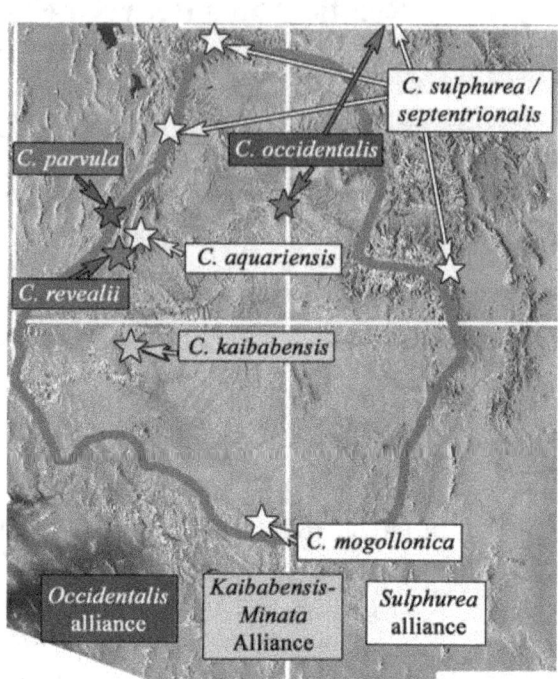

FIGURE 2: Distribution of members of the Septentrionales group of *Castilleja* in the Colorado Plateau region based on Holmgen (1973).

distributed widely in the Rocky Mountains. However, a taxonomist currently working with the genus holds that *C. mogollonica* is a valid species, and instead *C. sulphurea* should be synonymous with *C. septentrionalis* (Lindl.) (Egger 2004).

With the exception of retaining *C. mogollonica*, plant nomenclature used throughout this paper conforms to the PLANTS database (http://plants.usda.gov).

Some biologists have even questioned the status of the flagbearer of rare species in the White Mountains, the Apache trout. Some taxonomists contend that this trout should be designated merely as a subspecies (i.e., *Oncorhynchus gilae* ssp. *apache*) (Behnke 2002). These trends reflect in part the vicissitudes of taxonomy. However, they also may reveal a growing recognition that the White Mountains have not been entirely

isolated from other high mountain ranges during the time in which new species have evolved.

SIGNIFICANCE OF GEOLOGY TO PLANT DISTRIBUTIONS

Reconstructing the geologic evolution of landscapes helps to explain the distributions of endemic species. Geology not only explains the past conditions an organism has withstood, but it also regulates present aspects of habitat including climate (through orographic effects), hydrology, and soil chemistry. However, many ecologists studying rare biota in the White Mountains of Arizona have either ignored geologic variation or oversimplified it. For example, in discussing the biogeography of the endemic Mogollon paintbrush, Bainbridge and Warren (1992) described the region as "basaltic." Similarly, the conservation agreement for the Arizona willow asserted that all but one population of the plant occur on "basaltic (volcanic) soils" (AWITT 1995). These statements are incorrect, and they mislead readers to assume that the White Mountains are monolithic.

The geologic formations underlying populations of Arizona willow and Mogollon paintbrush in Arizona originated from felsic Tertiary volcanism, which formed several other montane regions in the Southwest. Some researchers have considered the importance of variation among these volcanic landforms as well as the influence of glaciation in evaluating the habitat of rare species in the White Mountains. Ladyman (1996) reported that the endemic Mogollon Clover (*Trifolium neurophyllum* Greene) appeared "to be positively associated with basalt soils and negatively associated with datil soils" [Datil Group volcanics are predominantly felsic pyroclastic rocks containing pumice and ash located east of Mount Baldy in New Mexico (McIntosh and Chamberlin 1994)]. Other researchers have argued that Pleistocene glaciation had been a primary factor controlling the distribution of Arizona willow and other willow species (Price et al. 1996). Rinne (2000) hypothesized that both mineral composition and glacial history could account for reported differences in trout productivity between streams derived from rocks close to the Mount Baldy volcano and those farther away.

Geologic Associations of Arizona Willow

White Mountains, Arizona

A complex series of volcanic flows created the White Mountains, but the central massif of Mount Baldy was formed from felsic volcanic flows during the late Miocene period (Merrill 1974). Mudflows and lahars down the young volcano created extensive deposits of colluvium that are known as the Sheep Crossing Formation (Merrill 1974). During the Quaternary, four distinct glacial events sculpted the two highest remnant peaks of the volcano, Mount Baldy and Mount Ord. The earliest glaciation carved out five U-shaped valleys that flowed to the west, north, and east (Merrill 1974). Within the past 3000 years, a very small glacier occurred on Mount Ord, while periglacial activity formed talus deposits in northeastern drainages of the Mount Baldy volcano and also shaped some of its south-facing slopes (Merrill 1974).

Populations of Arizona willow in Arizona are concentrated on landforms derived from the felsic Mount Baldy volcanics (Long and Medina, this proceedings, Geologic Associations of the Arizona Willow in the White Mountains, Arizona). The four populations on glacial deposits are the largest and highest density populations in Arizona, with estimated populations in the hundreds or thousands (AWITT 1995). Nearly half of the subpopulations are located on sites mapped as the Sheep Crossing Formation, which is a sedimentary formation also derived from Mount Baldy volcanics. Most of the remaining populations occur within four kilometers downstream of outcrops of this formation. The Sheep Crossing Formation is texturally indistinguishable from glacial tills in the area, although it was deposited millions of years earlier from debris fans and mudflows from Mount Baldy (Merrill 1974). Comparisons of plant densities to substrates show that alluvium, glacial

61

deposits, and Sheep Crossing Formation represent the prime habitat for Arizona willow in the White Mountains. Small populations occur on surfaces mapped as basaltic flows, although these deposits may be thin enough that underlying felsic formations yield water and substrates to the inhabited areas.

High Plateaus, Utah

The Utah populations occur in the High Plateaus region (Fig. 1) which is capped by andesitic and dacitic Tertiary volcanics of the Marysvale volcanic field as well as some younger basaltic flows (Stokes 1986; Luedke 1993; Rowley et al. 1994). Thus, the petrology and age of the High Plateaus of Utah are similar to the White Mountains volcanic field of Arizona. The populations of Arizona willow in Utah are scattered across the plateaus, with the greatest concentration on the Markagunt Plateau around Brian Head, a geologic cousin of Mount Baldy. Several drainages on the eastern side of this peak were glaciated. Nearly 100 kilometers to the northeast lie two populations in glacial deposits along Seven Mile Creek on the Fish Lake Plateau, which is also derived from Tertiary volcanics (Mead 1996). Those Tertiary lava flows once connected the Fish Lake and Markagunt Plateaus, although drainages have since cut down between them.

An isolated population has been reported from the Wasatch Plateau, representing the currently known northern limit for the species. Another small population occurs on the East Fork of the Sevier River on the Paunsaugunt Plateau where Tertiary volcanics have been eroded away. This population lies in Quaternary alluvium derived from Wasatch limestone and Kaiparowits Formation (Doelling et al. 1989), and it appears to be the only one in Utah occurring in a watershed devoid of Tertiary volcanics. However, at least six other populations have diverse substrates in their watersheds, leading Mead (1996) to characterize them as being derived in part from sedimentary formations.

Southern Rocky Mountains, New Mexico and Colorado

In northern New Mexico, the Arizona willow occurs in at least 21 populations in the Sangre de Cristo Mountains and four populations in the Jemez Mountains (Atwood 1996; Atwood 1997; Dorn 1997). The rocks underlying these areas are more varied and much older than those in the White Mountains of Arizona or the High Plateaus of Utah due to the tremendous uplift of the Rocky Mountains. Substrates for Arizona willow habitat appear to become more diverse in these taller mountains. In the Sangre de Cristo Mountains, eight populations in the Pecos drainage are found on areas that have been mapped as Pennsylvanian undifferentiated sedimentary deposits (Miller et al. 1963). Thirteen populations near the northern border of New Mexico coincide with a jumble of upper Oligocene volcanic rocks and glacial deposits (Green and Jones 1997). Populations in the San Pedro Parks of the Jemez Mountains are underlain by lower Proterozoic plutonic rocks (Green and Jones 1997). A recently discovered population in the southern San Juan Mountains of Colorado (Colorado Natural Heritage Program 2001) is located on Oligocene silicic volcanics (Steven 1975) that were sculpted by glaciers during the Quaternary.

GEOLOGIC ASSOCIATIONS OF MOGOLLON PAINTBRUSH AND RELATED SEPTENTRIONALES

Stream reaches harboring Mogollon paintbrush were reported by Bainbridge and Warren (1992) and Carl-Eric Granfelt (unpublished data). Approximately 12 populations of Mogollon paintbrush found in the White Mountains occur on surfaces derived from Mount Baldy volcanics and four more are within five kilometers downstream of such outcrops. Four more populations occur on areas mapped as younger basalts in drainages of Snake Creek that do not flow downstream from Tertiary volcanics. However, the basalt layers in this area are thin and contain porous cinder deposits. Consequently, there are likely to be subsurface hydrologic connections to the slopes of Mount Baldy.

Mogollon paintbrush occurs at approximately 15 sites with Arizona willow, with five more sites occurring within three kilometers of Arizona willow populations. This association suggests that habitat for the two species are quite similar, although the paintbrush typically occurs in drier portions of meadows. However, the paintbrush has been observed only in north or northeast-trending drainages in areas that were above tree-line during the last glacial maximum (Merrill 1974).

Although *C. mogollonica* appears to be a distinct species, it has several relatives in the Septentrionales group that occur in the Intermountain and Southern Rocky Mountain regions (Fig. 2). *Castilleja aquariensis* N. Holmgren is a related species that grows in subalpine sagebrush meadows on the Aquarius Plateau. Other paintbrushes isolated in southern Utah include *C. revealii* N. Holmgren on the Paunsaugunt Plateau, *C. kaibabensis* N. Holmgren on the Kaibab Plateau, *C.*

parvula Rydb. on the Tushar Plateau, and *C. occidentalis* Torr. in the La Sal mountains. The closest relative to both *C. aquariensis* and *C. mogollonica* appears to be the yellow-bracted *C. sulphurea*, which grows throughout the Rocky Mountains from Alberta to southern New Mexico (Holmgren 1973). These three species form a group intermediate in morphology between the "occidentalis alliance," which includes *C. revealii* and *C. parvula*, and an alliance of *C. kaibabensis* and *C. miniata* (Dougl. ex Hook.) (Holmgren 1973).

GEOLOGIC FACTORS GOVERNING THE DISTRIBUTION OF ARIZONA WILLOW AND MOGOLLON PAINTBRUSH

Many interrelated factors may constrain habitat for the Arizona willow and Mogollon paintbrush. Factors such as high elevation, cold temperatures, and increased precipitation are associated not only with glaciers, but also with the volcanic formations that cap most of the plateaus and mountain peaks of the Southwest. These correlations and the limited fossil evidence of pre-glacial conditions complicate attempts to infer the role of glaciation in distributing the modern flora. The effects of glaciation appear to have interacted with the composition of underlying formations to produce the habitats presently occupied by these plants.

Glaciation

Glaciation unquestionably had dramatic effects on the habitat currently occupied by Arizona willow in Arizona, since most of that area would have been above treeline during the three major glaciations (Merrill 1974). The cooler and moister climate during the Pliocene-Pleistocene glacial periods would have created more favorable conditions at low elevations, while proglacial erosion would have deposited favorable substrates far downstream in the three major glaciated river valleys where Arizona willow occurs (Black River, White River, and Little Colorado River).

Periglacial activity also shaped non-glaciated drainages, including Becker Creek, which has prominent talus deposits (Merrill 1974). Becker Creek also has some of the densest populations of Arizona willow and Mogollon paintbrush in Arizona. Price et al. (1996) noted that heavy snows and rock slides help to rejuvenate willow stands. These responses suggest that periglacial activity could stimulate expansion of willow populations.

In Utah, glaciation affected many of the locations harboring Arizona willow. Mead (1996) classified seven sites, including the largest and healthiest stands, as being partially derived from glaciated materials. Two of them, Sidney Valley and Castle Valley, have extensive accumulations of glacial till (Gregory 1950). The Fish Lake and Wasatch plateaus, where isolated populations of Arizona willow occur, were also glaciated (Stokes 1986). The Paunsaugunt Plateau, a third area harboring Arizona willow, was not glaciated, although many slopes show effects of nivation in past and present (Gregory 1950). Moreover, deposits of Quaternary unconsolidated debris are found at the top of the drainage where the Arizona willow occurs (Doelling et al. 1989). Frost action has fractured lava rocks on Brian Head and sandstone blocks on the Markagunt Plateau, forming talus piles at the base of slopes that supply substrates to the alluvial systems (Gregory 1950).

All populations in New Mexico and Colorado are found well above 3000 m in areas that were shaped by glaciers throughout much of the Plio-Pleistocene. Frost action has greatly affected these high altitude areas, since the southern part of the Sangre de Cristo Mountains has the highest incidence of freezing and thawing of any area in North America (Miller et al. 1963).

The retreat of glaciers appears to have created optimal habitat for the Arizona willow; however, many smaller populations of Arizona willow are found in unglaciated areas shaped by periglacial activity such as nivation, frost action and talus formation. Rock slides, exposure of mineral soil, and stream braiding are mechanisms that would have created willow habitat. Glacial and periglacial activity alone do not explain the distribution of Arizona willow, since the plant has not been reported from many other glaciated mountains in the region (e.g., San Francisco Peaks, La Sal Mountains, and Tushar Mountains) and since its distribution is narrow even within areas affected by glacial activity. Therefore, other factors such as mineralogy and hydrologic connections should be considered to explain the biogeography of this species.

Volcanics

Analysis of distributions suggests that the Arizona willow presently has a strong affinity for substrates derived from Tertiary felsic volcanics. The Tertiary volcanics of Mount Baldy in Arizona and the High Plateaus of Utah are dominated by andesitic to dacitic rocks with silica contents ranging from 54 to 70% (Nealey 1989; Luedke 1993). Tertiary volcanics in the Sangre de Cristo Mountains where Arizona willow occurs include a mixture of rhyolitic-pyroclastic rocks, andesites and basaltic andesites with local felsic flows, and felsic flows and pyroclastic rocks (Green and Jones 1997). The area containing the lone identified population in Southern Colorado appears on a small-scale map (Luedke 1993) to be underlain by Tertiary dacite (62-70% silica). Throughout its range, Arizona willow seems to be rarely associated with basaltic rocks, which have less than 50% silica content.

Many factors that vary between the different mineralogies influence plant distributions, including age of formation, topography, soil texture, hydrology, pH, and nutrient levels. As silica-rich volcanics weather, they form relatively deep, acidic soils with low clay content and low organic matter content (Freeman and Dick-Peddie 1970). Flatter-lying basaltic landforms, on the other hand, tend to form fine-textured soils. At several of the sites in Arizona where Arizona willow does occur on basalt, the rocks are highly fractured (pers. observation). Such fractured substrates may allow greater aeration than is typical of most meadows formed from basalts.

Volcanic-derived Sedimentary Formations

Because felsic volcanics tend to form steep domes (Stokes 1986), erosion of these landscapes may accumulate coarse substrates in alluvial and colluvial valleys. In the White Mountains, these deposits include glacial tills and the Sheep Crossing Formation, which are texturally indistinguishable (Merrill and Péwé 1971). These "gravelly sands" promote hydraulic conductivity and serve as shallow aquifers by conducting flow from Mount Baldy to contact areas

where less permeable basalts force the water to the surface (Merrill 1974). Arizona willow and other willows congregate at these seeps and springs at the base of the mountain.

Non-volcanic-derived Sedimentary Formations

Although Arizona willow appears to favor volcanic substrates in Arizona and in Utah, it does occur in soils derived entirely from sedimentary substrates, including the Claron Formation and Kaiparowits Formation (Mead 1996). However, these substrates appear to share the coarse textures found in the volcanics. Many of the sedimentary formations of southern Utah weather to fairly coarse cobbles and gravels (Doelling et al. 1989). Limestone gravels derived from the Claron Formation resist abrasion and deterioration (Doelling et al. 1989). The Kaiparowits Formation is predominantly sandstone, with occasional conglomeratic beds appearing in the western exposures where Arizona willow occurs (Doelling et al. 1989). Thus, this formation has potential to weather into coarse, silica-rich substrates as well. In New Mexico's Sangre de Cristo Mountains, sedimentary formations bearing Arizona willow include undifferentiated Pennsylvanian formations. The stratigraphy of these formations is complex and hard to discern due to extensive vegetative cover, but they are generally comprised of quartzite-rich sandstones and limestones of widely varying ages (Miller et al. 1963).

Edaphic Characteristics

Many of the geologic formations where Arizona willow grows produce coarse-textured mineral soils. Good hydraulic conductivity and aerobic conditions provide favorable habitat, particularly for the tallest and most productive willow plants (Long and Medina, this proceedings, Geologic Associations of the Arizona Willow in the White Mountains, Arizona). However, other soil factors, including soil chemistry, may govern the physiologic factors that lead to this association.

No studies have described soil preferences of Mogollon paintbrush, but one should expect correspondence to those of Arizona willow given their close association. Other members of the Septentrionales group also inhabit coarse-textured soils. *C. revealii* inhabits "limestone gravelly soil," and *C. aquariensis* grows in "rocky soil" (Holmgren 1973), although neither occurs in wetlands. *C. septentrionalis* inhabits "damp, rocky soil" (Pennell 1935). Given their relatively narrow distributions, some members of the Septentrionales group appear to be more edaphically constrained than Arizona willow.

While Arizona willow and members of the Septentrionales group do not appear to be strict substrate specialists, they both show affinity for coarse-textured soils. The sands and gravels may be derived from a variety of parent materials, including extrusive volcanic and sedimentary deposits from the Precambrian, Paleozoic, and Cenozoic eras. However, populations are small or absent from fine-textured soils derived from Pliocene or Pleistocene basalts. The La Sal, Henry, and Abajo Mountains represent a very different landscape type because they are relatively steep, laccolithic mountains composed of igneous rocks penetrating up through shales and sandstones (Stokes 1986; Betancourt 1990).

Ecologists have reported many examples of glacial-pluvial flora whose distributions are governed by differences in substrates. Several willow species may reach their southern limits in the igneous White Mountains of New Mexico because the coarse-textured geology maintains adequate soil water (Freeman and Dick-Peddie 1970). Several conifer species extend their lower elevation limits in sandstone-derived soils (Betancourt 1990). On the other hand, shale and limestone substrates may impose higher elevation limits, where only specially-adapted species may survive (Betancourt 1990). Bristlecone pine (*Pinus longaeva* D.K. Bailey) enjoys a competitive advantage on dolomite in the Sierra Nevada due to its tolerance for low water and nutrient conditions (Wright and Mooney 1965). These examples reveal the importance of geology in determining suitable refugia for subalpine plants in the Southwest.

EVOLUTIONARY HISTORY OF THE ARIZONA WILLOW AND MOGOLLON PAINTBRUSH

The distributions of the Arizona willow and the Mogollon paintbrush could yield insights into the broader landscape evolution of the Colorado Plateau. If the presence of these plants were tightly linked to the Pleistocene glaciations, then continued warming might portend rapid doom for these species. On the other hand, if the plants had dispersed across the Colorado Plateau far earlier, then they would have demonstrated resilience to the dramatic climatic swings of the Pleistocene.

Opportunities for a Quaternary Dispersal

During the Pleistocene, the range of Arizona willow may have been larger and more contiguous (Price et al. 1996). A cooler and moister climate during the Pleistocene would have created more favorable conditions at low elevations. Increased rainfall, glacial and periglacial processes would have accelerated erosion, invigorating populations of the willow and exposing new areas for colonization on gravel-rich fan deposits. Frost action and erosion may have broken up thin basalt deposits at the edges of the volcanic outcrops, exposing new microsites. Headwater stream captures also may have provided yet another avenue for dispersal into unoccupied habitats.

Biogeographers have contended that the mountains of Central Arizona and the High Plateaus of Utah were ecologically connected to the Southern Rocky Mountains of Colorado and New Mexico during the last glacial maximum (Moore 1965; Betancourt 1984). Bailey (1970) posited that *Pinus aristata* (Engelm.) descended the Sangre de Cristo Mountains, crossed the Rio Grande, traveled the high mountains of west-central New Mexico to the White Mountains of Arizona, and then spread across the Mogollon Rim to Flagstaff during the Pleistocene. This hypothesis is supported by pollen samples from Hay Lake in the White Mountains that reveal the presence of bristlecone pine during the Middle Wisconsin (Jacobs 1985). A nearly continuous range of mountains leads from the White Mountains of Arizona to the Sangre de Cristo Mountains of New Mexico, and these are dominated by Oligocene andesitic to basaltic-andesitic volcanics that might have provided suitable habitat for the Arizona willow. Endemic plants of the White Mountains, including the Mogollon clover, the Goodding onion (*Allium gooddingii* Ownbey), and the Gila groundsel (*Packera quaerens* (Greene) W.A. Weber & A. Löve), extend into the Mogollon Mountains of New Mexico. However, because those plants occur in lower elevation, drier microsites on mafic soils, they are less likely to share the evolutionary history of the Arizona willow and Mogollon paintbrush.

Populations of Arizona willow in Utah remain hydrologically connected through the drainages of the Sevier River, which flow into Sevier Lake, a vestigial Pleistocene pluvial lake. This distribution suggests that Arizona willow may have been more widely distributed throughout the Sevier watershed, perhaps extending to the shores of the Pleistocene Lake Bonneville along with other subalpine flora (Betancourt 1990). A colder and wetter Pleistocene climate would have promoted contiguity among the populations in Utah.

Arguments for a Tertiary Dispersal

An earlier dispersal of the species may be favored by the fact that populations of Arizona willow in Arizona and Utah are separated by vast expanses of basalt flows and sedimentary deposits across the Colorado Plateau, in addition to the chasm of the Grand Canyon. This separation has allowed bristlecone pine populations in the two states to form separate species, perhaps indicating isolation since the mid-Tertiary (Bailey 1970). Many theories concerning the origin of willows and other Arcto-Tertiary flora propose that diversification occurred during the Neogene (Wolfe 1997). Holmgren

(1971) suggested that various endemic species of *Castilleja* in the Southwest became isolated during the Pliocene.

The volcanism that formed Mount Baldy and Brian Head had ended by the start of the Pliocene (Fig. 3). Extensive erosion occurred as the Plateaus were elevated (Stokes 1986), and as Mount Baldy was reduced by 600 m from its peak elevation (Merrill 1974). Massive debris slides in the valleys below these mountains could have yielded ideal substrates for the willow to colonize. Similar geomorphic evolution transpired in New Mexico and Colorado at an earlier date. Extensive volcanism formed the San Juan mountains during the Oligocene (24-38 M yr) (Fig. 3). During the Miocene period, 14-15 M yr, the region appeared to have a mild winter climate (Axelrod and Bailey 1976), but

the climate then cooled (Wolfe 1997). The climate of the Southern Rocky Mountains then became more favorable to dispersal of subalpine plants. Formation of volcanic peaks and regional uplift promoted cooling and increased precipitation at high elevations. Even without changes in climate, peaks such as the White Mountains of Arizona would have been cooler than at present due to their higher elevation (Merrill 1974). The ancestral Rio Grande dates to the upper Pliocene, following rapid uplift and block-faulting of the Sangre de Cristo Range (Axelrod and Bailey 1976). Subalpine plants could have spread overland or along shifting rivers in the Rockies to occupy the uplifting Sangre de Cristo mountains.

Hydrologic Connections

Hydrologic connections between

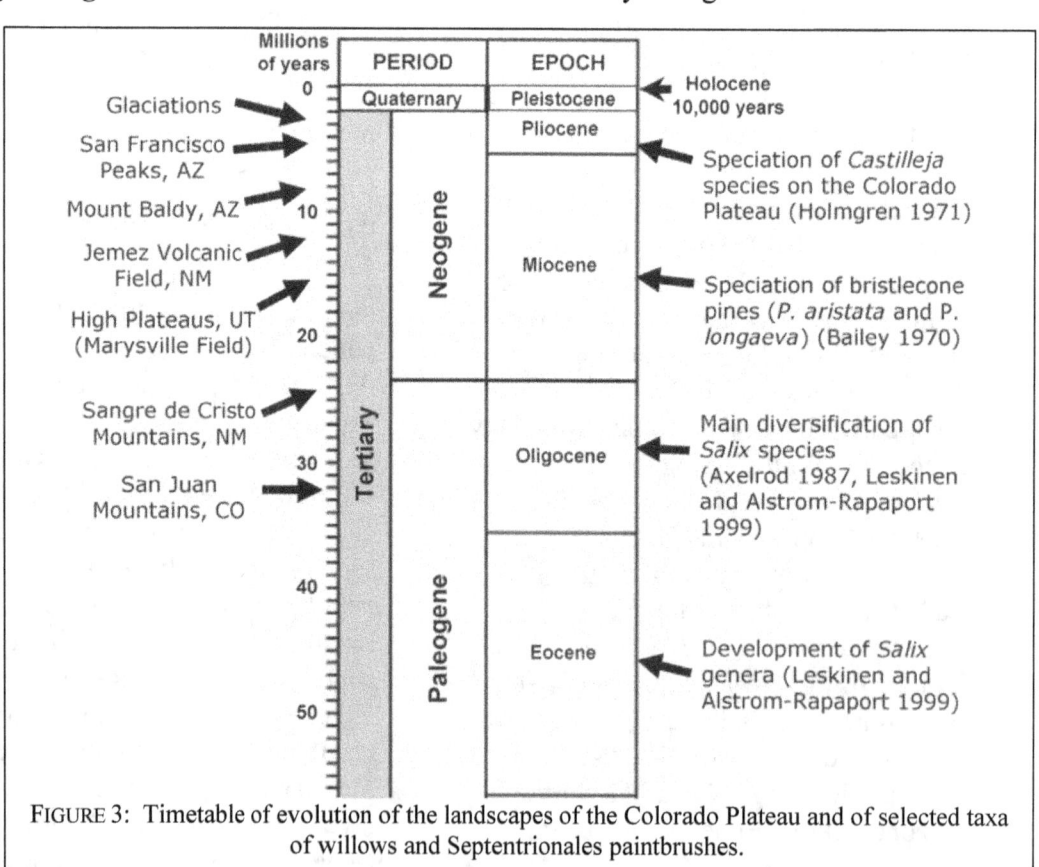

FIGURE 3: Timetable of evolution of the landscapes of the Colorado Plateau and of selected taxa of willows and Septentrionales paintbrushes.

Arizona's White Mountains and Utah's High Plateaus apparently existed during the mid-late Neogene (Fig. 4). In Arizona, the ancestral Little Colorado River from Mount Baldy toward the Colorado River. Along the way, the system was dammed in places to form the lacustrine/playa deposits of the Bidahochi Formation, or Hopi Lake, in northeastern Arizona (Fig. 4) (Scarborough 1989; Gross et al. 2001). The source drainages of this formation remain uncertain, but they included the ancestral Little Colorado River and may have at times included tributaries of the ancestral Colorado River from the Rocky Mountains (Dallegge et al. 2003). Fossil records of beaver and an ancestral pikeminnow (*Ptychocheilus*) in the formation indicate abundant wetland habitat, although the climate may have been relatively warm on average (Repenning and Irwin 1954; Scarborough 1989). Geologic evidence suggests that an arrangement of mountains and drainages similar to the present-day was in place within the region by the Mid-Miocene, except that the ancestral Colorado River had not yet breached the Kaibab Plateau (Gross et al. 2001). Instead, the river may have flowed north along the present-day course of Kanab Creek (Lucchita 1990). This course leads directly to the plateaus of Utah, coinciding with drainages of the Sevier River where Arizona willow occurs (Fig. 4). Consequently, during the Neogene, this drainage system may have linked the Rockies to the volcanic peaks of Mount Baldy and southern Utah.

Around 5 to 6 million years ago, the Colorado River changed its course to follow its present path to the Gulf of California, forming the Grand Canyon (Scarborough 1989). The Canyon cut

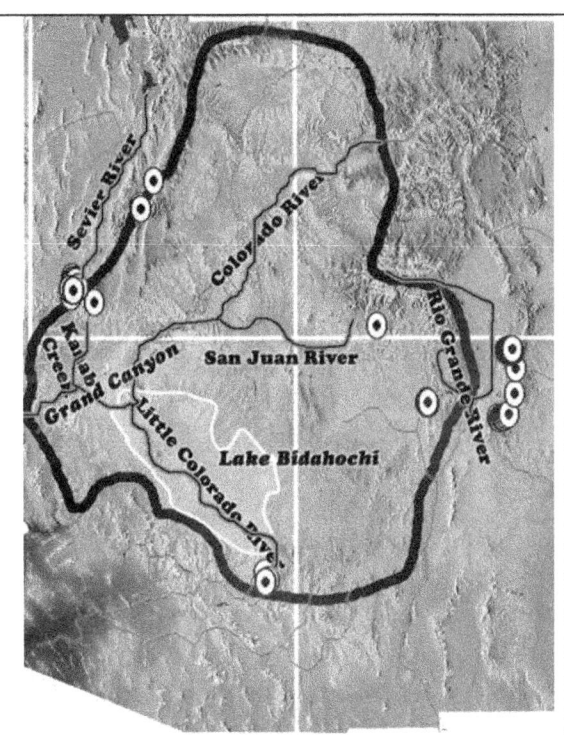

FIGURE 4: Hydrologic connections among features of the Colorado Plateau and Southern Rocky Mountains during the Neogene.

deeper as the area uplifted; simultaneously, the plateaus of southern Utah also rose (Doelling et al. 1989). The orogeny coincided with a change to a drier climate that may have been similar to the present (Scarborough 1989). During the late Pliocene and Pleistocene, the Springerville volcanic field reached its peak activity (Condit and Connor 1996). These relatively flat basalt flows overlaid parts of the Bidahochi formation and may have disrupted stream flow along the Little Colorado River from Mount Baldy. These formations may have restricted the Arizona willow to the areas close to the older and steeper slopes of Mount Baldy.

Arizona willow is well-distributed throughout the glacial tills and exposed Sheep Crossing Formation except on the western slopes of Mount Baldy and

Mount Ord. This asymmetrical distribution suggests that hydrologic connections played an important control on its dispersal. The imposing massif of Mount Ord and the deeply incised canyon of Big Bonito Creek appear to have blocked its spread to westerly-flowing drainages. The concentration of subpopulations along the Little Colorado River strongly suggests that this drainage first brought the plant to the White Mountains of Arizona. Headwater stream transfers and low drainage divides could have permitted extension to the White and Black River watersheds. Behnke (1979) presumed that headwater transfers during the Quaternary glaciations were important mechanisms in distributing fish species in the White Mountains.

In Utah, most populations of Arizona willow occur on tributaries of the Sevier River, which lies in the transition between the Great Basin and Colorado Plateau. Populations on the Fish Lake and Wasatch plateaus flow into tributaries of the Colorado, although these populations are located close to the divide with the Sevier watershed. The population on the East Fork of the Sevier River on the Paunsaugunt Plateau is found less than three kilometers from the drainage divide with Kanab Creek, indicating potential dispersal from the Colorado drainage.

Populations of Arizona willow in New Mexico extend across several major watersheds and occur on all aspects. This distribution supports the idea that the species might have dispersed through the southern Rockies via a shifting network of high-elevation drainages. Straddling the basins of the Colorado and Rio Grande, the San Juan Mountains were hydrologically connected during the Pliocene to all the areas where Arizona willow occurs in New Mexico, Utah and Arizona (Fig. 4).

The San Francisco Peaks and Mount Taylor are prominent peaks in the Southwest within the range of Arizona willow. The composition of these volcanoes range from basalt to dacite. However, the species has not been reported from those peaks. This absence could be explained by the fact that these volcanoes formed during the Pliocene and Pleistocene, possibly after Arizona willow had dispersed.

The Mogollon Mountains of New Mexico are older volcanoes of intermediate to felsic composition that include Sierra Blanca, which was the southernmost glaciated peak in North America during the Pleistocene. Arizona willow and Mogollon paintbrush have not been reported from those mountains, although it is unlikely that systematic surveys have been made of the region. A predominantly water-based journey from this region to the other Arizona willow populations would require a rather long path through either the relatively low, warm valley of the Rio Grande to the Sangre de Cristo Mountains or across mostly mafic plateaus via the San Francisco River.

Genetic Evidence

The time frame for the dispersal of Arizona willow and its closest relatives across the Southwest is a subject for debate. Arizona willow is similar in appearance and in genetics to Booth's willow (*Salix boothii* Dorn) (Thompson et al. 2003). Mead (1996) claimed that Argus, a taxonomic expert on willows, thought that Arizona willow may have diverged from *S. boothii* during Pleistocene glaciations. However, Argus has said that there is not sufficient evidence to draw conclusions about the timing or direction of evolution of these species (Argus 1999). Dorn (1976) asserted that nearly all American species originated "before or during glaciation." Glaciation influenced the regional distribution of some willow species, as Dorn (1975) suggested that *S. boothii* and *S. myrtillifolia* Anderss. may have been separated during the Wisconsin glaciation and then converged in the Northern Rocky Mountains of the United States. Because *S. arizonica* overlaps with *S. boothii* over such a large area, it seems unlikely that it could have evolved as a separate species in such a relatively short time. Based on flavenoid analyses (which are admittedly more primitive than DNA testing), Arizona willow appears chemically "very different" from *S. boothii* and instead appears more similar to the low-growing blueberry willow, *S. myrtillifolia* (Dorn 1975). Both *S. boothii* and *S. myrtillifolia* are identified as synonyms for *S. pseudomyrsinites* (Dorn 1975), the name originally applied to the 1913 collection of Arizona willow from Utah (AWITT 1995). These three species may share a complex evolutionary history, but DNA comparisons of Arizona willow populations (Thompson et al. 2003) did not include any *S. myrtillifolia*.

Those DNA tests did reveal that the populations of Arizona willow in Utah and Arizona were highly divergent (Thompson et al. 2003). Based on this finding, Thompson et al. (2003) hypothesized that the species was panmictic only as late as the Eocene (ca 50 M yr), when vast lakes connected the White Mountains of Arizona to the High Plateaus of Utah. The fact that the Saliceae family in general has a slow evolutionary rate (Leskinen and Alstrom-Rapaport 1999) lends some support to the hypothesis that the diaspora of Arizona willow may indeed be ancient. Yet, despite being one of the oldest genera of angiosperms, *Salix* itself dates only to the Eocene (55-65 M yr, Fig. 3) (Leskinen and Alstrom-Rapaport 1999). Furthermore, researchers believe that diversification of most species occurred after the Oligocene (post 38 M yr, Fig. 3) (Axelrod 1987; Leskinen and Alstrom-Rapaport 1999). The limited genetic evidence does not seem to support either a very recent dispersal of Arizona willow or a far more ancient one.

Palynological Evidence

Unfortunately, pollen samples provide little insight into the timing of the radiation of Arizona willow. Willow pollen is rarely identified to the species level, and it is not even reported from the handful of pollen records from the White Mountains of Arizona (e.g., P.S. Martin and R. Hevly unpublished data in (Whiteside 1965), (Merrill and Péwé 1977)). *Salix* pollen is also absent in reports from Hay Lake (Jacobs 1985) and from Dead Man Lake in the Chuska Mountains (Wright et al. 1973). This absence may be the result of low pollen production, insufficient identification, absence of willow in the sampled depressions, or the tendency of willow pollen to clump (Faegri and Iversen 1964). Regardless of these problems, the short time frame of most pollen records could not resolve whether the plant was present in the White Mountains of Arizona before the last glacial period.

Mechanisms of Dispersal

Arizona willow and various paintbrush species may have distributed along paths different from those of upland species such as bristlecone pine. Members of the *Saliceae* have the potential to disperse long distances due to their light seeds with long tails that catch the wind (Wells 1983). Moreover, suitable climatic conditions may have been lowered by 1000 meters or more in canyon bottoms on the Colorado Plateau during the last glacial maximum (Betancourt 1990). However, willow seeds are short-lived and usually must land in a sustained moist environment within days to germinate (Densmore and Zasada 1983). Thompson et al. (2003) argued that prevailing winds do not support seed flow between populations in Utah and Arizona. A Pleistocene dispersal across unfavorable habitat between Arizona and Utah appears less likely than a Pliocene voyage along favorable drainages. However, connections across the Arizona-New Mexico Mountains may have permitted dispersal into Arizona from the southern Rocky Mountains. Without a more detailed fossil record or DNA studies, the timing of the arrival of Arizona willow to the White Mountains will remain speculative.

Implications for Environmental Tolerance

Understanding how long Arizona willow has lived in its present regions may help resolve its environmental tolerances. Regardless of whether the species existed in Arizona and Utah before the last glacial maximum or after, it would have withstood the dramatic climatic change of the Altithermal warming period (about 8000-4000 year ago) as well as grazing by the large-bodied mammals that dominated the Pleistocene landscape. However, the unusually warm and dry climate experienced in the White Mountains in recent years (Lynch 2004) combined with increased ungulate abundance and more continuous grazing may have created novel habitat conditions. Herbivory by ungulates, particularly elk, has been linked to reduce plant vigor of Arizona willow (Maschinski 2001) and has been a contributing factor in the loss of individual plants (Granfelt 2004). Aided by construction of watering tanks, reduction of predator populations, and introductions of both domestic livestock and the Rocky Mountain subspecies of elk (*Cervus elaphus* ssp. *nelsoni*), ungulate behavior has changed in seasonality and extent from the conditions under which subalpine flora have evolved (Axelrod 1987; Burkhardt 1996).

Implications for Conservation and Future Research

This interpretation of the biogeography of Arizona willow has several implications. Conservation of the species should recognize that the glacial and Tertiary volcanic formations yield substrates that promote the highest densities of these plants and serve as natural refugia. Populations on basalt and other fine-textured formations may experience greater stress associated with warming and drying. Although different species may have dispersed at different times, similarities among the subalpine flora of the White Mountains of Arizona, High Plateaus of Utah, Southern Rocky Mountains of New Mexico, and San Juan Mountains of Southern Colorado point to parallel geologic origins and past linkages during both the Neogene and Pleistocene. Surveys in the San Juan

Mountains are likely to reveal additional populations of Arizona willow.

Future research may help to resolve questions concerning the evolution of these rare plants. Genetic comparisons of willow populations in New Mexico and Colorado with those in Utah and Arizona could help to resolve the sequence by which existing populations separated. For example, if the populations in Arizona are more similar to those in New Mexico, then a Quaternary dispersal to the White Mountains, like that of bristlecone pine, would seem plausible. However, if the Arizona, Utah, and Rocky Mountains populations are equally dissimilar, then an earlier Neogene dispersal would seem more likely.

ACKNOWLEDGMENTS

I thank Carl-Eric Granfelt for his dedication to understanding the rare plants of the White Mountains and for sharing his thoughts on this manuscript. I also thank Steve Overby for his review of this manuscript, and Mark Egger for providing an update on the taxonomy of the Mogollon paintbrush.

REFERENCES

Argus, George W. 1999. [E-mail to J. W. Long]. 11-17-1999.

Atwood, D. 1996. Final report for inventory of *Salix arizonica* on the Santa Fe National Forest. Unpublished report on file at Rocky Mountain Research Station, Flagstaff, AZ. 5 p.

_____ Survey of Arizona on the Carson National Forest. Unpublished report on file at Rocky Mountain Research Station, Flagstaff, AZ. 8 p.

AWITT (Arizona Willow Interagency Technical Team) 1995. Arizona willow conservation agreement and strategy. Ogden, UT: U.S. Forest Service, Intermountain Region; U.S. Forest Service, Southwest Region, Albuquerque, NM; National Park Service, Rocky Mountain Region, Denver, CO; U.S. Fish and Wildfire Service, Mountain-Prairie Region, Salt Lake City, UT; U.S. Fish and Wildlife Service, Southwest Region, Albuquerque, NM.

Axelrod, D. I. 1987. The late Oligocene Creede Flora, Colorado. University of California Publications in Geological Sciences, Volume 130. Berkeley: University of California Press. 235 p.

Axelrod, D. I. and H. P. Bailey. 1976. Tertiary vegetation, climate, and altitude of the Rio Grande depression, New Mexico-Colorado. Paleobiology 2: 235-254.

Bailey, D. K. 1970. Phytogeography and taxonomy of *Pinus* subsection *balfourianae*. Annals of the Missouri Botanical Garden 57: 210-249.

Bainbridge, S. J. and P. L. Warren 1992. Status report, April revision: *Castilleja mogollonica* (Mogollon paintbrush). Unpublished report submitted to U. S. Fish and Wildlife Service, Ecological Services, Phoenix, AZ.

Behnke, R. J. 1979. Monograph of the native trouts of the genus *Salmo* of Western North America., Denver, CO: U.S. Department of Agriculture, Forest Service, Rocky Mountain Region. 163 p.

_____. 2002. Trout and salmon of North America. New York, NY: The Free Press. 359 p.

Betancourt, J. L. 1984. Late Quaternary plant zonation and climate in southeastern Utah. The Great Basin Naturalist 44: 1-35.

_____ 1990. Late Quaternary biogeography of the Colorado Plateau. In: Betancourt, J. L., Devender, T. R. V., and Martin, P. S., eds. Packrat middens: The last 40,000 years of biotic change. Tucson, AZ: University of Arizona Press: 259-293.

Burkhardt, J. W. 1996. Herbivory in the Intermountain West: An overview of evolutionary history, historic cultural impacts and lessons from the past. Station Bulletin 58. Moscow, ID: Idaho Forest, Wildlife and Range Experiment Station, College of Forestry, Wildlife and Range Sciences, University of Idaho. 20 p.

Colorado Natural Heritage Program. 2001. Plant species of special concern survey form. Unpublished report on file at College of Natural Resources, Colorado State University, Fort Collins, CO. 2 p.

Condit, C. D. and C. B. Connor. 1996. Recurrence rates of volcanism in basaltic volcanic fields, an example from the Springerville volcanic field, Arizona. GSA Bulletin 108(10): 1225-1241.

Dallegge, T. A., M. H. Ort, and W. C. McIntosh. 2003. Mio-Pliocene chronostratigraphy, basin morphology and paleodrainage relations derived from the Bidahochi Formation, Hopi and Navajo nations, northeastern Arizona. The Mountain Geologist 40(3): 55-82.

Densmore, R. and J. Zasada. 1983. Seed dispersal and dormancy patterns in northern willows: ecological and evolutionary significance. Canadian Journal of Botany 61: 3207-3216.

Doelling, H. H., F. D. Davis, and C. J. Brandt. 1989. The geology of Kane County, Utah, geology, mineral resources, geologic hazards. Bulletin 124. Salt Lake City: Utah Geological and Mineral Survey. 192 p.

Dorn, R. D. 1975. A systematic study of *Salix* section *Cordatae* in North America. Canadian Journal of Botany 53: 1491-1522.

_____ 1976. A synopsis of American *Salix*. Canadian Journal of Botany 54: 2769-2789.

_____ 1997. Survey of Arizona willow on the Carson National Forest. Unpublished report to the U.S. Forest Service Region 2, on file at U.S. Department of Agriculture, Forest Service, Rocky Mountain Research Station, Flagstaff, AZ.

Egger, J. Mark. 2004. [E-mail to J. W. Long]. 4-19-2004.

Faegri, Knut and Iversen, Johs. 1964. Textbook of pollen analysis. NY: Hafner Publishing Company. 237 p.

Freeman, C. E. and W. A. Dick-Peddie. 1970. Woody riparian vegetation in the Black and Sacramento Mountain Ranges, Southern New Mexico. The Southwestern Naturalist 15: 145-164.

Granfelt, C. 2004. [Phone conservation with J. W. Long]. 4-19-2004.

Green, G. N. and Jones, G. E. 1997. The digital geologic map of New Mexico in ARC/INFO format. Open-File Report 97-52. Denver: U. S. Geological Survey.

Gregory, H. E. 1950. Geology of eastern Iron County, Utah. Bulletin 37. Salt Lake City: University of Utah Press. 153 p.

Gross, E. L.; P.J. Patchett,, T. A. Dallegge and J. E. Spencer. 2001. The Colorado River System and Neogene sedimentary formations along its course: Apparent Sr Isotopic connections. Journal of Geology 109(4): 449-461.

Holmgren, N. H. 1971. A taxonomic revision of the *Castilleja viscidula* group. Memoirs of the New York Botanical Garden 21(4): 1-63.

_____ Five new species of *Castilleja* (Scrophulariaceae) from the Intermountain Region. Bulletin of the Torrey Botanical Club 100(2): 83-93.

Jacobs, B. F. 1985. A middle Wisconsin pollen record from Hay Lake, Arizona. Quaternary Research 24: 121-130.

Ladyman, J. 1996. Distribution and biology of *Trifolium longipes* subsp. *neurophyllum* (Greene). In Maschinski, J., H. D. Hammond, and L. Holter, L., (eds.) Southwestern rare and endangered plants, second conference: proceedings; 9-11-1995; Flagstaff, AZ: 262-269.

Leskinen, E. and C. Alstrom-Rapaport. 1999. Molecular phylogeny of Saliceae and closely related Flacourtiaceae, evidence from 5.8 S, ITS 1 and ITS 2 of the rDNA. Plant Systematics and Evolution 215: 209-227.

Lucchita, I. 1990. History of the Grand Canyon and of the Colorado River in Arizona. In: Flagstaff, AZ: Museum of Northern Arizona Press: 311-332.

Luedke, R. G. 1993. Maps showing distribution, composition, and age of early and middle Cenozoic volcanic centers in Colorado and Utah. Miscellaneous Investigations Map I-2291-B.

Lynch, A. M. 2004. Fate and characteristics of *Picea* damaged by *Elatobium abietinum* (Walker) (Homoptera: Aphididae) in the

White Mountains of Arizona. Western North American Naturalist 64(1): 7-17.

Maschinski, J. 2001. Impacts of ungulate herbivores on a rare willow at the southern edge of its range. Biological Conservation 101(1): 119-130.

McIntosh, W. C. and R. M. Chamberlin. 1994. $^{40}AR/^{39}AR$ geochronology of middle to late Cenozoic ignimbrites, mafic lavas, and volcaniclastic rocks in the Quemado Region, New Mexico. In Chamberlin, R. M.; B. S. Kues, S. M. Cather, J. M. Barker, and W. C. McIntosh, (eds).9-28-1994; New Mexico Geological Society, Inc.: 165-173.

Mead, L. L. 1996. Habitat characteristics of Arizona willow in Southwestern Utah. Provo, UT: Brigham Young University. Unpublished master's thesis.

Merrill, R. K. 1974. The late Cenozoic geology of the White Mountains, Apache County, Arizona. Tempe, AZ: Arizona State University. Ph.D. dissertation.

Merrill, R. K. and T. L. Péwé. 1971. Sheep Crossing formation, a new late Cenozoic epiclastic formation in East-central Arizona. Journal of the Arizona Academy of Science 6: 226-229.

_____ 1977. Late Cenozoic geology of the White Mountains, Arizona. Special Paper No. 1. Tucson, AZ: University of Arizona.

Miller, J. P., A. Montgomery and P. K. Sutherland. 1963. Geology of part of the southern Sangre de Cristo Mountains, New Mexico. Memoirs M-11. Socorro, New Mexico: New Mexico Bureau of Geology and Mineral Resources. 106 p.

Moore, T. C. 1965. Origin and disjunction of the alpine tundra flora on San Francisco Mountain, Arizona. Ecology 46: 860-864.

Nealey, L. D. 1989. Geology and petrology of the Late Cenozoic Mount Baldy trachytic volcanic complex, White Mountains volcanic field, Apache and Navajo Counties, Arizona. Albuquerque, NM: University of New Mexico. Ph.D. dissertation.

Pennell, F. W. 1935. The Scrophulariaceae of Eastern temperate North America. Monograph, 1. Philadelphia: Academy of Natural Sciences of Philadelphia. 650 p.

Pennell, F. W. 1951. A new Indian paint-brush from the Mogollon Plateau of Arizona (*Castilleja*: Scrophulariaceae). Notulae Naturae, no. 237. Philadelphia: The Academy of Natural Sciences of Philadelphia. 300 p.

Price, P. W., T. G. Carr and A. M. Ormond. 1996. Consequences of land management practices on willows and higher trophic levels. In Maschinski, J., H. D. Hammond, and L. Holter, L., (eds.) Southwestern rare and endangered plants, second conference: proceedings; 9-11-1995; Flagstaff, AZ 219-223.

Repenning, C. A. and J. H. Irwin. 1954. Bidahochi formation of Arizona and New Mexico. American Association of Petroleum Geologists Bulletin 38: 1821-1826.

Rinne, J. N. 2000. Fish and grazing relationships in southwestern National Forests. In: Jemison, R., and Raish, C., eds. Livestock management in the American southwest: ecology, society and economics. The Netherlands: Elsevier Science: 329-371.

Rowley, P. D., H. H. Mehnert, C. W. Naeser, L. W. Snee, C. G. Cunningham, T. A. Steven, J. J. Anderson, E. G. Sable, and R. E. Anderson. 1994. Isotopic ages and stratigraphy of Cenozoic rocks of the Marysvale Volcanic Field and adjacent areas, West-Central Utah. Bulletin 2071. Washington, DC: US Government Printing Office. 35 p.

Scarborough, R. 1989. Cenozoic erosion and sedimentation in Arizona. In: Jenney, J. P., and Reynolds, S. J., eds. Geologic evolution of Arizona. Tucson, AZ: Arizona Geological Society: 515-537.

Steven, T. A. 1975. Middle Tertiary volcanic field in the Southern Rocky Mountains. In: Curtis, B. F., ed. Cenozoic History of the Southern Rocky Mountains, Memoir, 144.The Geological Society of America, Inc. 94 p.

Stokes, William L. 1986. Geology of Utah. Salt Lake City, UT: Utah Museum of Natural History, University of Utah and Utah Geological and Mineral Survey Department of Natural Resources. 280 p.

Thompson, J. T.; R. Van Buren and K. T. Harper. 2003. A genetic analysis of the rare species, *Salix arizonica* (Salicaceae) and associated willows in Arizona and Utah. Western North American Naturalist 63(3): 273-282.

Wells, P. V. 1983. Paleobiogeography of montane islands in the Great Basin since the last glaciopluvial. Ecological Monographs 53: 341-382.

Whiteside, M. C. 1965. Paleoecological studies of Potato Lake and its environs. Ecology 46: 807-816.

Wolfe, J. A. 1997. Relations of environmental change to angiosperm evolution during the Late Cretaceous and Tertiary. In: Iwatsuki, K., and P.H. Raven, (eds.) Evolution and diversification of land plants. New York: Springer-Verlag: 269-290.

Wright, H. E. Jr., A. M. Bent, B. S. Hansen, and L. J. J. Maher. 1973. Present and past vegetation of the Chuska Mountains, northwestern New Mexico. Geological Society of America Bulletin 84: 1155-1180.

Wright, R. D. and H. A. Mooney. 1965. Substrate-oriented distribution of bristlecone pine in the White Mountains of California. American Midland Naturalist 73: 257-284.

Patterns of Growth and Mortality in the Endangered Nichol's Turk's Head Cactus (*Echinocactus horizonthalonius* var. *nicholii* L. Benson; Cactaceae) in Southeastern Arizona.

McIntosh, M.E.[1], L.A. McDade[1,2], A.E. Boyd[3] and P.D. Jenkins[1].

[1]Department of Ecology and Evolutionary Biology, University of Arizona, Tucson, Arizona 85721
[2]Academy of Natural Sciences, 1900 Ben Franklin Parkway, Philadelphia, Pennsylvania 19103
[3]Warren Wilson College, P.O. Box 9000, Asheville, North Carolina 28815.

ABSTRACT. Nichol's Turk's Head Cactus (*Echinocactus horizonthalonius* var. *nicholii* L. Benson; Cactaceae) occurs in a few isolated populations in the Sonoran desert of south-central Arizona (Pima and Pinal counties). The populations of this variety are disjunct from the more widespread variety that occurs in the Chihuahuan desert of Texas and Mexico. This species occurs only on limestone-derived soils, and the *nicholii* variety was federally listed as endangered in 1979. Since 1995 we have monitored study plots of this cactus in the Waterman Mountains (AZ), measuring growth and reproduction of about 175 tagged individuals. Growth rates were slow, averaging 0.3 cm in height and 0.2 cm in width per year. Plants usually began flowering when they reached around 4 cm high and 8 cm wide. Of the 52 deaths recorded since 1995, about half followed a visible decline in condition; the rest were unanticipated. There was a distinct jump in mortality during the past two years, possibly due to drought.

INTRODUCTION

Although *Echinocactus horizonthalonius* is widely distributed in the Chihuahuan desert of west Texas and Mexico, the variety *nicholii* only occurs in a few locations in southeastern Arizona. Variety *nicholii* thus forms a disjunct population. This cactus was federally listed as endangered in 1979, due to the limited range and known threats to its existence. Because it is endangered, demography information is of interest to land managers and conservationists.

Since 1995, we have monitored ca. 175 individuals in four study plots in the Waterman Mountains of SE Arizona. This population has been estimated at approximately 10,000 plants. Here we present some preliminary descriptive data on plant size, growth, and mortality.

METHODS

Six described species of *Echinocactus* grow in the southwestern U.S. and Mexico. Of the two varieties described by Benson (1969), variety *nicholii* is the only one that occurs in southeastern Arizona. Recent studies suggest that the two varieties may not be as distinct as was once thought (Chamberland 1995). Variety *nicholii* grows on limestone-derived soils in the Upland Division of Sonoran Desert Scrub at elevations ranging from 600 to 1,100 m (Turner et al. 1995). The perceived threats to this plant at the time of listing were mining of limestone deposits, off-road vehicle use and collection.

The study site is in the Waterman Mountains of southeastern Arizona, approximately 50 km WNW of Tucson (32°21′N, 111°28′W, elev. 975 m). The Waterman Mountains and surrounding area became part of the Ironwood Forest National Monument, administered by the Bureau of Land Management, in 2000.

For three of the four study plots, we selected a general location, and then determined the borders and the size of the plot using a random number generator, to avoid favoring plots with an unusually high density of plants. The fourth plot was selected for convenience along both sides of a trail. The study plots range in size from ca. 100 square meters to ca. 550 square meters (total area under study: 1,120 square meters, or about 0.11 hectare). The plots also differ from each other in slope and orientation.

Plants were marked with numbered aluminum tags at the initial survey in the fall of 1995. At each subsequent census, which usually occurred in January (but as late as March in 1999) we recorded height and width of each plant to the nearest 0.5 cm, noted presence/absence of fruits, and took notes on the condition of each plant. The plots were not censused in the winter of 2002-2003.

RESULTS

The density of plants in the study plots has ranged from 0.05 plants per m^2 to 0.29 plants per m^2 (range is across plots and years). Average density (pooled across sites, ranged across years) has ranged from 0.10 plants per m^2 to

0.12 plants per m^2, or from 9 to 10 m^2 per plant.

Plants are round disks when young, becoming cylinder- to pyramid-shaped as they grow. Width increases until it reaches ca. 15 cm, then levels off (Fig. 1). Height continues to increase throughout the life of the plant. Only in the very tallest plants does height ever exceed width (Fig. 1).

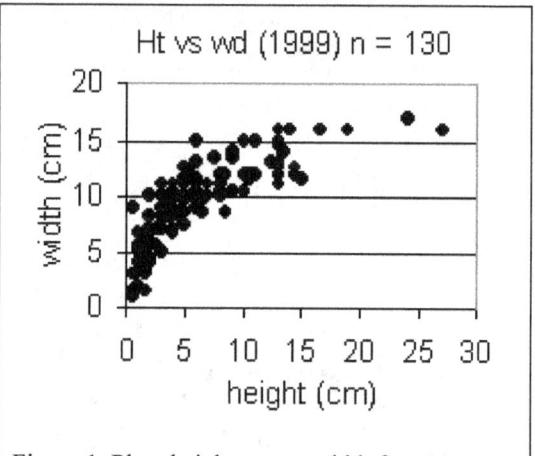

Figure 1. Plant height versus width for 130 plants in 1999. Each point represents one plant.

Because growth in height continues indefinitely whereas growth in width levels off, size classes based on height may be more useful than those based on width (however, it is easier to measure width accurately). We show both types of size classes in order to compare our data to that of Reid et al. (1983) (Fig. 2a, b). The distribution of individuals among size classes based on height is similar for 1995 and 2003, although there are more individuals in size class 3 (height = 6.0 to 8.5 cm) in 2003 than in 1995 (Fig. 2a).

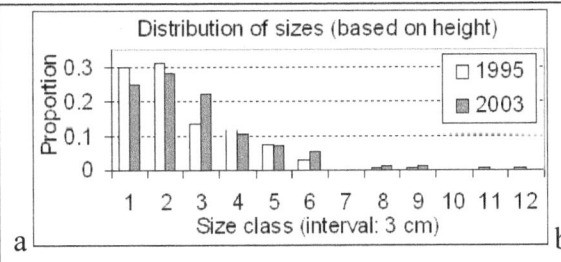
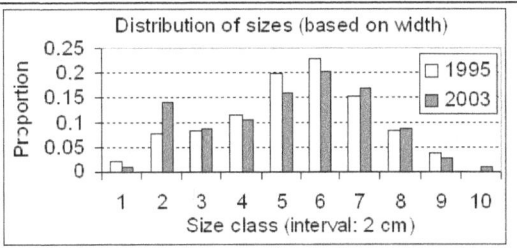

FIGURE 2. Proportion of individual plants in size classes. a) size classes based on plant height using equal intervals of 3 cm. b) size classes based on plant width using equal intervals of 2 cm.

Size at first reproduction is usually 8 cm in width and 4 cm in height, although a few individuals as small as 6 cm width and 2 cm height have flowered. Therefore, individuals in height size class 2 and up, and width size class 5 and up, may be considered adults (Fig. 2).

Growth is slow. From 1995 to 2003 (8 yr), plants grew about 2.3 cm in height and 1.5 cm in width, or 21 cm³ in plant volume (Table 1). Thus plants grow an average of 0.18 cm per year in width, and 0.29 cm per year in height. Growth rates for both height and width decrease gradually as size increases (Fig. 3a, b). The number of plants in our study plots (plots pooled) has declined during the survey, with a particularly sharp drop during the last two years, possibly as a result of prolonged drought (Fig. 4). The differences in mortality rates among the different size classes are not significant, suggesting that there is no size class that is particularly vulnerable (data not shown).

TABLE 1. Average growth of individual plants during the 8 yr period 1995-2003. $N = 78$ plants. Plant volume is calculated as the volume of a cylinder.

	Mean	SE	Range
Change in plant height (cm)	2.33	0.18	6.0 to -3.0
Change in plant width (cm)	1.45	0.15	4.0 to -3.0
Change in plant volume (cm³)	20.6	2.53	76 to -57

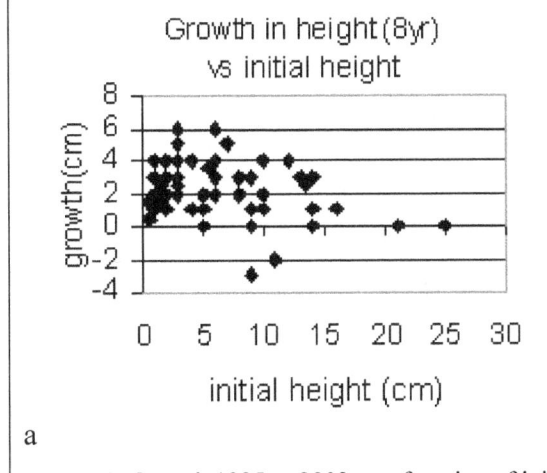
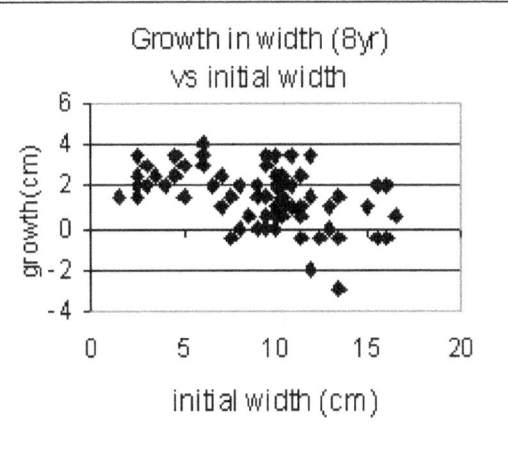

FIGURE 3. Growth 1995 to 2003 as a function of initial size. a) growth in height. b) growth in width.

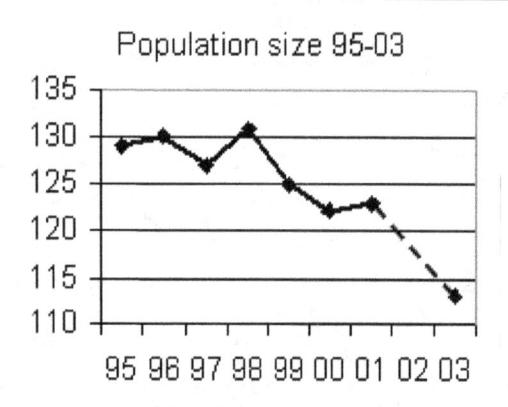

Figure 4. Population size (pooled across study plots) over time, 1995 to 2003. The population was not censused in 2002.

During our surveys, we note the condition of each plant. In some cases, plants sustain obvious damage such as gouging or being dug up. Other conditions noted include surface discoloration, which is quite common, desiccation evidence such as puckering or wrinkling, surface irregularities such as blistering or flaking, and patches of dead or rotting tissue. Some of these indicators are associated with the subsequent death of the plant, others less so. For example, signs of desiccation are relatively common among the "trouble reports," but are relatively rare as a precursor of death (Table 2). On the other hand, necrosis is not often mentioned, but when it is, the plant is very likely to die during the next year (Table 2). However, of plants that died, only about 48% showed signs of trouble the previous year, suggesting that "sudden death" is quite common.

DISCUSSION

Reid et al. (1983) measured 174 individuals of *E. horizonthalonius* in Texas just outside of El Paso, and created size classes based on 2 cm intervals of plant width (as we do here). Their distribution of individuals among size classes was more irregular than ours, but it is worth noting that in both studies, the proportion of individuals peaked in size class 6 (width = 10 to 12 cm) (Fig. 2b).

Table 2. Fatal versus non-fatal plant conditions. N = number of plants. Only plants that were recorded as having a problem or condition are included.

Condition	Percent plants with this condition that died (n)	Percent plants with this condition that lived (n)	No. plants with this condition (percent of all plants)
Necrosis (necrotic, rotting, dead flesh)	37% (3)	63% (5)	8 (7%)
Discoloration (cuticle red, yellow, brown, burned-looking)	30% (14)	70% (33)	47 (38%)
General poor condition (not specified)	20% (1)	80% (4)	5 (4%)
Damage (gouge, exit hole, torn open)	14% (3)	86% (19)	22 (18%)
Surface irregularity (cracks, blisters, dimples, peeling, flaking, "warts")	11% (1)	89% (8)	9 (7%)
Desiccation (wrinkled, puckered, shriveled)	9% (3)	91% (29)	32 (26%)
TOTAL	20% (25)	80% (98)	123

Dimension measurements such as height and width depend on the water status of the plant (some plants actually shrank in overall size over the eight years of the study). Previous studies have suggested that these plants require ten to thirty-two years to reach a height of 5 cm (cited in AGFD 1994). Extrapolating from our growth data would give an age of 17 years for a plant 5 cm high. These extrapolations are probably of limited value. For example, we found that size at first reproduction is about 8 cm wide and 4 cm high; extrapolating from our growth rates would give a cactus of this size an age of 14 yr (based on height) to 44 yr (based on width).

An alternate method for measuring growth is to count the number of new areoles that appear in a time period—this could be done by marking the central spine of each spine cluster (May et al. 1986). New areoles represent actual new tissue generated at the apical meristem. It has been suggested that plants of the same height and width can be very different ages (May et al. 1986), and the high variance in growth rates among individual plants that we found is consistent with that suggestion. If, as has been suggested (May et al. 1986), these plants generate one new areole per rib per year, counting areoles could be a much better method for correlating size with age. We plan to include this method in our further monitoring of these plants.

Our study was inspired in part by a monumental but somewhat obscurely published study of *Sclerocactus polyancistrus* following 350 individual plants over 15 years at six study sites (May 1994). Of particular interest was the author's detailed analysis of causes of mortality. Careful observation and dissection of carcasses enabled him to develop a unique system of carcass classification. Small mammal predation resulted in "open" carcasses, in which the flesh of the plant was chewed, torn apart, or completely consumed, with mammal scat being found nearby. "Closed" carcasses could be attributed to insect infestation, indicated by bore holes, exit holes, and the remains of pupal cells in the soil directly below the plant. Mammal predation was much more common than infestation.

Without further study, our condition notes cannot accurately inform us about the ultimate or even proximate causes of death of the plants in our study. For example, we classified wrinkling and puckering as signs of desiccation, but other signs such as surface discoloration may also be due to desiccation. May (1994) found stem discoloration to be associated with insect infestation. A distinction can also be made between proximate and ultimate causes of mortality; for example, a plant weakened by drought may be more susceptible to insect infestation. Finally, about half of the plants that died during our study showed no signs of trouble in the previous year; this could be more suggestive of predation than of environmental factors. However, environmental stressors such as frost damage can lead rapidly to necrosis and death.

Many plants that have died are found as intact, standing corpses, which may suggest infestation. For example, of the 20 plants that died between the 2001 census and the 2003 census, eight were found as intact carcasses. Of the rest, three were found as shreds of a carcass, for four we found only scattered spine clusters, four were gone without a trace (although we found the tags), and one was buried under a pile of soil at the entrance to a rodent burrow. Dissection of living and dead plants would be needed to confirm the possible presence of burrowing insects such as the cactus beetle (*Moneilema* spp., Cerambycidae).

ACKNOWLEDGMENTS

We wish to thank those who assisted us in the field: Sandy Adondakis, Betsy Arnold, David Hearn, Michael Chamberland, and Pat Penn.

LITERATURE CITED

Arizona Game and Fish Department (AGFD). 1994. *Echinocactus horizonthalonius* var. *nicholii*. Unpublished abstract compiled and edited by the Heritage Data Management System. Phoenix, Arizona: Arizona Game and Fish Department.

Benson, Lyman. 1969. The cacti of Arizona. Third edition. Tucson, Arizona: University of Arizona Press.

Chamberland, M. 1995. Cactaceae, Part 2. Cactus Family *Echinocactus* Link & Otto. Journal of the Arizona-Nevada Academy of Science 29(1): 13-14.

May, C. J., T. R. Van Devender, T. C. Gibson, M. Butterwick, and P. Olwell. 1986. Recovery plan for the Nichol turk's head cactus (*Echinocactus horizonthalonius* Lemaire, var. *nicholii* L. Benson). Prepared for the U.S. Fish and Wildlife Service, Albuquerque, New Mexico.

May, R. W. 1994. The ecology of *Sclerocactus polyancistrus* (Cactaceae) in California and Nevada. Desert Plants 11(1): 6-22.

Reid, W., R. Lozano, & R. Odom. 1983. Non-equilibrium population structure in three Chihuahuan desert cacti. Southwestern Naturalist 28(1): 115-117.

Turner, Raymond M., J.E. Bowers, and T. L. Burgess. 1995. Sonoran desert plants: an ecological atlas. Tucson, Arizona: The University of Arizona Press.

Initial Response of *Arabis johnstonii* Munz to Fire

NAROG, MARCIA G[1], CHRISTIE J. SCLAFANI[1], CHRISTINA ESCOBAR[1], KATE A. KRAMER[2]
AND JAN L. BEYERS[1]
[1]USDA Forest Service, Pacific Southwest Research Station, Riverside, CA 92507
mnarog@fs.fed.us, [2]San Bernardino National Forest, San Jacinto Ranger District,
Idyllwild, CA 92549 kakramer@fs.fed.us

ABSTRACT. *Arabis johnstonii* Munz (Johnston's rock cress) is a small herbaceous perennial plant endemic to the San Jacinto Mountains of southern California. It is considered rare by the California Native Plant Society and is a Forest Service Sensitive species. Three *A. johnstonii* occurrences grow within an area that the San Bernardino National Forest plans to burn for hazardous fuel reduction. Prior to this study little was known about fire effects on *A. johnstonii*. We used a 1.1 m diameter cylindrical stainless steel wire "fire cage" within which we conducted small-scale experimental burns on twenty clusters of *A. johnstonii*. Weather, fuel conditions, and fire behavior were recorded during burns conducted in September 2003 and January 2004. *A. johnstonii* survival, growth and recruitment will be measured twice a year for up to three years after the fires. About five months after the first experimental burn, most *A. johnstonii* were still alive, but they were generally smaller and shorter than unburned individuals. Burned *A. johnstonii* showed no change in numbers of individuals compared to pre-burn counts, however unburned plot numbers increased by 15 percent over the same time period.

INTRODUCTION

Hazardous conditions persist in many areas of the Southwest as decades of fire suppression now coalesce with drought to produce dangerous accumulations of flammable fuels. The firestorms that burned southern California during 2003 vividly illustrate how wildland areas, now intertwined with urban sprawl, create perilous zones of extreme fire risk. Land managers labor to reduce fuels for both ecosystem health and human safety. Ironically, prescription burning may be the tool that could most effectively reduce fuel and thus fire danger over relatively large areas. The trick is to apply it under thoughtfully prescribed and operationally safe conditions.

Even when conditions are appropriate, the presence of rare species may complicate attempts to implement any desirable fuels treatments, prescribed burning included. Resource managers hesitate to place a rare species or its habitat in jeopardy when nothing is known about how the disturbance will affect it (e.g. when positive or negative fire effects are unknown for a species of concern). But failure to treat accumulated fuels could lead to habitat disturbance by wildfire, with equally unknown impacts. Prescribed burns can be accomplished with complex boundaries designed to exclude rare species. However, some rare species benefit from fire and would then be excluded from this positive management practice. Obviously, information is urgently needed to resolve this predicament without exposing already vulnerable populations to harmful perturbation or to chance.

Arabis johnstonii Munz (Johnston's rock cress), a small herbaceous perennial in the mustard family (Brassicaceae), occurs in the San Jacinto Mountains of western Riverside County, California (California Native Plant Society 2001, Rollins 1993) (Fig. 1). *A. johnstonii* is a Forest Service Sensitive species and is listed as rare by the California Native Plant Society (California Native Plant Society 2001). *A. johnstonii* grows on various soil types near Garner Valley within the San Bernardino National Forest (SBNF) (Berg and Krantz 1982, California Natural Diversity Database 2001). The SBNF wants to use prescribed fire in Garner Valley and vicinity for fuel hazard reduction to protect nearby mountain communities. A prescribed fire was conducted in the general area in the early 1980s, but no specific information was collected on whether any *A. johnstonii* actually were burned at that time. No historic fire effects data exist for the locations within the proposed prescribed fire perimeter where three *A. johnstonii* occurrences grow. No fire effects have been documented for *A. johnstonii* at other sites either.

FIGURE 1--*Arabis johnstonii* (Johnston's rock cress) in bloom on the pebble plain-like soil at McGregor Flat, San Jacinto Mountains, California in April 2004.

Fire, prescribed or accidental, and related activities harbor many challenges and could have possible unknown consequences for tenuous species or populations such as *A. johnstonii*. Multiple fuel breaks would have to be built within the proposed burn to isolate the three populations. Site disturbance for fuel break construction could incidentally harm some *A. johnstonii* or promote invasion by nonnative plants. The consequences of such perturbation could be worse for the species than impacts from fire itself. Prescribed burning may promote open tree and shrub canopies where these plants occur. Total fire exclusion may allow canopy closure, which may have negative consequences for this plant.

Overriding concerns about escalating fire hazard evolving from an extended drought and accumulating dead fuels were paramount in the decision to risk the injury or sacrifice of a limited number of *A. johnstonii*. Information obtained for another rare California *Arabis* species suggests that fire would not unduly harm *A. johnstonii*. *Arabis Shockleyi* Munz., (Shockley's rock cress) growing on the Angeles National Forest, survived the Williams Fire in 2002. *A. johnstonii* has similar growth habits, with basal leaves, tuberous root and aboveground parts that may undergo drought or summer dormancy, and growing in openings in chaparral where fire may burn less intensely. These characteristics suggest that *A. johnstonii* may survive fire given the appropriate fire weather conditions (SBNF botanist M.A. Lardner, personal communication).

In southern California, safe prescribed or controlled burning must occur during narrow windows of opportunity when fuel and weather conditions allow optimal fire safety and containment. These conditions typically occur during winter and spring when fuel moisture is high and there is little chance for fire to escape. The impacts of out-of-season prescribed fire can be different from those of summer fire (reviewed in Beyers and Wakeman 2000), adding further complication to the job of prescribing fire in rare plant habitat. Summer or fall may be an ecologically more appropriate time to burn because many species have passed their peak growth periods and reproductively vulnerable stages. At this time, vegetation may naturally ignite from lightning strikes during mountain thunderstorms

Because fuel reduction is needed in Garner Valley, the SBNF decided that small field trials would be an appropriate risk for this situation: sacrifice a few plants rather than risk decimation of the entire population to wildfire. Consequently, we designed an experiment to test the simulated effects of fire on a limited number of individual *A. johnstonii*. The study compares fire applied during the historic fire season – late summer – to fire applied in winter, when prescribed fire would normally be used. By evaluating plants burned in both seasons, we hope to determine the general response of *A. johnstonii* to fire, as well as its reaction to fire applied outside the "normal" burning window. Fire effects are currently being monitored and evaluated for *A. johnstonii* after two seasons of burning. Initial evidence shows that individual *A. johnstonii* survived and will reproduce after a September fire.

Study Sites

The three *A. johnstonii* occurrences in Garner Valley that could be affected by the proposed fuel reduction program

grow among varying fuel types. These include several plant associations: 1) pebble plain-like with chaparral, 2) open sage/chaparral, and 3) logged yellow pine forest. Although all sites have 10 percent slope or less, they differ in exposure and topographic position. Site 1, near McGregor Flat (hereafter "McGregor"), is located on and near the crest of a slope at an elevation of nearly 2,200 m. Vegetation at the site is composed of chaparral, including species of *Adenostoma*, *Ceanothus*, *Arctostaphylos*, and *Quercus*. At this site, sizeable inter-shrub spaces have high clay/gravel/rock soil components that limit herbaceous fuels. *A. johnstonii* is found scattered in and around the chaparral shrubs, along a dirt access road, and near a water catchment basin used for livestock. Plants grow in full sun and in shade under shrub canopies. Livestock and rabbit grazing activity is high in this area. Fire would burn hot in clusters of chaparral fuels but probably would not carry in inter-shrub spaces because of absence of fuels.

Sites 2 and 3 are located at about 1,200 m in elevation. Site 2, near Kenworthy Station (hereafter "Kenworthy"), faces west, while Site 3, near Quinn Flat (hereafter "Quinn"), faces northwest. At both sites *A. johnstonii* grows in rocky areas on slopes under and around mature *Pinus jeffreyi* Grev. & Balf. (Jeffrey pine) with various amounts of herbaceous and pine litter. The pines that formerly shaded Kenworthy died and were recently logged to reduce fire hazard. Quinn has a mixture of *Artemisia tridentata* Nutt. (big sagebrush), *Adenostoma fasciculatum* Hook & Arn. (chamise), and a few *P. jeffreyi* unevenly scattered across the slope. During certain times of the year sufficient fine fuels are available at Kenworthy and Quinn to carry fire.

There were two other rare plant species growing at Quinn: *Penstemon californicus* [Munz & I.M. Johnston] Keck (California penstemon) and *Calochortus palmeri* S. Watson var. *munzii* F. Ownbey (Munz's mariposa lily). Because no fire effects information is available for these species, they were incorporated into our burn trials. The higher elevation McGregor site had fewer and smaller *A. johnstonii* individuals than the others. Quinn appeared to have more favorable growing conditions, based on the higher *A. johnstonii* population density, greater plant size and increased diversity (Beyers et al. 2004). *Penstemon californicus* and *C. palmeri* grow later in the year than *A. johnstonii*. Therefore, from the September 2003 burns only fire effects data for *A. johnstonii* was available in winter, and data for it alone will be presented here.

METHODS

At each study site, twelve 1-m^2 areas supporting at least five *A. johnstonii* were identified as our study plots. An extra plot was established at Quinn Flat to obtain a larger sample of *P. californicus* and *C. palmeri* var. *munzii*. Each plot was mapped, permanently marked and photographed. Within each plot, all plants of the three study species were mapped and measured (height, two canopy diameters, and phenological attributes – number of flowers, stalks and seed pods). We established 37 plots with a total 382 *A. johnstonii*, 52 *P. californicus*, and 66 *C. palmeri* var. *munzii* observed during pre-burn counts.

To conduct small scale burns with realistic fire intensity and severity of effects, we constructed a capped cylindrical "fire cage" (1.1 m diameter x 0.62 m tall) using 8x8 mesh stainless steel woven wire cloth to use as a firewall to contain the flames during burns (Beyers et al. 2004) (Fig. 2). The fire cage was large enough to cover a 1 m^2 plot with a 10 cm buffer around the edges. Testing of the fire cage in a burn building allowed us to determine how well the cage worked to contain the fire, sparks and fire brands. We also determined how much and what type of fuel was needed for appropriate fire behavior, heat transfer and cooling (Beyers et. al. 2004).

Burning treatments were conducted on September 4, 2003 to imitate a "normal" summer season fire, and late January 22, 2004, to simulate a typical winter prescribed fire. Burn treatments were randomly assigned to 6 plots per site (3 each for September and January), and were paired with 3 grazed and 3 ungrazed control plots. The entire *A. johnstonii* population at Quinn is fenced from grazing so does not have an ungrazed treatment. This allowed us to burn an additional plot on each burn day.

Each burn plot was instrumented with

FIGURE 2--Operational 1 m^2 fire-cage burn of *Arabis johnstonii* conducted during January 2004 at Quinn Flat, San Jacinto Mountains, California.

two thermocouples attached to a digital thermometer: one was at the soil surface, with the other 2 cm or more below the soil surface. In addition, three ceramic tiles treated with temperature sensitive Omega-marker crayons (with maximum melting temperatures of 93, 149, 260 and 399°C) were randomly placed within each plot. Natural fuel was so sparse on most of the plots at the time we conducted the experiment that fuels would not burn sufficiently to carry fire or increase below ground temperatures at the plant root zone. For a successful heat and combustion treatment, 1 kg of pre-weighed excelsior (0.5 kg) and chaparral (0.5 kg) fuels were added to each burn plot at all three sites. A scratch line to inorganic soil and fire shelters were placed around the fire cage to serve as a fuel break. Bricks supported the fire cage above the ground so that a butane torch could be used to ignite fuels. A Forest Service fire engine and crew were on site during all ignitions.

Weather, fuel and soil moisture, and fire behavior variables were recorded prior to and during burns. Three soil and three fuel samples were collected at each site. These samples were later weighed and dried at the laboratory to determine percent moisture. The random placement of thermocouples and thermal tiles were mapped. Tiles were individually labeled and placed with half of the tile above and the other half under ground (at least 2 cm). Ignition time for each plot took about 30 seconds. Active flame duration was about 2 to 3 minutes. The thermal pulse into the soil was monitored until the soil temperature began to decrease, which was generally within 30 minutes after ignition.

Survival, growth, and recruitment of *A. johnstonii*, *P. californicus* and *C.*

palmeri will be measured twice a year for three years. In this paper, we report only the effects of the September 4, 2003 burns on *A. johnstonii* because of its earlier emergence, growth and reproduction.

RESULTS

The data reported here were obtained from the burns conducted on September 4, 2003 at all three sites. Air temperatures ranged between 23 and 29°C (74 and 84°F) during the burns. Relative humidity was appropriate for burning until a storm blew in. The storm front brought rain and sleet and interrupted our last two burns at Quinn. Maximum wind speed (gusts) varied between 1 and 12 miles per hour and changed directions over the course of the day. Fire behavior varied among plots with maximum flame height ranging between 1.3 and 2.2 m with an average height of 1.8 m. During the burns, flame angles varied with the wind--maximum flame angles on plots ranged between 25 and 45 degrees. Burning of the fuels within the fire cage took about 3 minutes and averaged 95 percent combustion for all trials (table 1).

Prefire fuel and soil moisture varied among plots and sites (Fig. 3). Thermocouple depth varied by 3 cm among all plots. Temperature profiles showed peaks within the first 5 minutes

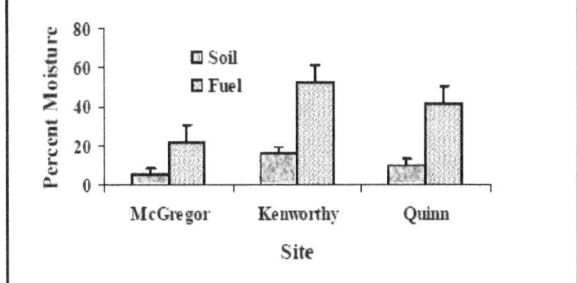

FIGURE 3 Average percent moisture content for on-site soils and fuels at study sites prior to the September 4, 2003 burns. Error bars are the standard error of the means. N=27 for fuel & soil.

TABLE 1--Abiotic conditions recorded during experimental burns conducted September 4, 2003, at the three study sites on the San Bernardino National Forest, San Jacinto, California.

Site	Plot #	Air °C	RH %	Wind mph	NSEW	Fuel % consumed	Flame height m	[a]Flame < degrees	[b]T1 depth cm
McGregor	1	27	48	7	N	98	1.5	30	2.2
	3	29	36	3.6	NE	98	2.2	45	3.7
	6	27	36	6.9	NE	95	1.5	30	4.2
Kenworthy	2	31	49	7.9	SE	99	2	25	5.4
	11	31	38	2.7	SE	92	1.3	30	3.2
	12	27	49	3	S	98	2.0	30	3
Quinn	3	29	44	8.3	SE	95	1.7	45	4.6
	4	24	65	12	SSW	95	1.7	45	4.5
	6	23	58	7	NW	95	2.0	45	3.2
	13	24	100	1.5	N	85	1.5	30	5.2

[a] Flame angle (<) in degrees
[b] T1=buried thermocouple

after ignition (Fig. 4a). Maximum temperatures reached 400°C on the soil surface and were highly variable among plots. Below ground temperatures remained below 40°C (Fig. 4b). The thermal crayon tiles did not show any change below ground. However, most tiles registered increased temperatures above ground throughout each plot. The lowest tile temperature of 93°C was reached on all (26) except two tiles at the McGregor site. Twenty-two tiles registered temperatures between 149 and 260°C; only one tile from Quinn, two from McGregor, and three from Kenworthy did not reach these temperatures. Seven tiles (four at McGregor and three at Quinn) reached temperatures between 260 and 399°C. One tile at the Quinn site reached a temperature of over 400°C

Pre-burn counts of *A. johnstonii* varied among plots and sites. Quinn had the most individuals per plot overall, while McGregor had the least (Fig. 5). Data collected in January after the September burn show that post-fire *A. johnstonii* populations were similar to pre-burn counts (Table 2). However, over this same period of time the unburned plots increased in plant abundance (table 2). Overall, the average number of plants found per square meter was slightly lower in the burned compared to the unburned plots for all sites (Fig. 6). Post-fire mean plant heights were less than in unburned plots (Fig. 7). The average cover for burned plots was only about one third (12.8 cm^2) of the cover observed in unburned plots (31.4 cm^2) (Fig. 8). At this time, results have not been tested for significance.

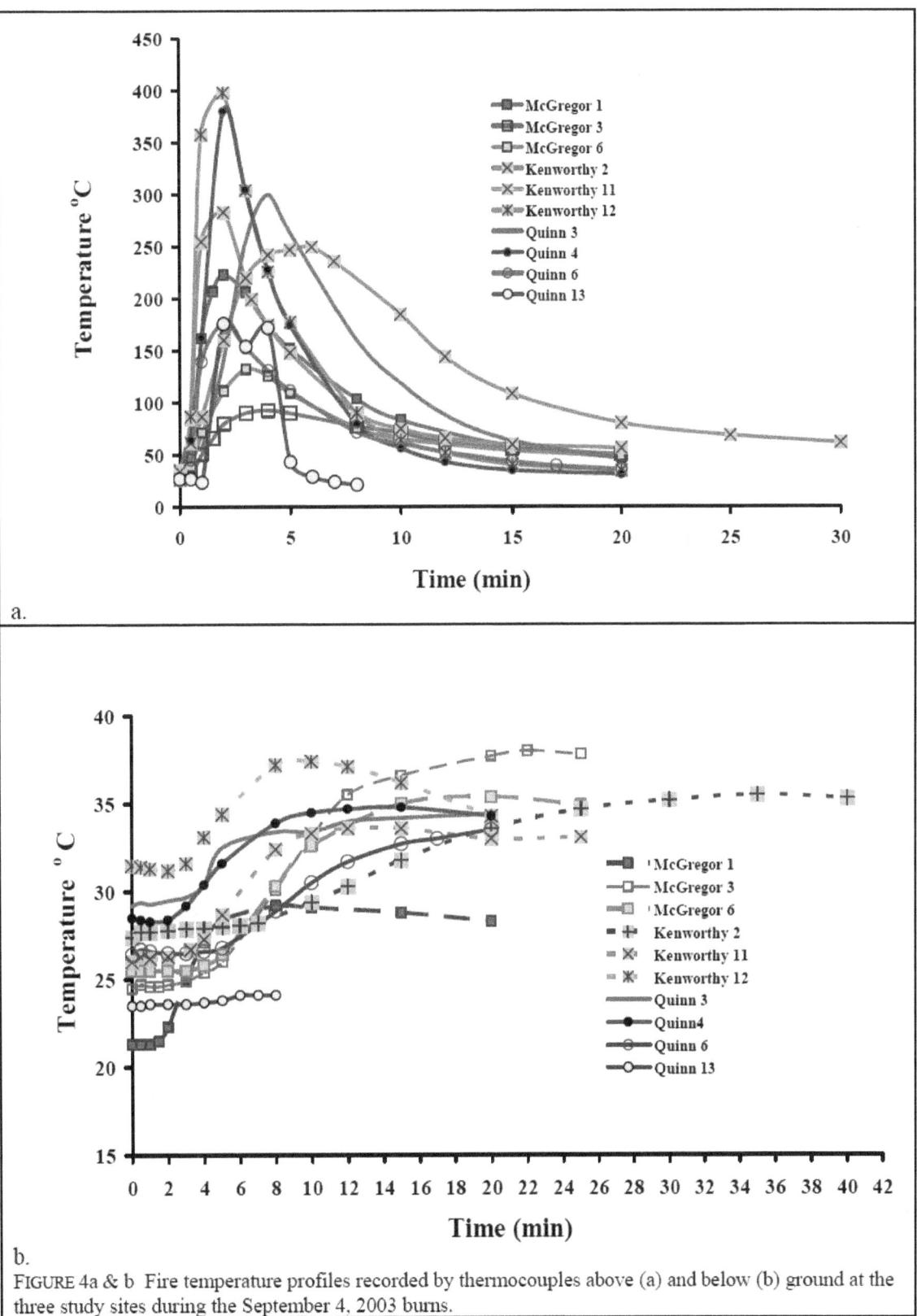

a.

b.

FIGURE 4a & b Fire temperature profiles recorded by thermocouples above (a) and below (b) ground at the three study sites during the September 4, 2003 burns.

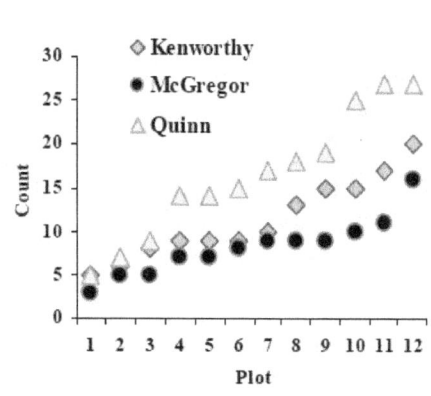

FIGURE 5 -Number of *Arabis johnstonii* plants per plot recorded in pre-burn counts at three study sites on the San Bernardino National Forest, California.

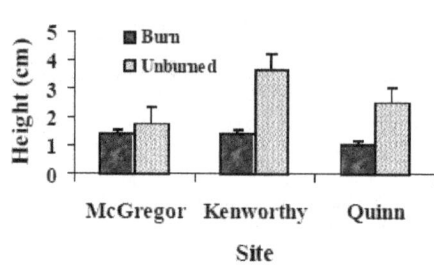

FIGURE 7 Average height of *Arabis johnstonii* plants in burned and control plots recorded 4.5 months after the September 2003 burns on the San Bernardino National Forest, California. Height of unburned plants included dead flower stalks from the previous year; all flower stalks burned in treated plots. Error bars represent standard error of mean.

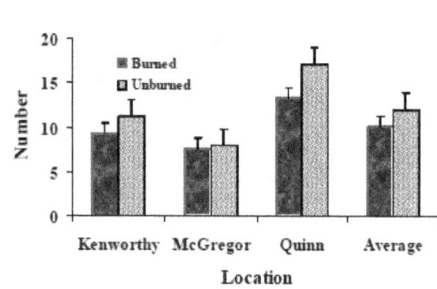

Figure 6 Average number of *A. johnstonii* plants per square meter recorded January 22, 2004 at each study site on the San Bernardino National Forest, CA. Error bars represent standard error of mean.

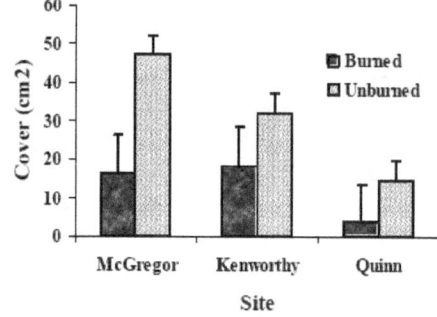

FIGURE 8 Average cover of *Arabis johnstonii* plants in burned and unburned plots 4.5 months after the September 2004 burns. Error bars represent standard error of mean.

TABLE 2 Total number of *Arabis johnstonii* plants recorded within all plots at each site before (Pre) and 4.5 months after (Post) the September 04, 2003 experimental burns on the San Bernardino National Forest, California.

Treatment	Kenworthy		McGregor		Quinn	
	Pre	Post	Pre	Post	Pre	Post
Burn 1	25	28	23	23	42	40
Unburned	85	103	87	102	118	129

DISCUSSION AND MANAGEMENT IMPLICATIONS

Based on the temperatures recorded by the thermocouples and thermal tiles, we are confident that all *A. johnstonii* within a plot were burned or exposed to realistically intense heat above the soil surface. Abiotic factors among the sites although variable, were moderate. The lower elevation Quinn and Kenworthy sites had higher fuel and soil moisture than the higher elevation McGregor site.

Based on the fire weather conditions recorded, the 1 kg of standardized fuels that was added to each plot aptly normalized the fire behavior, treatment and combustion among all plots on all sites. By adding fuel, we were able to test if *A. johnstonii* would survive fire under conditions that might occur when precipitation promoted more herbaceous fuels or when *A. johnstonii* grew with heavier fuels, such as under shrub canopies. Plots at McGregor recorded somewhat lower maximum fire temperatures above ground during the burns. Several factors that may have contributed to this are: it is higher in elevation, it was the first site burned in the early morning, soil composition had a higher rock content which may have also affected thermocouple placement.

The placement of the thermocouples and thermal tiles or the character of the soil substrate may have contributed to variable temperatures recorded. Even still, adequate heat was dispersed within the fire cage to assure that all plants received some high thermal challenge. Duration of heat was shorter and more intense above than below ground. Below soil temperature increases took longer, but did not exceed maximum thermal threshold ranges (40-52°C or 104-127°F) reported for temperate zone herbaceous species during growing seasons for plant injury (Larcher 1975). This increased the likelihood that the tuberous root of the *A. johnstonii* would survive a fire of this intensity. *A. johnstonii* that occur in the immediate proximity of very heavy fuels supplied by chaparral or yellow pine may experience higher or more prolonged temperatures than what we applied.

Plant number increased 4.5 months after the fire in control plots but remained relatively static in the burn plots. Two *A. johnstonii* were obviously lost during the burns at Quinn, but among all sites, there was a net gain of one plant between pre- and post-burn observations. However, this net increase in the burned population numbers is considerably less than the 15 percent increase observed in the unburned population during the same growth period. As expected, plant size and cover were less in burned plots. In all cases, the entire plant was measured, which included all leaves, stalks and flowers without differentiating dried stalks that remained from previous seasons. These dried stalks all burned in the test fires. Loss of these stalks in the burn plots somewhat exaggerates the difference in dimensions between burned and unburned *A. johnstonii*. Long-term observations will show if fire intensity or soil heating affect plant vigor or viability. Results from the September 2003 fire indicate that mature *A. johnstonii* can survive and grow after being exposed to fire. Future plot measurements will determine what effect fire has on seed production and germination, seedling establishment, and population dynamics. Comparisons between grazed and ungrazed plots will be evaluated after one year to determine if this additional level of disturbance affected the plant density, size or reproduction.

The known fire dynamics of the associated vegetation suggests that *A. johnstonii* also evolved with fire as an environmental component. The initial response of *A. johnstonii* to fire in this experiment is encouraging since it was resilient enough to produce flowers within 5 months of being exposed to a late summer fire. This plant may be fire tolerant and we are hopeful that it one day can be easily incorporated into future fire management programs. The results from the January burn, to be collected later this year, will indicate whether *A. johnstonii* can also survive fire during a less phenologically optimal season.

ACKNOWLEDGEMENTS

This project was funded by the Joint Fire Science Program and was made possible by the cooperation of the San Bernardino National Forest staff and fire crew. Field and lab operations were expedited through the help of many individuals, including Lynne Casal, Joey Chong, Eugene Hanson, David Kisor and Rosie Martinez. We also appreciate the editorial improvements made by Melody Lardner and Tim Paysen.

LITERATURE CITED

Berg, K., and T. Krantz. 1982. A survey of two endemic species of plants in the San Jacinto Mountains: *Arabis johnstonii* Munz and Layia ziegleri Munz. Unpublished report prepared for the San Bernardino National Forest.

Beyers, J. L. and C. D. Wakeman. 2000. Season of burn effects in southern California chaparral. Pp. 45-55 in J. E. Keeley, M. Baer-Keeley, and C. J. Fotheringham (eds.), 2nd interface between ecology and land development in California. Open-File Report 00-62. Sacramento, CA: U.S. Geological Survey.

Beyers, Jan L. Marcia G. Narog, Christie J. Sclafani, and Christina Escobar, 2003. Using a "Fire Cage" to test the response of *Arabis johnstonii* to fire. Unpublished extended abstract #P2-16. Second International Wildland Fire Ecology and Fire Management Congress and Fifth Symposium on Fire and Forest Meteorology, 16-20 November 2003, Orlando, Florida. Conference CD-ROM. Available from American Meteorological Society, 45 Beacon Street, Boston, MA 02108-3693.

California Natural Diversity Database. 2001. RareFind 2, Version 2.1.2 (September 5 2001, update). Sacramento, CA: California Department of Fish and Game.

California Native Plant Society. 2001. Inventory of rare and endangered plants of California (sixth edition). Rare Plant Scientific Advisory Committee, David P. Tabor, convening editor. Sacramento, CA: California Native Plant Society.

Larcher, Walter. 1995. Physiological Plant Ecology, Ecophysiology and stress physiology of functional groups, 3rd edition. Springer, New York, N.Y. 506p.

Rollins, R. C. 1993. Brassicaceae. In Hickman, James C. (ed.), The Jepson manual: higher plants of California. Berkeley, CA: University of California Press: 392-404.

USDA Forest Service, Pacific Southwest Region Forest Sensitive Species by Forest. 2001.

Effects of a Natural Fire on a Kuenzler's Hedgehog Cactus (*Echinocereus fendleri* var. *kuenzleri*) and Nylon Hedgehog Cactus (*Echinocereus viridiflorus*) Population in Southeastern New Mexico

ROBERT C. SIVINSKI

New Mexico Forestry Division, P.O. Box 1948, Santa Fe, NM 87504

ABSTRACT. During the summer of 1992, a natural wildfire burned 250 acres of juniper savanna on Rawhide Ridge in the Guadalupe Mountains of southeastern New Mexico. This fire burned through the center of a Kuenzler's hedgehog cactus population. This threatened cactus is locally sympatric with the more abundant nylon hedgehog cactus, which has similar growth form and stature. The local populations of both cacti were assessed within equal areas of burned and unburned habitats in May 1999. Burn area density of Kuenzler's hedgehog cactus was about one-third the density of unburned habitat. Nylon hedgehog cactus density in the burn area was about one-fifth the density of adjacent unburned habitat. The majority of individuals of both species found in the burned habitat appeared to be new recruits after the fire. Therefore, mortality was extremely high during this fire and population recovery is very slow for both species.

INTRODUCTION

Echinocereus fendleri (Englem.) Engelm. ex Rümpler var. *kuenzleri* (Castetter et al.) L. Benson (Kuenzler's hedgehog cactus), a taxon listed as threatened under the Endangered Species Act, occupies arid grassland and piñon-juniper woodland at sporadic locations in the Sacramento and Guadalupe mountains of southeastern New Mexico. The effects of human impacts (livestock grazing, roads, collection, etc.) and ecological processes, such as fire, on this endangered grassland plant are of interest to land management agencies within its range. During the summer of 1992, a wildfire burned approximately 100 hectares (250 acres) of juniper savanna and desert grassland on Rawhide Ridge in the Guadalupe Mountains of southeastern New Mexico. This fire burned through the center of a population of Kuenzler's cactus. A brief 1996 search of part of the burned area by the author failed to locate any surviving Kuenzler's cactus or the more common *Echinocereus viridiflorus* Engelm. (nylon hedgehog cactus). A subsequent intensive survey of the area was conducted in May 1999 and is the subject of this report. The purpose of this survey was to thoroughly assess the burned area and comparable adjacent unburned areas in an attempt to document the impacts of fire on these *Echinocereus* populations.

STUDY AREA

The study area is in the Guadalupe Mountains of Eddy County, New Mexico and is located on the lower part of Rawhide Ridge in the Lincoln National Forest at T23S R21E Sections 3 SW¼, 4 SE¼, 9, and 10 NW¼. The elevation ranges from 1610-1650 m (5,280-5,410 ft). This ridge top has slopes ranging from 0-15%, but most of the survey occurred on gradients of less than 5%. The soils have a silty, sandy loam texture and are tan to reddish in color. Limestone gravel and cobble make up to approximately 50% cover and the barren limestone bedrock is frequently exposed at the surface.

Vegetation aspect is of a shrubby grassland and juniper savanna. Tree cover varies from 2-25% and is predominantly composed of one-seed juniper (*Juniperus monosperma*). A few piñon (*Pinus edulis*) and alligator juniper (*Juniperus deppeana*) contribute to the overstory. The relatively low-growing Pinchot's juniper (*Juniperus pinchotii*) is nearly as abundant as *J. monosperma* and could be classified as either a small tree or large shrub. Other common shrub species include banana yucca (*Yucca baccata*), New Mexico agave (*Agave parryi* var. *neomexicana*), sacahuista (*Nolina texana*), sotol (*Dasylirion leiophyllum*), cholla (*Cylindropuntia imbricata*), prickly pear (*Opuntia phaeacantha*), squawbush (*Rhus trilobata*), algerita (*Berberis haematocarpa*), and Apache plume (*Fallugia paradoxa*). Grasses are the dominant ground cover (25-40%) and are mainly represented by curlyleaf muhly (*Muhlenbergia setifolia*), blue grama (*Bouteloua gracilis*) and black grama (*Bouteloua eriopoda*). Tabosa grass (*Pleuraphis mutica*) is localized, but densely covers silty swales in Karst depressions. Herbaceous species are fairly diverse, but comprise less than 5% of the ground cover. Common species include bladderpod (*Physaria fendleri*), globe mallow (*Sphaeralcea leptophylla*), vervain (*Verbena perennis*), and baby white aster (*Chaetopappa ericoides*). Species of low-growing, cylindrical cacti growing in this habitat include Kuenzler's hedgehog cactus, nylon hedgehog cactus, pincushion cactus (*Escobaria vivipera*), Heyder's pincushion (*Mammillaria heyderi*), and

Chihuahuan fish-hook cactus (*Sclerocactus uncinatus* ssp. *wrightii*).

METHODS

Field surveys were conducted on May 11-13, 1999, which coincides with the early blooming period for Kuenzler's hedgehog in the Guadalupe Mountains. Surveyors included the author and three U.S. Forest Service employees. The first day was spent by a single observer establishing the perimeters of the burned and unburned study areas and flagging any observed Kuenzler's hedgehog cacti. All four participants worked the following days. A total of 60 man hours were devoted to this field survey. Exactly one-half of this time was spent surveying the burned area and the other 30 hours surveying the adjacent unburned areas.

Care was taken to ensure that the burned and unburned surveys were comparable. The same amount of time was spent in each treatment and roughly equal acreages were covered in the burned and unburned areas. Unburned area surveys were conducted on both sides of the burned area to determine if the original pre-fire population was continuous across the ridge top. Also, a few small areas of unburned habitat were located within the fire area. The survey was conducted by four men walking abreast at approximately 15 meter intervals. The outside man placed occasional strips of red flagging along his route so the inside man could keep a proper interval on the return trip across the study area.

The most abundant and evenly distributed small cactus species in the area is a brownish red- flowered species of nylon hedgehog cactus (*E. viridiflorus*). This species is comparable to Kuenzler's hedgehog in a fire impact study since they occur in the same grassy habitat and have approximately the same morphological stature. Therefore, all nylon hedgehog cacti were also counted in this study to corroborate the fire impact findings for Kuenzler's hedgehog.

RESULTS AND DISCUSSION

Gross vegetation changes within the burned area (after seven years of recovery) were not especially dramatic. The line between burned and unburned habitats was often difficult to detect. Grass and forb cover were similar in both the burned and unburned treatments and most of the burned woody species (yucca, Pinchot's juniper, squawbush, Apache plume, etc.) had sprouted from their root crowns. The most significant visual change in the burned area was the nearly complete elimination of sotol from the post-fire flora and the standing dead remains of one-seed juniper and cholla.

Detection of young, non-flowering Kuenzler's hedgehog cacti in grass-covered habitat is extraordinarily difficult. Only one non-flowering juvenile was located during the entire survey (burned area). All others cacti seen were adults and most of these had flowers or large flower buds. Since the juvenile fraction of the population could not be assessed by this field survey, it is reasonable to assume the proportionality of juvenile to adult individuals is similar in burned and unburned treatments.

Kuenzler's hedgehog is distributed nearly throughout the entire study area. The area of greatest density is the unburned habitat just east of the fire line. Its greatest density within the burn area is also near the east fire line. Density begins to peter-out in the unburned area west of the fire line and only a single cactus was located in the eastern-most transect of the study area. Likewise, there are very few plants at the tip of the ridge in the eastern-most part of the study area. Therefore, it is reasonable to assume that the fire impacted a large portion (possibly half) of the Kuenzler's hedgehog population on Rawhide Ridge and comparison of the burned and unburned areas is valid (Table 1). At the time of this survey (seven years post-fire), there were two-thirds fewer Kuenzler's hedgehog cacti in the burned area than in the comparable unburned habitat (43 vs. 110 respectively). The difference in nylon hedgehog densities was more dramatic with almost four-fifths fewer plants in the fire impacted area than the unburned area (74 vs. 342 respectively).

Only two of the more than 20 Kuenzler's hedgehog cacti seen by the author in the burned area appeared to be survivors of the 1992 wildfire. One was at the fire line (3 meters inside the burn area) where the fire intensity may have been low. It appeared to have been damaged because it had pupped three additional heads from the side of the

TABLE 1. 1999 densities of Kuenzler's hedgehog and nylon hedgehog cacti in equivalent areas of burned and unburned habitat on Rawhide Ridge, Guadalupe Mountains, NM.

	Kuenzler's Hedgehog	Nylon Hedgehog
Unburned - East Side	70	116
Unburned - West Side	34	223
Unburned inclusions (within fire area)	6	3
Total within unburned habitat	110	342
Total within burned habitat	43	74

plant facing the fire. The other survivor was within a large barren area of rock outcrop where it had escaped the flames. All other Kuenzler's hedgehog cacti seen by the author within the burned area lacked the gray epidermis on the lower stem, which marks older cacti. Therefore, approximately 90% of Kuenzler's hedgehog cacti seen in the fire-impacted area were probably less than seven years-old and had only recently reached reproductive age. Most cactus species of this type require at least four to five years to become large enough to flower and make fruit. These new individuals apparently germinated from the soil seed bank within a year or two after the fire. Seed dispersal from mature cacti in adjacent unburned habitat is also a possible source of these new individuals, but less likely, since dispersal over a distance is probably a slower process.

The majority of the approximately 60 Kuenzler's hedgehog cacti seen by the author in the unburned area had gray lower stems and appeared relatively old. Since nearly all of the Kuenzler's hedgehog cacti seen in the burned area were relatively young, it is reasonable to assume that mortality during the 1992 fire was almost complete. Severe mortality also occurred in the fire-impacted population of nylon hedgehog cactus. The dead remains of several nylon hedgehog cacti were still visible in 1996 and no live plants were seen during a brief walk through the burned area. Although relative age is difficult to determine for nylon hedgehog, the assumption that the majority of nylon hedgehog cacti in the burned area were less than seven years-old is probably also reasonable. The greater number of nylon hedgehog cacti than Kuenzler's

hedgehog cacti (74 and 43 respectively) in the burned area may be explained by the fact that the nylon hedgehog is a more abundant species and had established a larger soil seed bank for the germination of new plants in the post-fire habitat.

CONSERVATION CONSIDERATIONS

Fire appears to have an immediate and severe effect on Kuenzler's hedgehog populations. These cacti usually grow in grassy areas and are frequently found within clumps of grass. This proximity to highly flammable fine fuels results in the death of most cacti when fire sweeps through the habitat.

The impact of fire over the long-term is not so bleak. The Rawhide Ridge population of Kuenzler's hedgehog was apparently large enough to establish a soil seed bank capable of immediately colonizing the post-fire habitat. Germination and establishment may have been enhanced by nutrients released from burned vegetation. Total recovery, however, appears to be a slow process. Seven years after the Rawhide Ridge Fire, the adult population within the burned area was rather spotty and significantly less numerous than in the adjacent unburned habitat. The soil seed bank in the burned area was probably depleted after the first flush of germinants and will probably need many years of reproductive success by new adults to become sufficient to colonize a subsequent fire. Population density and an uneven age structure will also take many more years to normalize to pre-fire levels. At least two more generations similar to the first flush of post-fire recruitment will be needed to bring this species back to pre-fire density.

Prescribed fire is an important land management tool. Its use need not be eliminated from areas containing Kuenzler's hedgehog populations, but its impact could be significantly reduced if two considerations are included in the prescription:

1. An entire population of Kuenzler's hedgehog population should not be burned in any single prescribed fire event. The distribution of this plant is spotty and patch densities are usually very low (often less than five individuals). Low density patches may not have a sufficient soil seed bank to recover, and colonization of a particular patch of post-fire habitat may be entirely reliant upon seed dispersal from plants in adjacent unburned habitats.

2. Sufficient time between fire events should be allowed for the burned population to recover from the first fire and establish a soil seed bank capable of colonizing a subsequent burn. This is a very slow process and requires several generations to regain the pre-fire density of adult, seed-producing cacti. Therefore, fire frequency should not be less than 25 year intervals, and 50 year intervals may be a more prudent choice.

This survey should be repeated in another 10-15 years to test the assumptions made in this report on the time period needed for post-fire recovery. Fire frequency prescriptions could be refined and adjusted when additional information is available.

ACKNOWLEDGEMENTS

This study was funded by the Lincoln National Forest. The field survey was assisted by the sharp eyes of Alex Camero, Sam Fragua, and Duane Ross. This population of Kuenzler's hedgehog was initially discovered by Dan Baggao (BLM-Roswell) while fighting the Rawhide Ridge fire in 1992.

Knowlton's Cactus (*Pediocactus knowltonii*): Eighteen Years of Monitoring and Recovery Actions

ROBERT C. SIVINSKI[1] AND CHARLIE MCDONALD[2]

[1]New Mexico Forestry Division, P.O. Box 1948, Santa Fe, NM 87504
[2]USDA-Forest Service, 333 Broadway Blvd., SE, Rm. 209, Albuquerque, New Mexico 87102

ABSTRACT. *Pediocactus knowltonii* is a rare, endemic cactus that is presently known to occur on a single 10-hectare hill in northwestern New Mexico near the Colorado border. It was listed as federally endangered in 1979. Population monitoring and recovery actions were initiated when the Recovery Plan was adopted in 1985. The land at the type locality has been donated to The Nature Conservancy and long-term monitoring plots have been annually studied since 1986. This population reached peak density in 1994 and is presently in decline. A total of 301 clones were made and transplanted to two nearby habitats above the Los Pinos arm of Navajo Lake, beginning in 1985. Transplant survival and flowering were good, but natural recruitment has been slow. Seeding trials were also conducted at both locations in 1985 and 1991. Only 4% of seeds planted became established as adult plants and no new recruitment has yet been observed.

INTRODUCTION

Pediocactus knowltonii L. Benson (Knowlton's cactus), listed as endangered by U.S. Fish & Wildlife Service (USFWS) on November 28, 1979, is one of the rarest cacti in the United States. It was discovered in 1958 by the late Fred Knowlton and named by Lyman Benson (1961). Knowlton's cactus is known to occur only at its type locality on a small hill of about 10 hectares in San Juan County, New Mexico just south of the Colorado/New Mexico border above Navajo Lake. Extensive searches of this region in New Mexico and adjacent Colorado have failed to locate additional natural populations.

Shortly after its discovery, this *P. knowltonii* population was repeatedly visited by cactus collectors to obtain plants for the succulent hobbyist trade. This population was severely impacted by the New Mexico Cactus and Succulent Society in 1960, which was under the mistaken perception that this site would be flooded by the newly constructed Navajo Reservoir. Field trips were organized to salvage the cacti from the type locality. Several thousand *P. knowltonii* plants were reportedly taken by this group of hobbyists (Paul Knight, personal communication, 1984). This rare cactus is presently available as plants or seeds from licensed commercial growers, which has relieved some of the collection pressures on the natural population.

In an effort to protect the only natural population of this rare cactus, the landowner (Public Service Company of New Mexico) donated the 10-hectare type locality to The Nature Conservancy (TNC). This small preserve was fenced to exclude livestock. A few cacti (<100) occur on adjacent BLM land, which is also enclosed by a livestock-proof fence.

A recovery plan was developed for Knowlton's cactus and approved by USFWS in March, 1985 (USFWS, 1985). A reintroduction program into adjacent suitable habitats was identified as the primary effort towards recovery of this species. Monitoring at the type locality was also initiated to obtain information on growth and phenology from the natural population for comparison to the transplant efforts.

HABITAT AND POPULATION CHARACTERISTICS

Pediocactus knowltonii habitat occurs on Tertiary alluvial deposits overlying the San Jose Formation. These deposits form rolling, gravelly hills covered with piñon pine (*Pinus edulis* Englem.), Rocky Mountain juniper (*Juniperus scopulorum* Sarg.) and black sagebrush (*Artemisia nova* A.Nels.). A relatively dense soil cover of foliose lichen (*Parmelia* sp.) is an unusual aspect of the habitat. This cactus grows in full sun between cobbles and in the understory of sagebrush and conifers. Average annual precipitation is 30 cm, arriving mostly during late summer and winter months.

The only known natural habitat is the top and slopes of a single small hill. Knowlton's cactus density is variable at this location, but can be surprisingly high in some areas with up to13 cacti per square meter. The total population in 1992 was estimated to be 12,000 plants by using a series of belt transects across the hill where this species occurs. Individual plants can become reproductive adults when they are 10 mm, or more, in diameter. Flowering peaks in early May and fruits ripen in June and July. This small cactus has

contractile roots, which can pull the entire plant below the soil surface during periods of severe drought. All Knowlton's cacti begin with a single stem and most retain that morphology throughout their lives. However, plants that are damaged or buried for a long period will often become multi-stem plants. Approximately one-quarter of the natural population have 2-15 heads per plant.

MONITORING AND POPULATION TRENDS

Twenty-four circular monitoring plots (4 m diameter) were established in 1986 at the natural population of Knowlton's cactus in the TNC preserve. These plots have all conditions of slope, aspect, soil type, and associated vegetation on the small hill at the type locality. Only 11 of these plots contained Knowlton's cactus during the term of this study. One of these occupied plots (including rebar, tags, and an undetermined number of cacti) was removed by cactus poachers in 1995, so the final data set consists of a ten-plot total. Each plant within an occupied plot was measured and marked with a numbered tag held in the ground by a 8-penny nail. Stem diameter, and number of flowers or fruits have been recorded during the last eighteen years.

The total numbers of *P. knowltonii* within the study plots at the type locality between 1986 and 2003 are shown in Figure 1. The 1989 monitoring was incomplete (only 5 of 11 plots) and has been deleted from this analysis. Overall, the population trend increased by 78% from 1986 to 1994, then continuously decreased from 1995 to 2003 to a final number slightly below the original 1986 density. The steep decline and increase between 1995 and 1997 is an artifact of detectibility. Many cacti had pulled into

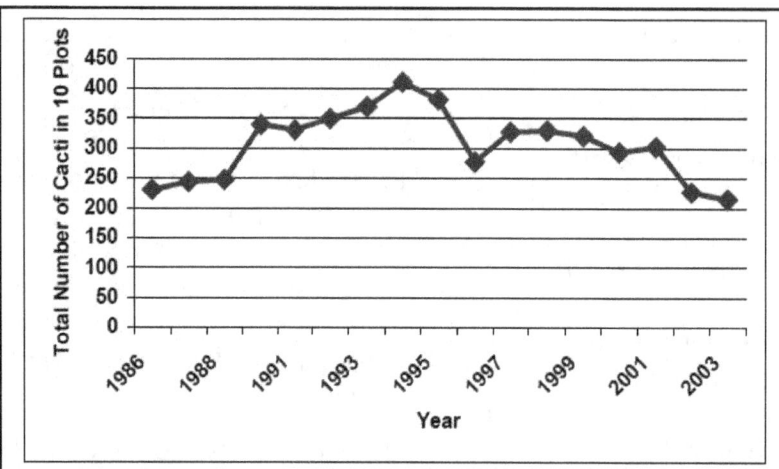

FIGURE 1. Total numbers of *Pediocactus knowltonii* in the ten monitoring plots at the TNC Preserve, New Mexico. Each plot is circular with a 4m diameter

the ground during the extreme drought year of 1996 and could not be accurately counted until 1997. Therefore, the trend line between 1995 and 1997 should, actually, be more gradual than shown in Figure 1.

There are no weather stations near the TNC Preserve, but a severe, long-term drought has been apparent in the Four Corners Region for the last several years and is probably the driving force behind the recent decline of this population. These small cacti are very drought tolerant, however, dry conditions cause an increase in rabbit and rodent attacks, which are frequently fatal. Recruitment to this population is not consistent over time and several years can pass between episodes of significant germination and establishment. A great many seedlings were observed during the early- and mid-1990s, but relatively fewer new plants were found in the monitoring plots during the years after 1995.

TRANSPLANTING PROGRAM

A ten-mile radius south of the *P. knowltonii* type locality was searched in

1985 and again in 1991 for suitable habitats that are similar to the natural habitat of this species. Suitability criteria were cobbley substrates in piñon-juniper woodland with a dominant shrub component of black sagebrush. Two locations were selected as potential reintroduction sites. One on Bureau of Land Management land approximately two miles south of the type locality and another on Bureau of Reclamation land approximately 5 miles to the south at Navajo Lake.

The reintroduction (transplant) program began in May, 1985, when 250 stem cuttings were taken from multi-stem plants at the type locality. These clones were taken to a greenhouse and grown in pots over the summer until fully rooted. One hundred fifty of these adult clones were placed at the transplant location on the Los Pinos arm of Navajo Lake, which is hereafter referred to as the Navajo #1 Site. They were planted in fall of 1985 in a grid pattern at two-meter intervals along 15 lines of ten plants each (Olwell et al, 1987). This site was supplemented with another 102 cuttings planted on the south side of this grid in the early spring of 1995. These later transplants are in the same general area, but are referred to as the Navajo #2 Site.

An additional 250 cuttings were taken in the spring of 1991. Each of the parent plants used for the 1991 cuttings were marked so that they could be monitored for any mortality that resulted from the stem cut. In September 1991, a total of 149 five month-old clones where planted on the BLM's Reese Canyon Area of Critical Environmental Concern (ACEC), which is referred to as the BLM #1 Site. This transplant effort differed from the Navajo Lake site by method of planting and placement pattern. The Navajo Lake plants were transplanted with the rooting medium still attached to the roots. The BLM #1 transplants were entirely bare-root plantings. The BLM #1 Site contains three lines of fifty plants each and spaced two meters apart (Fig. 2). Ten clusters of five plants (3-4 dm apart) are spaced at two-meter intervals along each line. The northern-most line is Line 1 and the southern-most Line 3:

1A	1B	1C	1D	1E	1F	1G	1H	1I	1J
2A	2B	2C	2D	2E	2F	2G	2H	2I	2J
3A	3B	3C	3D	3E	3F	3G	3H	3I	3J

FIGURE 2. Placement Pattern for Transplants at BLM #1 Site, arrangement of blocks.

Each five-plant cluster is arranged with the center plant being No. 1, the northern-most plant as No. 2, then clockwise to No. 5 (Fig. 3).

	1A2	
1A5	1A1	1A3
	1A4	

FIGURE 3. Placement Pattern for Plants within blocks.

These cacti do not all flower simultaneously. Therefore, the rationale for planting five-plant clusters is to increase the number of flowering plants in close proximity to one another and, hopefully, increase the potential for pollination and seed set.

Impacts of Cloning Operations

On 7 May 1991, Steve Brack, independent horticultural contractor, took 250 single-stem cuttings of Knowlton's cactus from multiple-stemmed individuals at the type locality population. After removing a cutting from the base of each cactus, a small rock was placed against the wound and a number was assigned to the donor plant.

This number was inscribed on an aluminum tag, which was anchored to the ground near the plant with a nail. Unfortunately, these tags were soft aluminum and 40 were torn away from their anchor nails (by wind?) and were lost.

A total of 210 secure marker tags were relocated in May of 1992. Of these, 185 donor plants that were still alive. Another 25 indicated dead plants or an area were no plant could be located and was assumed to be dead. This sample of 210 donor cacti experienced a 12 percent rate of mortality from May 1991 to May 1992. During this same period of time, unmolested, multiple-stemmed cacti in adjacent study plots experienced a natural mortality rate of 12.9 percent (n= 101). Therefore, no increase in mortality resulted from the stem damage incurred during the Knowlton's cactus cloning operation.

Transplant Survival

The clones at the transplant sites have persisted very well. Eighteen years after planting, 62 (41%) of the original Navajo #1 transplants were still surviving in 2003 (Table 1). An additional 102 cacti were transplanted to the Navajo Lake site in 1996 (Navajo #2), but immediately faced severe drought conditions that killed one-fifth of the new plants. The Navajo #2 transplant site had 66 (65%) of the original plants surviving in 2003, nine years after planting. Of the 149 cacti planted at the BLM #1 site in September 1991, 66 (44%) were still alive in May of 2003. This demonstrates the hardiness and suitability of this plant for establishing new populations through transplantation. The severe drought year 1996 cause many of these transplants to contract below the soil surface. These were not counted again until the following year (Table 1).

A significant problem with the method of autumn planting was encountered at the BLM #1 site. During the first winter after the September planting, approximately one third of the cacti were frost-heaved from the ground. These plants were found lying on the surface in a desiccated condition and were immediately replanted in March 1992. Several factors many be responsible for this problem. Unlike the Navajo Lake site, these cacti were planted bare-root and may have lacked the additional anchor of artificial potting soil. The late season planting also did not allow sufficient time for root development prior to winter dormancy. Soils at the BLM #1 site also have a finer texture and retain water that could contribute to frost heaving. Fortunately, root development during the growing season of 1992 allowed these plants to remain anchored in the soil during the following winters.

Flowering and Fruiting

Comparison of Knowlton's cactus reproductive activity in the natural population at the type locality and transplant sites is difficult because the transplants are cohorts of aging adults while the natural population contains all age classes. Therefore, the type locality data is modified to exclude all < 10 mm

TABLE 1. Total number and percent survival of *Pediocactus knowltonii* transplants counted at the Navajo Lake and BLM #1 transplant sites.

	Navajo #1		Navajo #2		BLM #1	
	N	% surviving	N	% surviving	N	% surviving
1986	150	100%				
1987	140	93%				
1988	125	83%				
1989	119	79%				
1990	116	77%				
1991	107	71%			149	100%
1992	107	71%			137	92%
1993	102	68%			121	81%
1994	98	65%			114	76%
1995	94	63%	102	100%	96	64%
1996	69	46%	76	75%	76	51%
1997	85	57%	81	79%	93	62%
1998	75	50%	76	75%	90	60%
1999	68	45%	73	72%	81	54%
2000	68	45%	68	67%	80	54%
2001	63	42%	75	74%	80	54%
2002	63	42%	68	67%	69	46%
2003	62	41%	66	65%	66	44%

diameter, single-stemmed, juvenile cacti from a 13-year reproductive comparison in Table 2.

Knowlton's cactus is reproductively unusual for cacti since it initiates most of its flower primordia in the early autumn months. Therefore, spring flowering is greatly influenced by the condition of the plant during the previous growing season and the intervening winter months.

During the severe drought years of 1996 and 2002, very few plants attempted flowering and less than 10% of the flowers produced fertile fruits at the type locality and transplant sites. Even during years of good precipitation, this plant is not a prolific bloomer. In 1992, the natural population had flowers or fruits on only 51% of adult-size cacti, which was the greatest percentage of reproductive effort at that location during this 13-year period. The transplant sites are uniformly older, more mature cohorts that usually show higher reproductive effort than the natural population, which has uneven age classes. Seed production was not monitored at any of these sites.

TABLE 2. Reproductive activity of *Pediocactus knowltonii* at the type locality and transplant sites. (* Excludes < 10 mm, single-stem plants.)

	Type	Nav #1	Nav #2	BLM #1
Sample Size*				
1991	306	107		
1992	337	107		
1993	358	102		121
1994	410	98		114
1995	366	94		96
1996	231	76	58	68
1997	263	85	80	92
1998	258	75	76	90
1999	272	68	73	81
2000	228	68	69	80
2001	256	62	72	79
2002	152	59	62	67
2003	173	64	66	66
No. Plants in Flower (%)				
1991	145 (47%)	52 (49%)		
1992	178 (51%)	59 (55%)		
1993	111 (31%)	25 (25%)		3 (2.4%)
1994	180 (44%)	42 (43%)		6 (5.5%)
1995	153 (42%)	52 (55%)		16 (17%)
1996	18 (8%)	12 (16%)	2 (3%)	8 (12%)
1997	111 (42%)	51 (60%)	12 (15%)	36 (39%)
1998	77 (30%)	25 (33%)	11 (14%)	35 (39%)
1999	43 (16%)	9 (13%)	4 (5%)	23 (28%)
2000	66 (29%)	23 (34%)	16 (23%)	23 (29%)
2001	93 (36%)	26 (42%)	30 (42%)	43 (54%)
2002	9 (6%)	0 (0%)	0 (0%)	3 (4%)
2003	66 (38%)	33 (52%)	29 (44%)	30 (45%)
Flowers/Flowering Plant				
1991	1.8	1.5		
1992	2.2	1.7		
1993	1.5	1.4		1
1994	1.8	1.5		1
1995	1.8	1.9		1.4
1996	1.4	1	1.5	1.3
1997	1.8	2.2	1.2	1.4
1998	1.9	1.8	1.4	1.3
1999	1.4	1.9	1.3	1.3
2000	1.6	1.9	1.4	1.6
2001	1.7	2.3	1.6	1.9
2002	1.1	0	0	1
2003	1.7	2.6	1.9	1.8

SEEDING TRIALS

Direct seeding to the soil was attempted well outside the transplant grids at both the Navajo Lake and BLM locations. Very little Knowlton's cactus seed could be obtained from the natural population because most seeds are immediately harvested by rodents (probably *Peromyscus* sp.) from the maturing fruits. Few fruits reach a mature stage of dehiscence before being opened and emptied by rodents. Therefore, the majority of seeds used in seeding trials were obtained from greenhouse-grown plants.

Only 288 seeds were planted in the autumn of 1987 at the Navajo Lake seed plot. These were planted in one-meter grid intervals and at various depths at each grid point. A template was used that allowed seed placement in the three locations of 10 cm north, 10 cm south and 10 cm west of each grid point. Two seeds were placed in each hole at a predetermined depth. At the south axis location, seeds were left on the surface and lightly covered with a coating of fine soil. West axis seeds were planted at 0.5 cm depth, and north axis seeds were planted 1 cm below the surface.

This seed plot was monitored for germination every spring and autumn from 1988 to 1990 with no seedlings being detected. The 1991 assessment was not entirely complete because of the observer's unfamiliarity with the plot layout. In May of 1992, eight Knowlton's cactus seedlings were located. These seedlings appeared to be from 1-3 years of age. They were firmly established and represented all three planting depths. Although this sample is small, planting depths above 1 cm do not appear to make a difference in seedling establishment. Additional cacti continued to be found at this plot until 1997 for a total of 18 plants, which is a 6.25% establishment of seeds planted. Only 9 (50%) of these germinants remain as adult cacti in 2003.

Another seed plot was established at the BLM #1 site in January 1994. A total of 2,250 *P. knowltonii* seeds were purchased from a permitted vendor and planted in permanent plots. Each plot is a grid constructed with field fence laid flat on the ground and held in position with steel reinforcement rods. The mesh openings in the fence are 2x3 inches and a single seed was planted in each opening. There are three 4 x 15 foot lengths of fence, each with three

TABLE 3. Numbers of *Pediocactus knowltonii* seedlings in three replicate plots at BLM #1. Each plot has blocks of no treatment (NT), brushed (Brus.) and cultivated (Cult.) treatments.

	Plot #1			Plot #2			Plot #3			
	NT	Brus.	Cult.	NT	Brus.	Cult.	NT	Brus.	Cult.	TOTAL
1994	8	1	2	0	1	0	0	0	0	12
1995	24	4	19	12	1	4	0	5	8	77
1997	15	4	13	5	3	1	6	16	9	72
1998	10	3	10	2	2	3	5	1	8	44
1999	13	1	8	7	4	3	4	11	12	63
2000	17	4	7	5	4	3	6	9	10	65
2001	20	2	11	8	6	5	10	17	14	92
2002	20	2	11	8	5	4	10	22	14	96

different 4 x 5 foot treatments:

No Treatment: Native vegetation with no disturbance;

Brushed: Sagebrush clipped off at ground level, no surface disturbance;

Cultivated: All brush and herbaceous vegetation removed by hoeing the soil.

Each treatment within the three plot replications received 250 seeds. Seeds was planted at a depth of approximately 5 mm and a small amount of blasting sand was poured on each planting hole to control erosion.

Only 12 seedlings were observed to have germinated by June 1994. The new seedlings were very tiny and most did not survive the unusually hot summer of 1994. Only 4 of the original 12 survived to be counted again in May 1995. A total of 69 new germinants were counted in the 1995 assessment. The seedlings were not readily visible during the severe drought year of 1996 and a complete assessment was not made during that year. Only 30 (39%) of the 1995 seedlings survived to be counted again in May of 1997. The remaining 42 of the 1997 seedlings were recent germinants. A total 44 seedlings were observed in 1998 of which 20 were new germinants. This represents a significant number (48) of previous year's seedlings that failed to become established. By 2001, most of the seedlings were becoming larger and two had reached reproductive maturity and were flowering. Six were flowering in 2002, a severe drought year. Two new (2-year old) seedlings were found in 2003, which shows germination can still occur nine years after planting. A 2003 total of 97 cacti represents a 4.3% establishment of the 2,250 seeds planted (Table 3).

An analysis of variance for the random block design of this experiment showed no significant differences between plot treatments (F=2.88 with 2 and 4 degrees of freedom). Seedbed preparation is unnecessary and will, in fact, increase soil erosion when seed plots are placed on a slope.

RECRUITMENT

Survival of Knowlton's cactus cuttings at the reintroduction site has been surprisingly good, but cannot be considered a success until there are cacti becoming established from natural reproduction in sufficient numbers to offset mortality. Recruitment at the seed plots is difficult to assess because there may be a period of overlap for detecting the offspring of early germinants that became reproductive and shed seed into the plot and the late germinants that arise from the original seed planted in the plot. New plants at the transplant sites are difficult to find until they reach sufficient size to be readily seen by researchers.

The first evidence of recruitment was a single seedling found in 2002 at the Navajo #1 reintroduction site. This plant was an approximately 2-years old plant and was observed sixteen years after the first fruits were produced in this transplant population. Another two seedlings were observed at this location in 2003. A single new seedling was also found at the BLM #1 site in 2003, twelve years after the first reproductive efforts in this transplant population. To date, only four new cacti have been detected as new recruits to both transplant locations.

CONCLUSIONS

Eighteen years of monitoring at the *Pediocactus knowltonii* type locality have demonstrated that this population fluctuates in density, probably in response to climatic conditions. Only one serious episode of cactus poaching was detected in 1996 when an entire monitoring plot and an undetermined number of cacti were removed from the natural population at the type locality.

Survivorship and reproductive efforts of Knowlton's cactus clones at all transplant sites has been good during the coarse of this study and the multi-stem donor plants in the natural population did not suffer from the loss of a single stem. These plants are relatively long-lived for small cacti; however, they are gradually dying away at the transplant sites and are not yet being replaced by new recruits. Direct seeding into new locations is a viable option to transplanting adult clones; however, only about 5% of the seed becomes established as adult plants and they require a longer period to become reproductive than do transplanted clones.

The feasibility of establishing new populations of Knowlton's cactus by transplantation or seeding at the rates in this study is yet to be established since natural recruitment to these new populations has been an exceedingly slow process. It is possible that a large volume of seed is being banked in the soil, but suitable conditions for germination and establishment have not yet occurred. Another possibility is that the high rate of seed predation by rodents that is evident at the natural population could also be seriously depleting seed production at the transplant locations. These hypotheses can be tested when the next episode of significant germination and establishment occurs in the natural population. If the transplant populations are not similarly augmented by new recruits, then too little seed is surviving at these new locations to maintain viable populations. Larger transplanting or seeding efforts would be needed. Instead of a few hundred adult clones and a few thousand seeds, future efforts would need a few thousand adult clones or tens of thousands of seeds to have a chance for success.

Inadequate recruitment at these small, new populations at the transplant sites may offer some insight into the rarity of this species. How large must a founding population of Knowlton's cactus be to become established in new, suitable habitat? If it requires a few thousand plants, then the single, isolated, natural population of this cactus on one small hill is no longer a mystery. It would be unable to naturally attain such a high rate of dispersal to adjacent unoccupied habitats. If *P. knowltonii* were more widespread in the past and has suffered local extinctions, the surviving population could not repopulate those habitats. If, on the other hand, it evolved at this single location, it has simply been unable to colonize adjacent suitable habitats because the few seeds that may find their way to new locations are inadequate to found new populations.

Acknowledgements

These recovery and research efforts were funded by the New Mexico EMNRD-Forestry Division and the U.S. Fish & Wildlife Service. We also thank The Nature Conservancy of New Mexico for allowing us to monitor the natural population of Knowlton's cactus on their preserve and obtain cuttings and seeds from that location. Bureau of Reclamation and Bureau of Land Management allowed us to establish transplants on lands within their jurisdictions. We appreciate the many people who gave their time and helping hands during this 18-year effort. The principals among these are Steve Brack, Anne Cully, Bill Falvey, Paul Knight, Karen Lightfoot, Peggy Olwell, Phil Tonne, and Barney Wegener.

LITERATURE CITED

Benson, L. 1961. A revision and amplification of *Pediocactus* I. Cactus and Succulent Journal 33:49-54.

Knight, P. and A. Cully. 1987. Section 6 progress report: *Pediocactus knowltonii.* Submitted to U.S. Fish & Wildlife Service, Region 2, Albuquerque, New Mexico.

Olwell, P., A. Cully, P. Knight and S. Brack. 1987. *Pediocactus knowltonii* recovery efforts. In: Conservation and Management of Rare and Endangered Plants, pp. 519-522, The California Native Plant Society, Sacramento.

U.S. Fish and Wildlife Service. 1985. Recovery plan for the Knowlton Cactus (*Pediocactus knowltonii* L. Benson). Albuquerque, New Mexico: U.S. Fish and Wildlife Service. 53 pp.

Conservation Implications of Spur Length Variation in Long-Spur Columbines (*Aquilegia longissima*)

CHRISTOPHER J. STUBBEN AND BROOK G. MILLIGAN

Department of Biology, New Mexico State University, Las Cruces, New Mexico 88003

ABSTRACT: Populations of long-spur columbine (*Aquilegia longissima*) with spurs 10-16 cm long are known only from a few populations in Texas, a historical collection near Baboquivari Peak, Arizona, and scattered populations in Coahuila, Chihuahua, and Nuevo Leon, Mexico. Populations of yellow columbine with spurs 7-10 cm long are also found in Arizona, Texas, and Mexico, and are now classified as *A. longissima* in the recent Flora of North America. In a multivariate analysis of floral characters from 11 yellow columbine populations representing a continuous range of spur lengths, populations with spurs 10-16 cm long are clearly separate from other populations based on increasing spur length and decreasing petal and sepal width. The longer-spurred columbines generally flower after monsoon rains in late summer or fall, and occur in intermittently wet canyons and steep slopes in pine-oak forests. Also, longer-spurred flowers can be pollinated by large hawkmoths with tongues 9-15 cm long. Populations with spurs 7-10 cm long cluster with the common golden columbine (*A. chrysantha*), and may be the result of hybridization between *A. chrysantha* and *A. longissima*. Uncertainty about the taxonomic status of intermediates has contributed to a lack of conservation efforts for declining populations of the long-spur columbine.

The genus *Aquilegia* is characterized by a wide diversity of floral morphologies and colors that play a major role in isolating two species via differences in pollinator visitation or pollen transfer (Grant 1952, Fulton and Hodges 1999, Hodges et al. 2002). Since there are few post-zygotic reproductive barriers in the genus, populations with intermediate forms resulting from hybridization and introgression are very common (Payson 1918, Munz 1946, Taylor 1967, Whittemore 1997). In addition, many columbines occur in small, isolated populations, which results in reduced gene flow (Strand et al. 1996) and potentially increased morphological variability due to genetic drift and inbreeding.

Due to the complex nature of floral variation, many columbine populations are difficult to identify accurately in plant keys. For example, floral spurs lengths are a key character used to differentiate yellow columbine species in the Southwest. In early monographs of the genus by Payson (1918) and Munz (1946), yellow columbines with short spurs 4-7 cm long were included with *Aquilegia chrysantha* and yellow columbines with long spurs 10-16 cm long were included with *A. longissima*. Recently, yellow columbines with intermediate spurs 7-10 cm long have been collected. Some authors include these populations with the common *A. chrysantha* (Correll and Johnston 1979, Lott 1979). In the recent Flora of North America, these populations were grouped with *A. longissima* (Whittemore 1997).

Since the most recent taxonomy of southwestern yellow columbines groups intermediate spur length populations with long-spur columbines, we examined floral variation among 11 yellow columbine populations in the Southwest. In particular, we selected populations representing short, intermediate and long spur lengths, and then identified floral characters that clearly differentiated populations using bivariate scatterplots and multivariate analyses. Finally, we describe differences among southwestern yellow columbine identified by previous researchers and discuss the taxonomic status of intermediate-spur length populations.

METHODS

Five floral characters were measured on 211 pressed flowers collected from 141 plants in 11 populations (table 1). The locations included seven populations with short-spurs (*A. chrysantha* Gray), two populations with long spurs (*A. longissima* Gray ex Watson), and two populations with intermediate spurs of uncertain taxonomic status. Floral measurements included the petal spur length, petal blade (lamina) length and width, and the sepal length and width. Lengths were measured from the point of attachment to the tip of each structure. Measurements from multiple flowers on

a plant were averaged and statistical analyses where performed using R (R Development Core Team 2004). Bivariate scatterplots and principal components analyses were used to examine differences in floral characters among the 11 populations. The herbaria at New Mexico State University (NMC), University of Arizona (ARIZ) and Arizona State University (ASU) were visited to check for *A. chrysantha* hybrids and to measure specimens from noteworthy collections.

RESULTS

Spur lengths range from 4-16 cm long in southwestern yellow columbines and the only break in the distribution occurs at 10 cm (fig 1). The short-spur columbines in the San Andres and Bofecillos Mountains have spurs 4-7 cm long. This spur range is identical to the type locality of *A. chrysantha* in the Organ Mountains in southern New Mexico (based on 170 flowers measured over a three year period, unpublished data). In the Sierra Madres, Mexico, the spurs are 4.5-9.2 cm long and all three Mexico populations have some plants with spur lengths greater than the current 7.2 cm cutoff separating *A. chrysantha* and *A. longissima* in the Flora of North America.

Table 1. The number of plants collected and flowers measured in each population. The two long-spur populations are listed in bold and two populations of uncertain taxonomic status are listed in italics.

Mountain Range	Population	# Plants	# Flowers
Bofecillos, Texas	Madrid Falls	5	6
	Palo Amarillo Springs	5	17
Chisos, Texas	Cattail Falls	10	12
	Maple Canyon	14	19
	Pine Canyon	18	19
San Andres, New Mexico	Ash Springs	12	14
	Rope Springs	11	14
	San Nicholas Canyon	13	17
Sierra Madres, Chihuahua	Basaseachic Falls	8	18
	Cuarenta Casas	26	42
	El Salto de Babicora	19	33

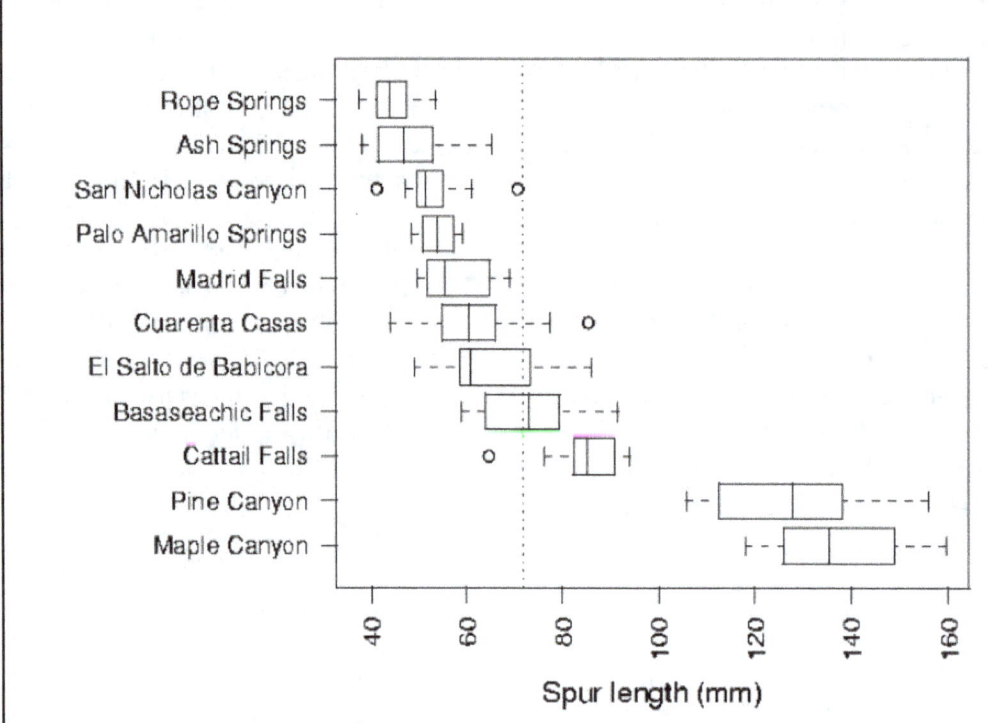

FIGURE 1. Side-by-side box plots displaying median spur length, interquartile range, smallest and largest spur lengths, and any outliers if present. The dotted line is the cutoff separating A. chrysantha and A. longissima in the Flora or North America.

A plot of spur length versus petal blade width clearly separates long-spur columbines at Pine and Maple Canyon from the remaining populations (Fig 2). For example, plants with intermediate-spur lengths at Cattail Falls cluster with other short-spur columbines due to the wider petals (mean = 1.5 cm wide, range = 1.0-1.7 cm) compared to Maple and Pine Canyon (mean=0.8 cm wide, range=0.4-1.2 cm). Also, spur lengths and petal widths are positively correlated in both groups, so the difference between petal widths is greatest when spur lengths from both groups are close to 10 cm long.

The principal component plot also separates the long-spur columbines from short-

and intermediate-spur populations (fig. 3). The first principal component is primarily an indicator of floral size, and the second principal component separates long-spur columbines based on increasing spur length and decreasing petal blade width and sepal width (Table 2). Again, the intermediate-spur populations at Basasiachic and Cattail Falls cluster with other short-spur columbines, and in the principal components plot their overall shape is similar to a very large *A. chrysantha*

TABLE 2. Loadings on the first three principal components which incorporate 90.9 percent of the variance.

Character	PC1	PC2	PC3
Sepal length	-0.565	-0.065	-0.140
Sepal width	-0.322	0.559	0.762
Petal length	-0.568	0.042	-0.272
Petal width	-0.030	0.734	-0.571
Spur length	-0.502	-0.378	0.012
% Variance	51.5	30.7	8.7

flowers.

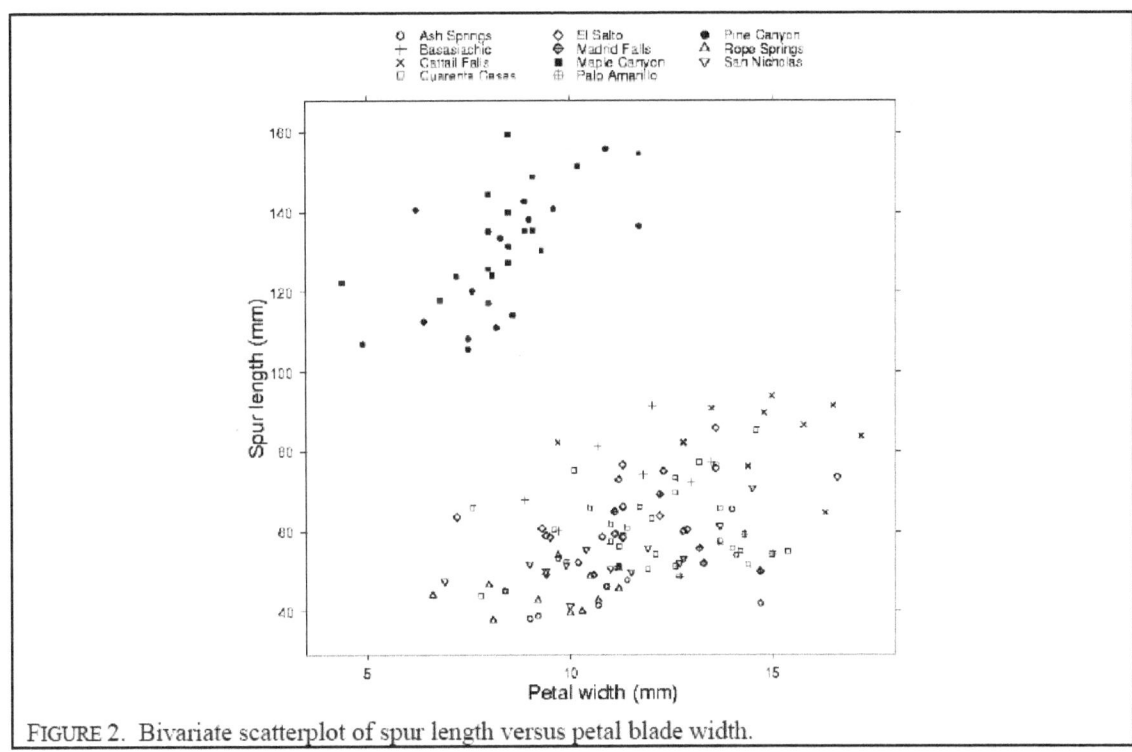

FIGURE 2. Bivariate scatterplot of spur length versus petal blade width.

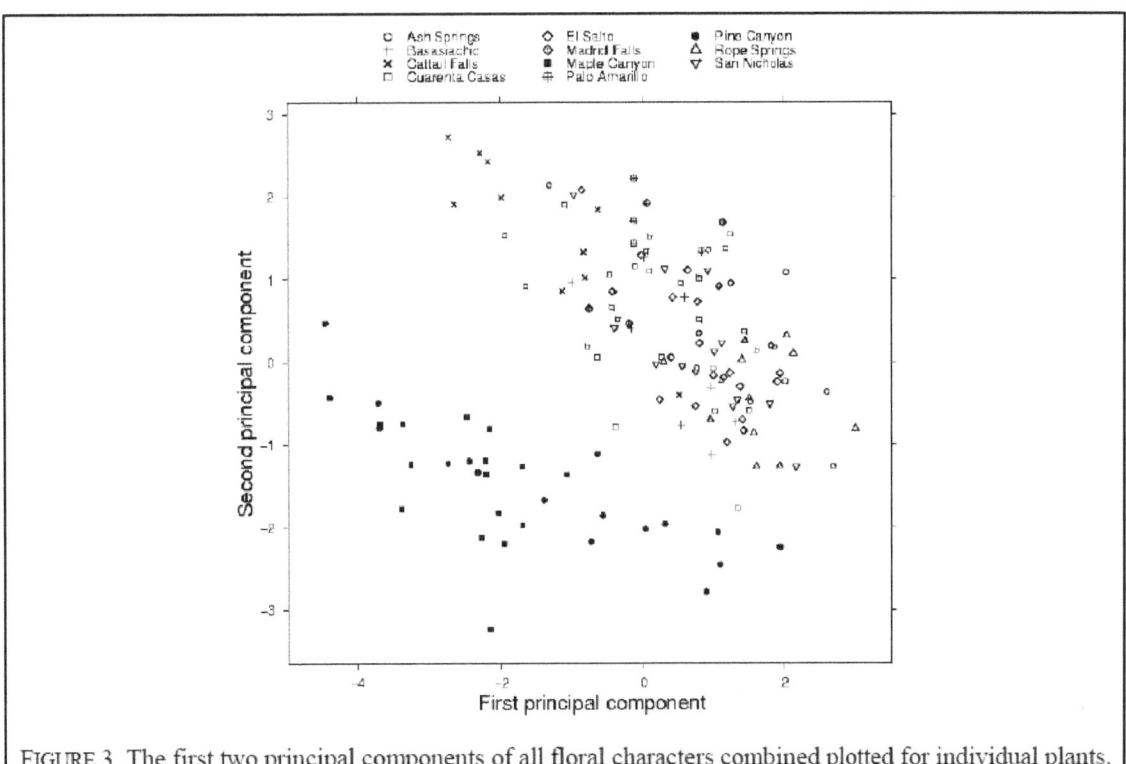

FIGURE 3. The first two principal components of all floral characters combined plotted for individual plants.

In the original species descriptions (Watson 1882 and Gray 1883), *A. longissima* is distinguished from *A. chrysantha* based on the extremely long, slender spur over 10 cm long, the narrow spatulate petals, and the very narrow opening at the base of the spur. In our multivariate analysis the combination of long spurs and narrow petal widths also differentiates long-spur columbines from other yellow columbines in the Southwest. Also, long-spur columbines at Pine and Maple Canyon have a very constricted opening at the base of the spur (mean= 2.4 mm wide, range=1.0-3.1 mm). Due to the narrow opening, the slender spurs usually hang straight down and the flower position is erect. In short- and intermediate-spur columbines, the spur opening is much wider and tapered. Due to the tapered opening, the spurs are often spreading and the position of the flower may vary from horizontal to erect.

There are a number of other potential reproductive barriers that maintain species boundaries between *A. chrysantha* and *A. longissima*, including temporal and ecogeographic isolating mechanisms and pollinator behaviors. The flowering phenology, ecology, and pollinators of southwestern columbines were discussed in detail by Lott (1979) who collected from a larger sample of mountain ranges in the Southwest, including long-spur columbines in the Davis Mountains, Texas and near the type locality in Coahuila, Mexico, and an intermediate-spur population in the Chinati Mountains, Texas. First, the long-spur columbines typically flower in later summer or fall after monsoon rains, while short- and intermediate spur columbines flower in spring and early summer. In some years, a few long-spur

columbines may flower early and some short-spur columbines may flower late during the monsoon rains. In our study the plants in the Chisos Mountains at Catttail Falls were collected in late March, while plants at Maple and Pine Canyon were collected in flower six months later in October. Second, long-spur columbines are usually found near intermittently wet substrates in oak-pine-juniper woodlands in shaded canyons or talus slopes. Short- and intermediate-spur columbines are usually found near permanent water by streams, pools, waterfalls, and springs.

The primary pollinators of *A. chrysantha* include small hawkmoths in the genus *Hyles*, *Eumorpha*, and *Sphinx* (Miller 1985, personal observations). The pollinators of *A. longissima* have not been recorded in the literature and we have not observed any pollinators on a number of visits to the Chisos Mountains. Trelease (1883) thought that the most likely pollinator of *A. longissima* would be the giant sphinx moth, *Cocytius antaeus*. The giant sphinx moth is a rare stray in the United States and has been collected near Pine Canyon (Van Pelt 1995). However, the most likely pollinators would be large hawkmoths in the genus *Agrius* and *Manduca* with tongues lengths 9-14 cm long (see Gregory 1964 for tongue measurements). These hawkmoths also pollinate other very long-tube flowers in the Southwest (Grant 1983, Grant and Grant 1983, Grant 1985).

There are three locations of intermediate-spur columbines in the United States and all have been collected near historical or recent collections of *A. longissima*. In Texas, a relatively large population is found at the base of Cattail Falls in the Chisos Mountains. There is a historical collection by Warnock (no collection number at ARIZ) of a long-spur columbine in 'Upper Cattail Falls' collected August 8, 1937 with spurs 13.4 cm long Two small populations of long-spur columbine can still be found nearby in Maple and Pine Canyon. Lott (1979) also surveyed a population with intermediate spurs at Tinaja Prieta in the Chinati Mountains, Texas and recently collected long-spur columbines in the same area (personal communication).

In Arizona, a population with intermediate spurs is found in Thomas Canyon in the Baboquivari Mountains. A collection by Toolin (#358 at ARIZ) is typical. The plant was collected 'About 1.0 mile above ranch house, on slope at west edge of main wash, under *Quercus arizonica* Sarg., *Juglans major* (Torr.) Heller, with *Rubus arizonensis* Focke. Thomas Canyon, Baboquivari Mountains, April 22, 1979'. The spur lengths from various flowers measured 7.0, 7.3, 8.0, 8.5, and 8.6 cm long. There is only one known collection of *A. longissima* in Arizona. Gentry (#3418 at ARIZ) collected a long-spur columbine in flower 'Near peak of Baboquivari Mountains, moist shade side of cliff; oak belt. October 1937'. The two spurs are 12.3 and 12.4 cm long, with narrow petals and a very narrow opening at the base of the spur 2.7 mm wide. This collection was probably from the western slope of the Baboquivari Mountains near the saddle above Thomas Canyon.

Contrary to the recent description in the Flora of North America, populations with intermediate spurs 7-9 cm long should not be included with *A. longissima*. In addition, these populations are also outside the typical range of spur lengths found in *A. chrysantha*. Although additional studies are needed, it is possible that long-distance pollen flow from *A. chrysantha* populations into isolated mountain ranges having only long-spur populations has resulted in hybrid populations of *A. chrysantha* x *A. longissima* near permanent water at lower elevations than the long-spur parent. In our survey of local herbaria *A. chrysantha* forms hybrids with *A. Formosa* Fisch. ex DC. in Zion National Park, Utah, with *A. coerulea* James in the San Francisco Peaks, Arizona, with *A. desertorum* (M.E. Jones) ex Heller in the Chiricahua Mountains, Arizona, and with *A. skinneri* Hook near Basasiachic Falls, Mexico. In Mexico, the columbine populations have spurs 4-9 cm long, which may be the result of local adaptations to larger hawkmoths or extensive backcrossing and introgression between both species in the same range.

ACKNOWLEDGMENTS

We thank federal and state agencies for permitting studies of *Aquilegia* in Big Bend National Park, Big Bend Ranch State Park, and the White Sands Missile Range. Allan Strand, Brook Milligan, and Rich Spellenberg collected columbines in Mexico. We also thank Kelly Gallagher and a group of students who measured floral characters on live and pressed plants over and over.

LITERATURE CITED

Correll, D.S., and M.C. Johnston. 1979. Manual of the vascular plants of Texas. University of Texas at Dallas, Richardson, Texas.

Fulton, M., and S.A. Hodges. 1999. Floral isolation between *Aquilegia formosa* and *A. pubescens*. Proceedings of the Royal Society of London B, Biological Sciences 266:2247-2252.

Grant, V. 1952. Isolation and hybridization between *Aquilegia formosa* and *A. pubescens*. Aliso 2:341-360.

_____ 1983. The systematic and geographical distributions of hawkmoth flowers in the temperate North American flora. Botanical Gazette 144:439-449.

_____ 1985. Additional observations on temperate North American hawkmoth flowers. Botanical Gazette 146: 517-520.

Grant, V., and K.A. Grant. 1983. Hawkmoth pollination of *Mirabilis longiflora* (Nyctaginaceae). Proceedings of the National Academy of Science 80: 1298-1299

Gray, A. 1883. *Aquilegia longissima*. Botanical Gazette 8:295.

Gregory, D.P. 1964. Hawkmoth pollination in the genus *Oenothera*. Aliso 5:385-419.

Hodges, S.A., J.B. Whittall, M. Fulton, and J.Y. Yang. 2002. Genetics of floral traits influencing reproductive isolation between *Aquilegia formosa* and *Aquilegia pubescens*. American Naturalist 159:S51-S60.

Lott, E.J. 1979. Variation and interrelationships of *Aquilegia* populations of Trans-Pecos Texas. Sul Ross State University, Department of Biology, Alpine, Texas. M.S. Thesis.

Miller, R.B. 1985. Hawkmoth pollination of *Aquilegia chrysantha* (Ranunculaceae) in southern Arizona. The Southwestern Naturalist 30:69-76

Munz, P.A. 1946. *Aquilegia*: the cultivated and wild columbines. Gentes Herbarum 7:1-150.

Payson, E.B. 1918. The North American species of *Aquilegia*. Contributions to the U.S. National. Herbarium 20:133-157.

R Development Core Team. 2004. R: A language and environment for statistical computing. Available: http://www.R-project.org.

Strand, A.E., B.G. Milligan, and C.M. Pruitt. 1996. Are populations islands? Analysis of chloroplast DNA variation in *Aquilegia*. Evolution 50:1822-1829.

Taylor, R.J. 1967. Interspeicific hybridization and its evolutionary significance in the genus *Aquilegia*. Brittonia 19:374-390.

Trelease, W. 1883. *Aquilegia longissima*. Botanical Gazette 8:319.

Van Pelt, A.F. 1995. An annotated inventory of the insects of Big Bend National Park, Texas. Big Bend Natural History Association, Big Bend National Park, Texas.

Watson, S. 1882. Contributions to American Botany. List of plants from southwestern Texas and northern Mexico, collected chiefly by Dr. E. Palmer in 1879-1880. Proceedings of the American Academy 17:37-318.

Whittemore, A. T. 1997. *Aquilegia* in Flora of North America. Volume 3: Magnoliophyta: Magnoliidae and Hamamelidae. Oxford University Press, New York.

A Tale of Two Cacti –The Complex Relationship between Peyote (*Lophophora williamsii*) and Endangered Star Cactus (*Astrophytum asterias*).

TERRY, M.[1], D. PRICE[2], AND J. POOLE.[2]

[1]Sul Ross State University, Department of Biology, Alpine, Texas 79832. [2]Texas Parks and Wildlife Department, Wildlife Diversity Branch, 3000 S. IH-35, Suite 100, Austin, Texas 78704.

ABSTRACT *Astrophytum asterias*, commonly called star cactus, is a federally listed endangered cactus endemic to the Tamaulipan thornscrub ecoregion of extreme southern Texas, USA, and Tamaulipas and Nuevo Leon, Mexico. Only three metapopulations totaling less than 4000 plants are presently known in Texas. Star cactus, known locally as "star peyote", is highly sought by collectors. This small, dome-shaped, spineless, eight-ribbed cactus is sometimes mistaken for peyote (*Lophophora williamsii*), which grows in the same or adjacent habitats. Peyote is harvested from native thornscrub habitats in Texas by local Hispanic people and sold to *peyoteros*, licensed distributors who sell the peyote to Native American Church members. Annual peyote harvests in Texas approach 2,000,000 "buttons" (crowns). Although the *peyoteros* do not buy star cactus from harvesters, they cultivate star cactus in peyote gardens at their places of business and give star cacti to their customers as lagniappe. If even 0.1% of harvested "peyote" is actually star cactus, the annual take of this endangered cactus approaches the total number of wild specimens known in the U.S. This real but unquantifiable take, together with information from interviews with local residents, suggests the existence of many more star cactus populations than have been documented.

ASTROPHYTUM AND *LOPHOPHORA* – SIMILARITIES AND DIFFERENCES

Astrophytum asterias (Zuccarini) Lemaire (star cactus) is a small, spineless cactus. Each plant usually has a single low, dome-shaped stem that becomes flat or depressed during dry conditions. In the wild, star cactus grows to 7 cm tall and 15 cm in diameter. Plants are green to grayish-green or goldish-brown, patterned with whitish to yellowish circular scales. Each normally has 8 triangular ribs separated by narrow grooves. The areoles follow a central line down each rib, bearing tufts of short, whitish hairs. The pale yellow flowers with orange-red bases appear in mid-March through May (Fig. 1) (Benson 1982; Damude and Poole 1990). Star cactus was listed as Endangered by the US Fish and Wildlife Service (USFWS) in 1993 due to its few populations and high degree of threat from collecting. It is also listed in the Convention on International Trade in

FIGURE 1. Endangered *Astrophytum asterias* (Star cactus), Starr County, Texas

Endangered Species (CITES) Appendix I. Star cactus is an extremely popular collector's item. Even though it is easily grown from seed, plants continue to be taken from the wild.

Lophophora williamsii (Lem. ex Salm-Dyck) Coult. (peyote) resembles star cactus in its size, shape and lack of spines. However, peyote is bluish-green and lacks the tiny whitish scales found on star cactus. Peyote has 5-13 (most often exactly 5, 8 or 13) ribs, the number increasing with age. Star cactus, in contrast, generally has 8 ribs throughout life. Peyote's ribs may extend toward the base in a spiral conformation not seen in star cactus. Mature specimens of *L. williamsii* may have pronounced tubercles, which may (particularly in spiral-ribbed individuals) give the ribs an irregular appearance not observed in *A. asterias* (Fig. 2). The flowers of peyote appear pale pink in color (Fig. 3). The outer tepals are white with a green stripe down the midline, but only the inner tepals, which are white with a pink stripe down the midline, are visible from above when the flowers are fully open. Peyote has a large (diameter ca. 70-90% of the diameter of the base of the stem),

FIGURE 2. *Lophophora williamsii (*Peyote), Starr County, Texas. Grandmother and younger plants showing variation in number of ribs.

FIGURE 3. Peyote in flower, Starr County, Texas

slowly tapering taproot with few lateral roots, while star cactus has a diminutive taproot (diameter ca. 10% of the diameter of the aerial portion of the stem) that branches into many slender roots suggestive of a fibrous root system (Fig. 4).

II. RANGE AND HABITAT OF *ASTROPHYTUM* AND *LOPHOPHORA*

The range of *Lophophora williamsii* includes both the Tamaulipan thornscrub and the Chihuahuan desert (Anderson 1996), while *Astrophytum asterias* has a much more restricted range in the Tamaulipan thornscrub only (Damude and Poole 1990; Martinez Avalos 2002; Sanchez-Mejorada et al.1986). The ranges

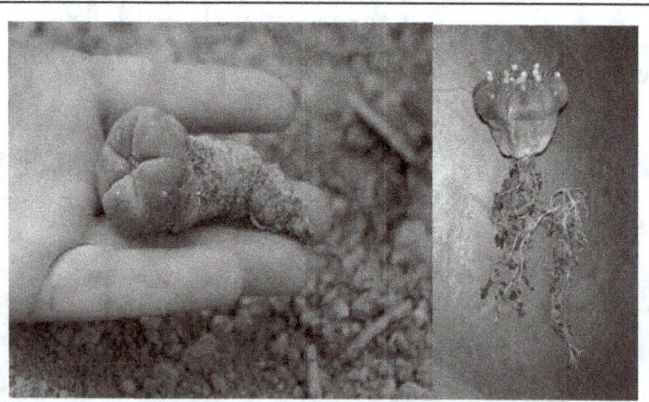

FIGURE 4. Taproot of Peyote (left) and star cactus fibrous roots (right). Star cactus has a fibrous root system with at most a diminutive taproot and cannot regenerate if the top is removed.

of the two species overlap in the Lower Rio Grande Valley of southern Texas, USA, and in northern Tamaulipas and Nuevo Leon, Mexico (Fig. 5).

Within the Tamaulipan thornscrub, star cactus grows in gravelly clays or loams, on gentle slopes in sparsely vegetated openings between shrub thickets within mesquite-blackbrush thorn shrublands (Fig. 6). Associates of both *Astrophytum* and *Lophophora* in Texas include the shrubs mesquite (*Prosopis glandulosa*), amargosa *(Castela erecta)*, blackbrush *(Acacia rigidula)*, lotebush *(Ziziphus obtusifolia)*, allthorn *(Koeberlinia spinosa)*, desert olive *(Forestiera*

angustifolia), guayacan *(Guaiacum angustifolium)*, coyotillo *(Karwinskia humboldtiana)*, saladillo *(Varilla texana);* native short grasses (*Bouteloua trifida, Monanthochloë littoralis, Aristida* spp., *Hilaria belangeri)*, and numerous other cacti (including *Opuntia leptocaulis, Echinocactus texensis,* and *Mammillaria heyderi*) (Damude and Poole 1990; Texas Parks and Wildlife Department and The Nature Conservancy of Texas unpublished field data).

Astrophytum and *Lophophora* may be found in close proximity within these habitats, sometimes growing together under the same nurse shrub (Fig. 7). More

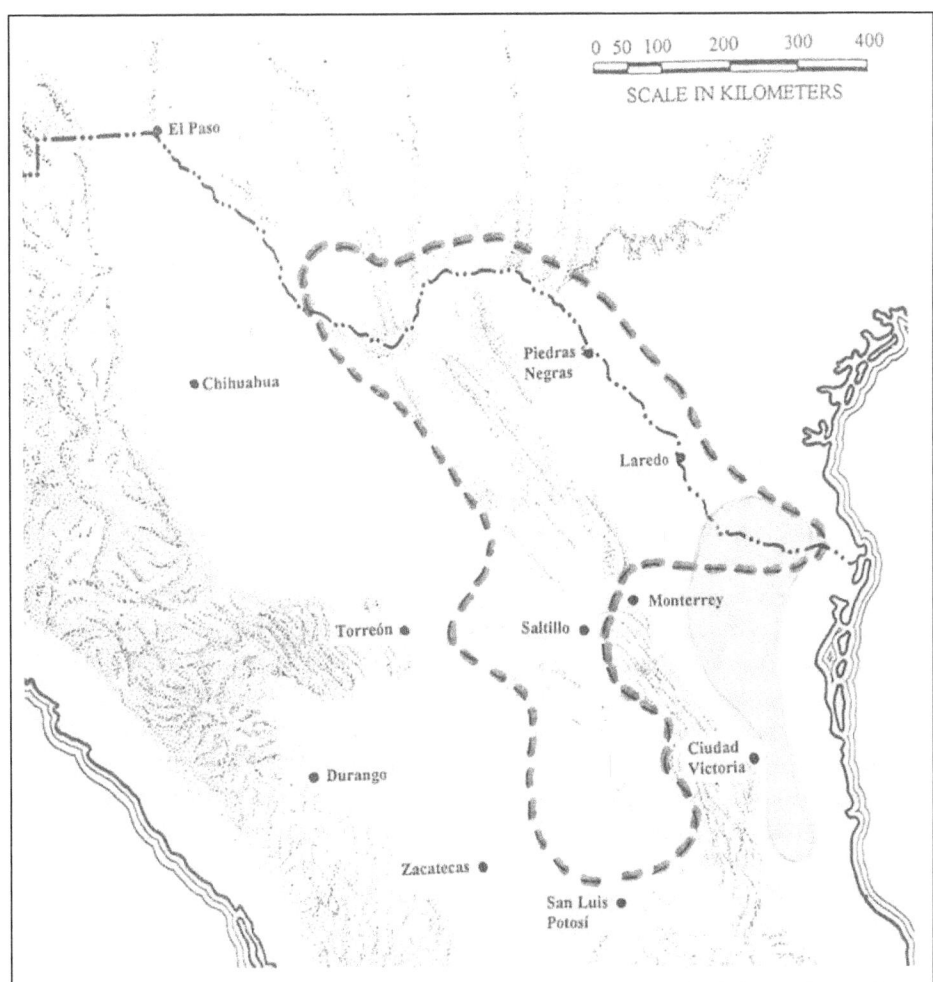

FIGURE 5. Distribution of peyote (dashed lines) and star cactus (shaded area) in southern Texas and northern Mexico. Adapted from Anderson (1996), with star cactus locality information from Martinez Avalos (pers. com.).

often, however, the two species appear to use slightly different microhabitats. For example, we have more often observed *Lophophora* near the base of shrubs while *Astrophytum* may grow farther out under the edge of the shrub's canopy or even in the open. The two cacti appear to show preferences (though not absolute requirements) for different soil types, as well. Further investigation is needed to determine whether and how these two cacti partition the habitat.

Castela erecta and *Opuntia leptocaulis* have been documented as important nurse shrubs for star cactus (Martinez Avalos, 2002).

III. COMMERCIAL PEYOTE HARVEST – HOW IT WORKS

Federal law provides protection for the use of peyote for bona fide religious ceremonial purposes by members of the Native American Church (NAC). The supply of peyote for such purposes is regulated by the Drug Enforcement Administration (DEA) and the Texas Department of Public Safety (2003). The regulated commerce in peyote begins with the harvest of peyote from wild populations by licensed peyote distributors or their agents. Commercial quantities of peyote occur in the U.S. only in Starr, Zapata, Webb and Jim Hogg Counties in South Texas, so all four currently licensed peyote distributors (*peyoteros*) are based in those counties, within 50 miles of the Rio Grande. Historically the *peyoteros* have gained access to harvestable populations of peyote through peyote-specific lease agreements with private landowners. Distributors normally tend to stay close to their places of business, where they can take orders from NAC members over the phone. Therefore, most of the actual harvesting of peyote is done by contract laborers who are paid by the number and size of freshly cut crowns ("buttons") of peyote they deliver to the licensed peyotero.

FIGURE 6. Area of Tamaulipan thornscrub, habitat for peyote and star cactus.

FIGURE 7. Star cactus and peyote growing under canopy of *Krameria ramosissima*

The proper technique for harvesting peyote is that the crown (i.e., the aerial stem) of the peyote cactus is cut off at the top of the root. Such harvesting of the commercially valuable crown of the cactus may be accomplished by cutting through the plant in cross section, parallel to the surface of the ground, at or near the interface of the green stem and the brown root, using a machete, a long-handled cutting tool with a broad flat blade (such as a hand edger), or virtually any kind of knife (Fig. 8).

When such traditional harvesting technique is adhered to, the decapitated taproot of the cactus (Fig. 9) remains intact in the ground, where it will normally begin to regenerate one or more new crowns within a few weeks after loss of the apical meristem (Fig. 10). These new crowns may themselves be harvested after they reach maturity in a few years (Fig. 11).

FIGURE 8. Cut peyote crown ("button"), showing proper harvesting technique.

FIGURE 10. Peyote "pups" (new stems) regenerating from cut crown

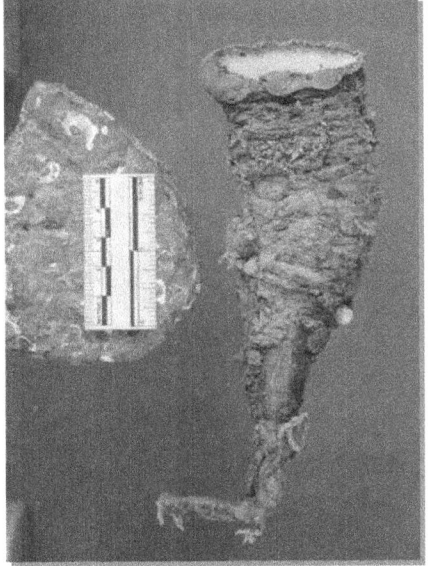

FIGURE 9. Harvested peyote taproot capable of regenerating.

FIGURE 11. Repeated harvest of peyote. Plant on left bears notches from having been harvested three times in the past; plant on right has never been harvested.

IV. INCIDENTAL HARVEST OF STAR CACTUS WITH PEYOTE: PROBLEM OR OPPORTUNITY?

Peyoteros maintain peyote gardens at their places of business, offering their Native American Church customers the opportunity to visit and pray. These gardens include specimens of both peyote and star cactus (Fig. 12). On rare occasions the NAC members take a specimen of star cactus back to their homes as a presumably nonconsumable souvenir from the "peyote gardens" of South Texas. Though the intention is to maintain these star cacti indefinitely in cultivation, damage to the root system that occurs in the collection process assures that most of these exiled plants will die in a few months. In any event, the act of removing such a plant from the population of which it was an element, renders it effectively dead in terms of its potential contribution to the genetics of the wild population.

Recent reports (Janssen 2004) from interviews with peyoteros indicate that the use of star cactus by some NAC members may not be of an exclusively nonconsumptive nature. NAC members are reported to ask the peyoteros specifically for "hard peyote" (*Astrophytum*), which they claim to be "stronger medicine" than "soft peyote" (*Lophophora*). This suggests that the desired effects of the "stronger medicine" are obtained by ingestion of the star cactus, as is the case with peyote, which is also called "medicine" by NAC members. However, whether the star cactus is being ingested to obtain the benefits of its "stronger" medicinal properties, or whether the effects can be perceived by NAC members without ingesting the plant (through its use as a religious amulet, for example), the detrimental effect of the loss of these plants at the population level is the same.

Star cactus is currently known from only three metapopulations in Texas and six in Mexico (Martinez Avalos 2002). The largest knownTexas population was estimated to total 2,000 individuals (Damude and Poole 1990). Peyoteros are familiar with star cactus and report that harvesters rarely bring it in; one distributor estimated that one plant in a thousand might be star cactus. In recent years, harvest of peyote in Texas has fluctuated around 2,000,000 buttons (Fig.13). Although rare, incidental harvest of star cactus at a rate of 0.1% of

FIGURE 12. Star cactus growing in a *peyotero*'s peyote garden.

FIGURE 13. Total peyote harvests reported by licensed distributors. (Source: Texas Department of Public Safety, 2003.)

120

peyote harvests would result in "take" of nearly 2,000 individuals, approaching the size of the known population.

Local people in the Lower Rio Grande Valley of Texas view star cactus or "star peyote" as a curiosity. On rare occasions botanists have encountered star cactus specimens being cultivated as potted plants or in home cactus gardens. These star cacti were collected locally from undisclosed private lands. Rumors of additional star cactus populations abound, yet in a landscape where over 90% of the land is privately owned (Anderson 1995), opportunities for botanists to survey are limited. Further, star cactus is extremely cryptic and easily overlooked during the long dry periods that are prevalent in South Texas.

We believe that peyote harvesters could significantly add to the number of known populations of star cactus, probably expanding the known extent of its distribution. Historically, there has been no incentive for them to do so. As we continue our fieldwork with these two species, we envision establishing working relationships with peyote harvesters. Collaboration with such important sources of local botanical knowledge will be crucial to the effective management of the endangered star cactus.

ACKNOWLEDGEMENTS

This work would not be possible without the collaboration of the Texas peyote distributors who generously allowed us to visit their businesses and discussed the peyote harvest with us, and the observations of the local people who shared their observations of "star peyote". We thank Guadalupe Martinez (Universidad Autónoma de Tamaulipas); Steve Van Heiden (Cactus Conservation Institute); Benito Treviño; Gena Janssen; Jody Patterson and Lesle Peloquin (Texas Department of Public Safety); Bill Carr and Lisa Williams (The Nature Conservancy); and Chris Best (USFWS): for inspiration, information and observations on star cactus and peyote in the field.

LITERATURE CITED

Anderson, E.F. 1995. The "peyote gardens" of South Texas: a conservation crisis? Cactus and Succulent Journal **67**: 67-73.

_____ 1996. Peyote: The Divine Cactus. Second edition. University of Arizona Press, Tucson.

Benson, L. 1982. The Cacti of the United States and Canada. Stanford University Press, Stanford.

Damude, N. and J. M. Poole. 1990. Status report on *Echinocactus asterias* (*Astrophytum asterias*). Report prepared for U.S. Fish & Wildlife Service, Albuquerque.

Janssen, G. 2004. email to authors, May 19, 2004. Texas Parks and Wildlife Department files, Austin..

Martinez Avalos, J.G. 2002. Distribución y estimación del tamaño de las poblaciones de *Astrophytum asterias* (Zucc.) Lem. (Cactaceae) a partir de la densidad, en la región noreste de Mexico. Proceedings of the Texas Plant Conservation Conference, Austin, Texas.

Sanchez-Mejorada, H., E.F. Anderson, N.P. Taylor and R. Taylor. 1986. Succulent plant conservation studies and training in Mexico. World Wildlife Fund, Washington, D.C.

Texas Department of Public Safety. 2003. Peyote sales totals and distributors of Texas. Unpublished data.

U.S. Fish and Wildlife Service. 1993. Endangered and Threatened Wildlife and Plants: Determination of Endangered Status for the Plant *Astrophytum asterias* (Star Cactus), Federal Register, Rules and Regulations 58 199: 53804-53807

The Importance of Competition in the Isolation and Establishment of *Helianthus Paradoxus* (Asteraceae)

Oscar W. Van Auken[1] and Janis. K. Bush

Department of Earth and Environmental Sciences, University of Texas at San Antonio, San Antonio, TX 78249 [1]Author for correspondence and reprints. FAX 210-458-5658; E-mail ovanauken@utsa.edu

ABSTRACT: *Helianthus paradoxus* (the Pecos or puzzle sunflower) is a threatened, federally listed annual species that is found in a few locations in west Texas and New Mexico. Two greenhouse experiments were conducted to evaluate the ability of *H. paradoxus* to compete with its progenitors and a with potential ecosystem competitor, *Distichlis spicata* (saltgrass) in simulated salt marsh and non-salt marsh environments. The results were usually dependent on soil salinity. *Helianthus paradoxus* was the better competitor in high saline soil and its progenitor *H. annuus* (common sunflower) was the better competitor in low saline soil. However, *H. paradoxus* was the better competitor in both high and low saline soils when compared to it progenitor *H. petiolaris* (plains sunflower) and to *D. spicata*, an ecosystem competitor. The ability of *H. paradoxus* to tolerate higher saline conditions, and perhaps even restrict the more geographically widespread *H. annuus* in saline soils may have allowed *H. paradoxus* to establish, become genetically isolated and survive as a species in inland salt marshes. Data presented here indicate that while *H. paradoxus* can grow in low saline soil, interference from *H. annuus* in low saline soils could restrict *H. paradoxus* to saline environments within salt marshes. The ability of *H. paradoxus* to out-compete *D. spicata* at high or low salt levels indicates that gaps in *D. spicata* vegetation would not be necessary in the salt marsh to allow the establishment and persistence of *H. paradoxus* in the saline soils of the salt marsh environment.

INTRODUCTION

It has been difficult to demonstrate that interspecific hybridization can be adaptive (Abbott 2003). Interspecific hybridization could produce a significant array of genotypes, including some with reasonable levels of fertility. If hybridization between two related species does occur, to be successful, some of the resulting offspring must survive and be fertile. In addition, the fertile hybrid must be isolated from the parents by a very strong post zygotic barrier. Thus, any subsequent mating between the parents and hybrid would result in few or no fertile offspring. In addition, if the hybrid individuals were found in a population of either parent, few fertile offspring would be produced because of the low probability of pollen from one hybrid plant reaching another hybrid plant. If the hybrids were adapted to a habitat different from that of either of the parents, the hybrids could be isolated from the parents and avoid any minority type disadvantages and possible negative effects of interspecific competition.

Hybridization between two common sunflowers (*Helianthus annuus* L. and *H. petiolaris* Nutt.) and the molecular genetics of the resulting hybrids between them have been recently reported (Rieseberg et al. 2003). They were interested in the mechanism that allowed the hybrid species, *H. paradoxus*, to become established and persist in unusual inland sulfate dominated salt marshes. They found that the chromosomal segments that were responsible for specific characteristics or traits in the parent species had at least one segment or trait with an effect in an opposite direction compared to the other segments. These specific traits were related to the parents' inability to survive in extreme habitats such as salt marshes. If the chromosomal segments should be separated during sexual reproduction, then potential recombinations could be created that might be successful in extreme environments. Thus, hybridization could result in recombinants with genes and traits producing extreme phenotypes and plants that could occupy unusual habitats.

Abiotic factors are often considered to be the main factors controlling establishment and patterns of vegetation. Salinity and flooding are often thought to be the key in determining zonation patterns in salt marshes. However, an important role for competition has been hypothesized in determining the limits of a species distribution along these salt marsh salinity gradients (Bertness 1991a, b; Bertness and Ellison 1987; Davy and Smith 1985; Snow and Vince 1984; Ungar 1998). For *H. paradoxus*, a narrowly distributed hybrid endemic, both abiotic factors (specifically soil salinity) and interference or competition between its progenitors may have contributed to its isolation and limited distribution. Its ability to tolerate higher saline soils, and even perhaps restrict the

more geographically widespread *H. annuus* in saline soils may allow it to survive in inland salt marshes where its progenitors are not found. Both *H. annuus* and *H. petiolaris* are found throughout the range of *H. paradoxus,* but not in its the salt marsh habitat.

Helianthus paradoxus is known to be more salt tolerant than *H. annuus* (Mendez 2001; Welch and Rieseberg 2002), but it is unknown if this salt tolerance is enough to promote the differential growth of *H. paradoxus* and *H. annuus* in the same habitats. *Helianthus paradoxus* does produce more biomass when grown with *H. annuus* or *H. petiolaris* at high salt levels, but at low soil salt levels, *H. annuus* produces more biomass (Bush and Van Auken 2004). In addition, it is unknown if *H. paradoxus* could establish and grow in a salt marsh in the presence of common species already established in the marsh such as *Distichlis spicata* (L.) Greene (saltgrass). *Helianthus paradoxus* is found with *D. spicata* in inland salt marshes (Figs. 1 and 2), but gaps could be required for establishment and maintenance (Van Auken and Bush 1998). It has been shown that the presence of neighbors reduces the growth of *H. paradoxus*, while disturbances promote its growth ((Bush and Van Auken 1997; Van Auken and Bush 2004). This certainly suggests that competition from neighbors could play a very important role in the ecology and management of this threatened species.

The purposes of the studies presented here are to examine the competitive abilities of *H. paradoxus* with its progenitors and the competitive abilities of *H. paradoxus* with *D. spicata*, a grass

FIGURE 1— Habitat photograph of the Diamond-Y Spring salt marsh looking to the north. A high-density stand of *Helianthus paradoxus* is on the right and a high-density stand of *Distichlis spicata* is on the left. *Helianthus paradoxus* is not present in the *Distichlis spicata* community, but *Distichlis spicata* is below the sunflowers although it cannot be seen in this photograph.

FIGURE 2—Habitat photograph of the Diamond-Y Spring salt marsh looking to the northwest. The foreground with the *Sporobolus airoides* grassland is slightly higher in elevation and slightly drier than the remainder of the salt marsh. *Helianthus paradoxus* and *Distichlis spicata* occur together at slightly lower and wetter parts of the salt marsh. *Scirpus americanus* is usually found in the wettest part of the salt marsh that usually has standing water.

and a potential major environmental competitor.

SPECIES ACCOUNT AND HABITAT

Helianthus paradoxus is estimated to be between 75,000 and 208,000 years old (Welch and Rieseberg 2002). It is an annual species based on distinct morphological characteristics (Correll and Johnston 1979). It was first described in 1958 and later distinguished as a species (Heiser 1965, 1958). F_1

hybrids between *H. paradoxus* and its progenitors are largely sterile with low pollen stainability and seed set (Heiser 1965, 1958; Heiser et al. 1969). Also, *H. paradoxus* has a stable karyotype and expresses no meiotic abnormalities (Chandler et al. 1986), and has a much larger genome than either of its parent species (Sims and Price 1985). Molecular tests indicated that *H. paradoxus* has combined rDNA repeat types of *H. annuus* and *H. petiolaris*, and has the chloroplast genome of *H. annuus*, confirming that *H. paradoxus* was derived through hybridization (Lexer et al. 2003; Rieseberg et al. 1990; Welch and Rieseberg 2002).

The genus *Helianthus* consist of approximately 67 species of annual and perennial herbs made taxonomically difficult by hybridization among its members (Correll and Johnston 1979). The genus has been divided into four sections based on fairly distinct phylogenetic lines (Heiser 1965). *Helianthus paradoxus* and its parent species *H. annuus* and *H. petiolaris* are annuals belonging to the same section, are obligate out-crossers, and have the same chromosome number (n = 17). In spite of these similarities, phenological, morphological, and habitat characteristics are different making identification relatively easy. *Helianthus annuus* and *H. petiolaris* flower in the spring and summer (depending on location), while *H. paradoxus* flowers in fall, usually late fall.

Morphologically, *H. paradoxus* is distinguished from the parent species by having smaller heads, nearly glabrous stems, longer and narrower leaves, narrower phyllaries, and fewer ray flowers (Correll and Johnston 1979; Heiser 1958). All three of these species of *Helianthus* differ in their habitat preference. *Helianthus annuus* occurs throughout North America on disturbed, heavy soils, that are wet in the spring but dry out by midsummer. *Helianthus petiolaris* occurs in western North America on sandy soil. *Helianthus paradoxus* is found in 25 locations in west Texas and New Mexico on brackish, saline, marsh soils (McDonald 1999). *Helianthus paradoxus* has been reported from two west Texas counties and two eastern New Mexico Counties in the Pecos River watershed and two western New Mexico Counties in the Rio Grande watershed (Fig. 3). The largest population of *H. paradoxus* is reported from a salt marsh associated with *Distichlis spicata* (saltgrass) at the Diamond-Y Spring Preserve near Ft.

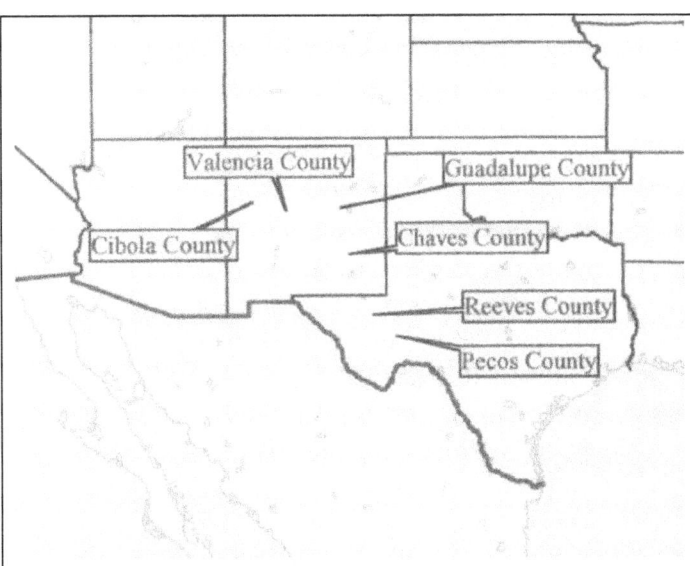

FIGURE 3—Distribution map of *Helianthus paradoxus* in western Texas and New Mexico. The counties were *H. paradoxus* is found are shown. The counties in eastern New Mexico and western Texas are in the Pecos River watershed. The counties in Western New Mexico are in the Rio Grande watershed.

Stockton, Texas (Van Auken and Bush 1998).

MATERIAL AND METHODS

Seeds of *Helianthus paradoxus*, *H. annuus* (common sunflower), and *H. petiolaris* (plains sunflower) were collected from native plants located north of Ft. Stockton, Texas in Pecos County, Texas (31° 0.54' N, 102° 55.49' W), in northwestern Bexar County, Texas (29° 37' N, 98° 36' W) and in central Bernalillo County, New Mexico (35° 5' N 106° 39' W), respectively. Seeds were placed on wet paper toweling in 5 cm deep trays covered with plastic wrap and placed at 4° C for three weeks to break dormancy. Deionized water was added as needed to keep the toweling moist. Clumps of *Distichlis spicata* were collected from the salt marsh at the Diamond-Y Spring Preserve near Fort Stockton, Texas. Clumps were approximately 15 x 15 x 15 cm and were collected by extraction with a shovel. Clumps were placed in large plastic bags for transport to the greenhouse in preparation for the experiment. Clumps were kept in the greenhouse for approximately one week prior to removal of the *D. spicata* rhizomes for placement into the experiment. Clumps were kept in open-top plastic tubs with several centimeters of water at the bottom. Deionized water was added as needed to keep the soil wet. Rhizomes were carefully removed from the soil by washing. Live rhizomes were cut into 3-cm lengths and placed in tap water and then randomly selected for transplanting. Aboveground parts and roots were trimmed to 5-cm lengths prior to transplantation.

Seedlings and saltgrass rhizomes were transplanted into pots containing 1400 g of Patrick series soil described as clayey-over-sandy, carbonatic-thermic, typic calciustoll, with the A horizon varying in depth from 25 to 41 cm (Taylor et al. 1966). The soil was air dried and sieved (6.4 mm mesh) prior to placement into pots lined with plastic bags (to prevent nutrient, salt and water loss). Soil analysis indicated 5-10 g/kg carbon, 11.6 g/kg calcium, 1.3 g/kg magnesium, 1.0 mg/kg total nitrogen, 12 mg/kg phosphorus, 138 mg/kg potassium, and 196 mg/kg sulfur. Each pot was supplemented with 0.2 g N as NH_4NO_3, 0.15 g P as Na_2PO_4, 0.1 g K as KCl, and 0.04 g S as $MgSO_4$.

A fiberglass greenhouse was used for plant growth with photosynthetically active photon flux density (PPFD, 400-700 nm) at 37% $\pm$ 12% of the outside mean PPFD (1,542 $\pm$ 18 $\mu mol/m^2/sec \pm$ SD averaged over the experiment). Light level was measured with a LI-COR® LI-188 integrating quantum sensor.

COMPETITION BETWEEN *HELIANTHUS PARADOXUS* AND ITS PROGENITORS

The growth of each species (*H. paradoxus*, *H. annuus* and *H. petiolaris*) grown alone was compared to growth with each of the other species. For each growth parameter evaluated: above ground, below ground and total dry mass or yield, (Van Auken & Bush 1997), a 2 x 2 analyses of variances was used which tested the main effects of soil salinity (two levels) and competition (two levels). The interaction term of the two main effects was also entered into the models. The two levels of salinity were 0 and 5 g/kg. The two levels of competition were growth alone and growth in mixture with one of the other species. There were five replications of each treatment. For example, an analysis of variance of *H. paradoxus* aboveground dry mass evaluated the effects of soil salinity, and the growth alone with growth with *H. annuus*. A separate analysis of variances of *H. paradoxus* aboveground dry mass evaluated the effects of soil salinity, and the growth with *H. petiolaris*. Because there were three growth parameters analyzed, there were a total of six ANOVA's performed for each species (SAS 1990). This was done because the competition between any species and a second species was independent of the other species. Total density in each pot was four plants, either four individuals of one species for growth in monoculture, or two of each species in mixture. This density was chosen because intraspecific experiments indicate that *H. paradoxus* and *H. annuus* compete at this density (Bush and Van Auken, unpublished data).

Soil was either native Patrick soil or native soil supplemented with creek water collected from the Diamond-Y Spring Preserve north of Ft. Stockton, Texas, one of only twenty-five locations where *H. paradoxus* occurs. Creek water was added to obtain a total soil salinity of 5 g/kg. The chemical composition of the creek water is presented in Table 1 (Veni 1991). Spatial and temporal

TABLE 1. Ions and their concentration found in the Diamond-Y Springs water, which was used to adjust the soil salinity in the experiment (analysis done by (Veni 1991).

Ion	Concentration (mg l^{-1})
Ca	500
Mg	300
Na	1250
Cl	1750
SO4	2450
HCO3	300
K	48
NO3	5

differences in total soil salt levels at the Diamond Y Spring Preserve have been reported between 5 and 40 g/kg (Van Auken and Bush 1998), which is mostly Cl and SO4. Current interest was in slight growth suppression of the test species with soil salts, and changes in their competitive abilities; thus, relatively low soil salt levels were tested.

Ten weeks after initiation of the experiment, after growth had stopped, plant tops were harvested by clipping at the soil surface, separating by species, and determining dry mass by drying at 100° C to a constant mass. Ash-free belowground dry mass (Bohm 1979) was measured by carefully washing the soil from the roots, separating by species, drying to a constant mass at 100° C, weighing, ashing at 650° C for 3 hours, reweighing, and subtracting the inorganic components. The roots were easily separated by species; however, since the inorganic matter was often difficult to remove without losing finer roots, ash-free dry mass was determined for the roots. Mean dry mass or yield per plant was determined by dividing the total mass by the density, and was used to compare growth in mixture and monoculture (Van Auken and Bush 1997). There were five replications of each treatment.

COMPETITION BETWEEN HELIANTHUS PARADOXUS AND DISTICHLIS SPICATA

Total density in each pot in the sunflower-saltgrass competition experiment was six plants, either six individuals of one species for growth in monoculture, or proportions of 4:2, 3:3, or 2:4 of the species in mixture. For the salinity treatment in this experiment, 5 g/Kg NaCl was added to each pot.

Twelve weeks after initiation of the experiment and after growth had stopped, plant tops were harvested by clipping at the soil surface, separating by species, and determining dry mass by drying at 100° C to a constant mass. As previously described, ash-free belowground dry mass (Bohm 1979) was measured. Mean dry mass or yield per plant was determined by dividing the total mass by the density, and was used to compare growth in mixture and monoculture (Van Auken and Bush 1997). There were five replications of each treatment.

As previously described, ANOVA's were performed separately for each species to test the effects of soil salinity and interference on aboveground, belowground, and total dry mass (SAS 1990). Main effects and their interactions were entered into the model.

RESULTS

When *H. paradoxus* aboveground, belowground, or total dry mass was compared with *H. annuus*, ANOVA's indicated that interference (competition, monoculture versus mixture), soil salinity, and their interaction were significant factors ($P \leq 0.05$). *Helianthus paradoxus* aboveground, belowground, and total dry mass was the same, regardless of the soil salinity. However, when grown with *H. annuus* in low soil salt conditions, *H. paradoxus* relative yield or relative total dry mass was 12% compared to monoculture (100%, Table 2). When grown in higher saline soil with *H. annuus*, *H. paradoxus* relative

yield or relative total dry mass was 150% or 50% higher compared to growth in monoculture (Table 2).

When *H. annuus* aboveground, belowground, or total dry mass was compared when grown with *H. paradoxus*, ANOVA's indicated that salinity was a significant factor influencing growth or relative yield. The effects of salinity, however, were dependent on interference or competition, as indicated by a significant interaction between interference and salinity. Interference was not a significant factor by itself. The growth or relative yield of *H. annuus* was essentially the reverse of the growth response of *H. paradoxus* when they were grown together. Growth of *H. annuus* was greater in the lower saline soil than the high saline soil. In low saline soil, *H. annuus* aboveground, belowground, and total dry mass when grown with *H. paradoxus* was higher compared to *H. annuus* growth in monoculture. Relative yield of total dry mass was 136% (Table 2) or 36% higher than relative yield in monoculture. In high saline soil, relative yield of *H. annuus* when grown with *H. paradoxus* was 8%, 3%, and 5% (aboveground, belowground, and total dry mass, respectively) compared to growth in monoculture (100%). Or, for

TABLE 2. Relative yields of *Helianthus paradoxus*, *H. annuus*, and *H. petiolaris* total dry mass when they were grown with each other in low and high saline soil. Relative yield in monoculture was 100% for each species and condition.

Salinity	Species	Competitor		
		H. paradoxus	H. annuus	H. petiolaris
-	H. paradoxus	—	12	100
	H. annuus	136	—	166
	H. petiolaris	80	20	—
+	H. paradoxus	—	150	160
	H. annuus	5	—	110
	H. petiolaris	0	0	—

total dry mass, the relative yield of *H. annuus* when grown with *H. paradoxus* was 5% of growth in monoculture (Table 2). In addition, it should be noted that in low saline soil the dry mass of *H. annuus* in monoculture was 92% higher than *H. paradoxus* in monoculture. In high saline soil, *H. paradoxus* dry mass was 7% higher than *H. annuus* growth in monoculture.

When *H. paradoxus* aboveground and total dry mass was compared with *H. petiolaris*, ANOVA's indicated that interference (competition), salinity, and their interaction were significant factors ($P \leq 0.05$). For belowground dry mass, only salinity was a significant factor. Growth of *H. paradoxus* in low saline soil was the same, regardless of the interference (monoculture or mixture). When grown in high saline soil with *H. petiolaris*, *H. paradoxus* relative yield of total dry mass was 160% or 60% higher compared to growth in monoculture (Table 2). *Helianthus paradoxus* belowground dry mass in the high saline soil was 16% higher when growth in mixture as compared to growth in monoculture (data not presented).

ANOVA's of *H. petiolaris* aboveground, belowground, and total dry mass when grown with *H. paradoxus* indicated that only salinity was a significant factor (data not shown). The interaction plots showed that growth in low saline soil was higher than growth in high saline soil; and as indicated by the ANOVA's, growth in monoculture or mixture with *H. paradoxus* was the same. In the high saline soil, there was 100% mortality of *H. petiolaris*.

ANOVA's of *H. annuus* aboveground and total dry mass when grown with *H. petiolaris* indicated that

interference (competition) and salinity were significant factors ($P \leq 0.05$). For belowground dry mass, salinity and the interaction of salinity and interference were significant factors. Aboveground, belowground, and total dry mass of *H. annuus* in lower saline soil was greater than in higher saline soil. For *H. annuus* when grown with *H. petiolaris* in the low saline soil, relative yield of total dry mass in mixture was 166% or 66% higher than growth in monoculture (Table 2). In high saline soil, relative yield of total dry mass in mixture was 110% or 10% greater than growth in monoculture (Table 2).

The ANOVA's of *H. petiolaris* when grown with *H. annuus* indicated that interference, salinity, and the interaction term were significant ($P \leq 0.05$). Growth of *H. petiolaris* was greater in low saline soil than in high saline soil. In the low saline soil, *H. petiolaris* relative yield of total dry mass when grown with *H. annuus* was 20% when compared with monoculture (Table 2). In the high saline soil, there was 100% mortality of *H. petiolaris*. There were no mortalities of *H. annuus* or *H. paradoxus* in any of the experiments at either level of soil salinity.

When *H. paradoxus* total dry mass was compared with *D. spicata*, ANOVA's indicated that interference (competition, monoculture versus mixture) was significant ($P \leq 0.05$); but, soil salinity and their interaction were not significant factors ($P > 0.05$). When grown in monoculture, *H. paradoxus* and *D. spicata* total dry mass was the same, regardless of the soil salinity. However, when *H. paradoxus* was grown with *D. spicata* in low soil salt conditions, relative yield or relative total dry mass of *H. paradoxus* was 181-

329% compared to monoculture (100%, Table 3), depending on the proportion. The greater the proportion of *H. paradoxus*, the greater the relative yield of *H. paradoxus*. In low salt soil conditions, relative yield of total *D. spicata* dry mass in mixture with *H. paradoxus* was 9-19% compared to monoculture (100%, Table 3), depending on the proportion. The greater the proportion of *H. paradoxus*, the lower the relative yield of *D. spicata*.

When *H. paradoxus* was grown with *D. spicata* in higher saline soil, relative yield of *H. paradoxus* total dry mass was 136-184% or 36-84% higher depending on the proportion, compared to growth in monoculture (100%, Table 3). The greater the proportion of *H. paradoxus*, the greater the relative yield of *H. paradoxus*. In high soil salt conditions, relative yield of *D. spicata* total dry mass grown with *H. paradoxus* was 24-39% compared to monoculture (100%, Table 3), depending on the proportion. The greater the proportion of *H. paradoxus*, the lower the relative yield of *D. spicata*. Growth of *D. spicata* was better in the higher salt treatments, but dry mass was reduced in the presence of *H. paradoxus*.

DISCUSSION

These west Texas and New Mexico salt marshes where *H. paradoxus* is found today (McDonald 1999) were probably very important in the past for the establishment and maintenance of new populations genetically isolated from the parent species (Abbott 2003;

Rieseberg et al. 2003). The hybridization event that led to the populations of *H. paradoxus* in this area apparently occurred between 75,000 and 208,000 years before the present (Welch and Rieseberg 2002). Ecological or spatial isolation in these salt marshes allowed the original population of *H. paradoxus* to escape any minority type disadvantages and avoid interspecific competition with the parent species (Abbott 2003). Thus, the hybrid species was able to establish in ecological isolation as a result of possessing a hybrid genotype adapted to the new habitat, the salt marsh. *Helianthus paradoxus* can produce more biomass and thus out-compete its parental species (*H. annuus* and *H. petiolaris*) in saline soils similar to those found in west Texas and New Mexico salt marshes (Bush and Van Auken 2004), (Table 2).

In addition, *H. paradoxus* grows faster and produces more biomass than *Distichlis spicata* (an environmental competitor) when both species are started together at the same time (Table 3). In greenhouse studies, *H. paradoxus* can out-compete a species found at high densities in these same salt marsh environments (Fig. 1). Furthermore, *H. paradoxus* should be able to establish and out-compete *D. spicata* in the salt marsh environment. In fact, we showed

TABLE 3. Relative yield of *Helianthus paradoxus* and *Distichlis spicata* total dry mass when grown with each other in low and high saline soil. There were three different proportions of *Helianthus paradoxus* to *Distichlis spicata* (4:2, 3:3, 2:4) at a constant density of 6 plants per pot. Relative yield in monoculture was 100% for each species and condition.

Salinity	Species	Competitor					
		Helianthus paradoxus Proportion			*Distichlis spicata* Proportion		
		4:2	3:3	2:4	4:2	3:3	2:4
-	*H. paradoxus*	---	---	---	329	219	181
	D. spicata	19	17	9	---	---	---
+	*H. paradoxus*	---	---	---	184	164	136
	D. spicata	39	32	24	---	---	---

that neighbors including *D. spicata* reduce the growth of *H. paradoxus* in the salt marsh (Bush and Van Auken 1997) and that disturbances promote the growth of *H. paradoxus* (Van Auken and Bush 2004). Others have reported low competitive ability of *D. spicata* in coastal marine environments where it is also found (Bertness 1991a).

Helianthus paradoxus has characteristics like some other halophytes in that it can apparently actively exclude sodium and some other mineral ions (Lexer et al. 2003), it can sequester other ions (Rieseberg et al. 2003) and has increased leaf succulence (Welch and Rieseberg 2002). In addition, *H. paradoxus* is competitively superior to the parent species in slightly saline soils (Bush and Van Auken 2004, Table 2).

Hybrid species, such as *H. paradoxus*, are often shown to be more tolerant of harsh conditions than parental species. Salt tolerance of hybrid species relative to parental species is one way that that hybrid species may escape parental competition, and may determine the sites where hybrids colonize (Abbott 2003). *Helianthus anomalus*, another diploid hybrid of *H. annuus* and *H. petiolaris*, has also been shown to be a mosaic of parental-like and transgressive phenotypes (Schwarzbach et al. 2001). The fitness effects of the transgressive characters, however, are not known. In addition, some hybrids of *H. annuus* and *H. petiolaris* appear to have the genetic 'architecture' which allows these individuals to colonize in salt marsh habitats (Lexer et al. 2003). It has been shown that segregating hybrids commonly show traits that are extreme relative to those of their progenitors (Anderson and Stebbins 1954; Lewontin

and Birch 1966; Rieseberg et al. 1999; Rieseberg et al. 2003; Welch and Rieseberg 2002). Specifically, *H. paradoxus* is more tolerant of NaCl than its parental species, and *H. paradoxus* was found to have traits commonly associated with salt tolerance in plants (Welch and Rieseberg 2002). They found that leaf sodium concentrations and leaf succulence were statistically higher in *H. paradoxus* than its progenitors. In addition, *H. paradoxus* is also found to be more tolerant of soil salts, especially sulfate, than *H. annuus* (Mendez 2001). On the other hand, not all hybrids are found to show increased salt tolerance or phenotypic plasticity. Working with native, exotic, and hybrid species of the genus *Carpobrotus* (Aizoceae) found in coastal plant communities throughout California, Weber and D'Antonio (1999) showed that the parental species and their hybrids were very similar in their ability to adjust to saline environments.

Some endemic species like *H. paradoxus* have morphological traits that enables them to survive in harsh environments. *Solidago shortii* Torr.& Gray, another member of the Asteraceae family, is a narrow endemic found in Kentucky. This species was shown to have morphological traits that enabled it to tolerate drier habitats than its widespread congener, *S. altissima* L. (Walck et al. 1999). While it is evident that there is a strong relationship between endemic plant species and unusual edaphic characteristics (Kruckeberg and Rabinowitz 1985), the relative role of these species response to the abiotic factors and competition in influencing distributions is debated.

In the current study with the endemic hybrid species *H. paradoxus* and its progenitors *H. annuus* and *H. petiolaris*, the progenitors were better competitors, but only in low saline conditions. Under harsh condition (high saline soils), *H. paradoxus* reduced *H. annuus* growth indicating it has a competitive advantage (Table 2). *Helianthus petiolaris* growth was restricted in both monoculture and mixture, indicating that its lack of growth under high saline conditions results from its intolerance of the abiotic conditions rather than competition.

The role of abiotic conditions in influencing plant distributions and communities has long been recognized, and the distribution of vegetation in marshes as been shown to be dependent on species' varying tolerances to physical factors (Cooper 1982; DeJong 1978; Etherington 1984; Ewing 2000; Mahall and Park 1976a; Mendelssohn et al. 1981; Naidoo et al. 1992; Rand 2000; Schat 1984; Snow and Vince 1984; Valiela et al. 1978; Vilarrubia 2000). While water has often been found to be one of the most critical factors in determining the growth and distribution of species in marshes (El-Ghani 2000; Mahall and Park 1976a, 1976b; Onkware 2000; Rogel et al. 2001; Vilarrubia 2000), differential species tolerance to salinity has also been shown to contribute to broad zonation of coastal vegetation (Oosting and Billings 1942; Rogel et al. 2001; Vilarrubia 2000; Vince and Snow 1984). Data from this study suggests that these three *Helianthus* species do respond differently to salinity; and, that these differences may be important, in part, in determining the out-come of competition between them. The relative competitive ability of these three species in saline conditions similar to those found where *H. paradoxus* occurs is *H. paradoxus* >

H. annuus > *H. petiolaris*. The data indicate that *H. petiolaris* absence from these areas may result from its inability to grow in the higher saline conditions. However, for *H. annuus*, while the soil salinity by itself will not prevent its growth, when grown in competition with *H. paradoxus*, interference interacts with soil salinity to reduce its growth. *Distichlis spicata* does not seem to be able to prevent the establishment and growth of *H. paradoxus* in saline or non-saline soils. Based on greenhouse and limited field studies, *H. paradoxus* should be able to establish in mature stands of *D. spicata* although this has not been conclusively demonstrated.

ACKNOWLEDGMENTS

We thank John Karges of the Texas Nature Conservancy for his help on various aspects of this study.

LITERATURE CITED

Abbott, R.J. 2003. Sex, sunflowers, and speciation. Science. 301(5637): 1189-1190.

Anderson, E., G.L. Stebbins. 1954. Hybridization as an evolutionary stimulus. Evolution. 2(4): 378-388.

Bertness, M.D. 1991a. Interspecific interactions among high marsh perennials in a New England salt marsh. Ecology. 72(1): 138-148.

_____ 1991b. Zonation of *Spartina patens* and *Spartina alterniflora* in a New England salt marsh. Ecology. 72(1): 125-137.

Bertness, M.D., A.M. Ellison. 1987. Determinants of pattern in a New England salt marsh community. Ecological Monographs. 57(2): 129-147.

Bohm, W. 1979. Methods of studying root systems. In: Billings, W.D., F. Golley, O.L. Lange, and J.S. Olson, (eds.), Ecological Studies. New York, NY: Springer-Verlag. p. 126-127.

Bush, J.K., and O.W. Van Auken. 1997. The effects of neighbors and grazing on the growth of *Helianthus paradoxus*. Southwestern Naturalist. 42(4): 416-422.

_____ 2004. Relative competitive ability of *Helianthus paradoxus* and its progenitors, *H. annuus* and *H. petiolaris* (Asteraceae), in varying soil salinities. International Journal of Plant Sciences. 165(2): 303-310.

Chandler, J.M., C.C. Jan, and B.H. Beard. 1986. Chromosomal differentiation among the annual *Helianthus* species. Systematic Botany. 11(2): 354-371.

Cooper, A. 1982. The effects of salinity and waterlogging on the growth and cation uptake of salt marsh plants. New Phytologist. 90(2): 263-275.

Correll, D.S., and M.C. Johnston. 1979. Manual of the vascular plants of Texas. Richardson, TX: University of Dallas Press. 1881 p.

Davy, A.J., H. Smith. 1985. Population differentiation in the life-history characteristics of salt-marsh annuals. Vegetatio. 61(1-3): 117-125.

DeJong, T.M. 1978. Comparative gas exchange and growth responses of C_3 and C_4 beach species grown at different salinities. Oecologia. 36(1): 59-68.

El-Ghani, M.M.A. 2000. Vegetation composition of Egyptian inland salt marshes. Botanical Bullentin of Academa Sinica. 41(4): 305-314.

Etherington, J.R. 1984. Comparative studies of plant growth and distribution in relation to waterlogging. X. Differential formation of adventitious roots and their experimental excision in *Epilobium hirsutum* and *Chamerion angustifolium*. Journal of Ecology. 72(2): 389-404.

Ewing, K. 2000. Environmental gradients and vegetation structure on South Texas coastal clay dunes. Madroño. 48(1): 10-20.

Heiser, C.B. 1958. Three new annual sunflowers (*Helianthus*) from the southwestern United States. Rhodora. 60(3): 272-283.

Heiser, C.B. 1965. Species crosses in *Helianthus*: III. delimitation of "sections". Annals of the Missouri Botanical Garden. 52(3): 364-370.

Heiser, C.B., D.M. Smith, S.B.Clevenger, and W.C. Martin Jr. 1969. The north American sunflowers (*Helianthus*). Memoirs Torrey Botanical Club. 22(1): 1-218.

Kruckeberg, A.R., and D. Rabinowitz. 1985. Biological aspects of endemism in higher plants. Annual Review of Ecology and Systematics. 16: 447-479.

Lewontin, R.C. and L.C. Birch. 1966. Hybridization as a source of variation for adaptation to new environments. Evolution. 20(3): 315-336.

Lexer, C., M.E. Welch, J.L. Durphy, and L.H. Rieseberg,. 2003. Natural selection for salt tolerance quantitative loci (QTLs) in wild sunflower hybrids: Implication for the origin of *Helianthus paradoxus*, a diploid hybrid species. Molecular Ecology. 12(5): 1225-1235.

Mahall, B.E. and R.B. Park. 1976a. The ecotone between *Spartina foliosa* Trin. and *Salicornia virinica* L., in salt marshes of northern San Francisco Bay II. Soil, water and salinity. Journal of Ecology. 64(3): 793-809.

_____ 1976b. The ecotone between *Spartina foliosa* Trin. and *Salicornia virinica* L., in salt marshes of northern San Francisco Bay III. Soil aeration and tidal immersion. Journal of Ecology. 64(3): 811-819.

McDonald, C. 1999. Endangered and threatened wildlife and plants; determination of threatened status for the plant *Helianthus paradoxus* (Pecos sunflower). Federal Register. 64: 56582-56590.

Mendelssohn, I.A., K.L. McKee, and W.H. Patrick. 1981. Oxygen deficiency in *Spartina alterniflora* roots: metabolic adaptation to anoxia. Science. 214(4519): 439-441.

Mendez, M.O. 2001. A comparison of the effects of salinity and light levels ont he growth of *Helianthus paradoxus* and *Helianthus annuus*. San Antonio, TX: UT San Antonio. 237 p. Thesis.

Naidoo, G., K.L. McKee, and I.A. Mendelssohn. 1992. Anatomical and metabolic responses to waterlogging and salinity in *Spartina alterniflora* and *S. patens* (Poaceae). American Journal of Botany. 79(7): 765-770.

Onkware, A.O. 2000. Effect of salinity on plant distribution and production at Lobura delta, Lake Bogoria National Reserve, Kenya. Austra Ecology. 25(2): 140-149.

Oosting, H.J. and W.D. Billings. 1942. Factors affecting vegetational zonation on coastal dunes. Ecology. 23(2): 131-142.

Rand, T.A. 2000. Seed dispersal, habitat suitability, and the distribution of halophytes across a salt marsh tidal gradient. Journal of Ecology. 88(4): 608-621.

Rieseberg, L.H., M.A. Archer, and R.K. Wayne. 1999. Transgressive segregation, adaptation and speciation. Heredity. 83(4): 363-372.

Rieseberg, L.H., R. Carter, and S. Zona. 1990. Molecular tests of the hypothesized hybrid origin of two diploid *Helianthus* species (Asteraceae). Evolution. 44(6): 1498-1511.

Rieseberg, L. H., O. Raymond, D.M. Rosenthal, Z. Lai, K. Livingstone, T. Nakazato, J.L. Durphy, A.E. Schwarzbach, L.A. Donovan, and C. Lexer. 2003. Major ecological transitions in wild sunflowers facilitated by hybridization. Science. 301(5637): 1211-1216.

Rogel, J.A., R.O. Silla, and F.A. Ariza. 2001. Edaphic characterization and soil ionic composition influencing plant zonation in a semiarid Mediterranean salt marsh. Geoderma. 99(1-2): 81-98.

SAS, I. 1990. SAS/STAT User's Guide, 1. Cary, NC: SAS Institute, Inc. 890 p.

Schat, H. 1984. A comparative ecophysiological study of the effects of waterlogging and submergence on dune slack plants: growth, survival and mineral nutrition in sand culture experiments. Oecologia. 62(2): 279-286.

Schwarzbach, A.E., L.A. Donovan, and L.H. Rieseberg. 2001. Transgressive character expression in a hybrid sunflower species. American Journal of Botany. 88(2): 270-277.

Sims, L.E. and H.J. Price, 1985. Nuclear DNA content variation in *Helianthus* (Asteraceae). American Journal of Botany. 72(8): 1213-1219.

Snow, A.A. and S.W. Vince. 1984. Plant zonation in an Alaskan salt marsh II. An experimental study of the role of edaphic conditions. Journal of Ecology. 72(2): 679-684.

Taylor, F.B., R.B. Hailey, and D.L. Richmond. 1966. Soil survey of Bexar County, Texas. Washington, D. C.: USDA Soil Conservation Service. 126 p.

Ungar, I.A. 1998. Are biotic factors significant in influencing the distibution of halophytes in saline habitats? Botanical Review. 64(2): 176-199.

Valiela, I., J.M. Teal, and G. Deuser. 1978. The nature of growth forms in the salt marsh grass, *Spartina alterniflora*. American Naturalist. 112(4): 461-470.

Van Auken, O.W. and J.K. Bush. 1997. Growth of *Prosopis glandulosa* in response to changes in aboveground and belowground interference. Ecology. 78(4): 1222-1229.

_____ 1998. Spatial relationships of *Helianthus paradoxus* (Compositae) and associated salt marsh plants. Southwestern Naturalist. 43(3): 313-320.

_____ 2004. Growth of *Helianthus paradoxus*, puzzle or pecos sunflower (Asteraceae), in response to disturbances In: Delmatier, C., F. Oxley, K. Clary, and J. Poole (eds.), Texas Plant Conservation Conference - 2002 Proceedings; Austin, TX: Lady Bird Johnson Wildlife Center and United States Fish and Wildlife Service:1-21.

Veni, G. 1991. Delineation and preliminary hydrogeologic investigation of the Diamond Y Spring, Pecos County, Texas. San Antonio, TX. Nature Conservancy of Texas.

Vilarrubia, T.V. 2000. Zonation pattern of an isolated mangrove community at Playa Medina, Venezuela. Wetlands Ecology and Management. 8(1): 9-17.

Vince, S.W. and A.A. Snow. 1984. Plant zonation in Alaskan salt marsh I. Distribution, abundance, and environmental factors. Journal of Ecology. 72(2): 651-657.

Walck, J.L., J.M. Baskin, and C.C. Baskin. 1999. Relative competitive abilities and growth characteristics of a narrowly endemic and a geographically widespread *Solidago*

speices (Asteraceae). American Journal of
Botany. 86(6): 820-828.

Weber, F. and C.M. D'Antonio. 1999.
Germination and growth responses of
hybridizing *Carpobrotus* species (Aizoaceae)
from coastal California to soil salinity.
American Journal of Botany. 86(9): 1257-
1263.

Welch, M.E. and L.H. Rieseberg. 2002. Habitat
divergence between a homoploid hybrid
sunflower species, *Helianthus paradoxus*
(Asteraceae), and its progenitors. American
Journal of Botany. 89(3): 472-478.